Henry VI

In this new assessment of Henry VI, David Grummitt synthesises a wealth of detailed research into Lancastrian England that has taken place throughout the last three decades, to provide a fresh appraisal of the house's last king. The biography places Henry in the context of Lancastrian political culture and considers how his reign was shaped by the times in which he lived.

Henry VI is one of the most controversial of England's medieval kings. Coming to the throne in 1422 at the age of only nine months and inheriting the crowns of both England and France, he reigned for thirty-nine years before losing his position to the Yorkist king, Edward IV, in the early stages of the Wars of the Roses. Almost a decade later, in 1470, he briefly regained the throne, only for his cause to be decisively defeated in battle the following year, after which Henry himself was almost certainly murdered. Henry continues to perplex and fascinate the modern reader, who struggles to understand how such an obviously ill-suited king could have continued to reign for nearly forty years and command such loyalty, even after his cause was lost.

From his coronation at nine months old, to the legacy of his reign in the centuries after his death, this is a balanced, detailed and engaging biography of one of England's most enigmatic kings and will be essential reading for all students of late medieval England, and the Wars of the Roses.

David Grummitt is Head of the School of Humanities at Canterbury Christ Church University. Hi~ ~~~~~~~ ~~~~~~~ include

The Calais Ga. 　　　　　　　　　　　　　　　 ᴐ–*1558*
(Boydell & Br　　　　　　　　　　　　　'*he Roses*
(I.B. Tauris, 2

ROUTLEDGE HISTORICAL BIOGRAPHIES

Series Editor: Robert Pearce

Routledge Historical Biographies provide engaging, readable and academically credible biographies written from an explicitly historical perspective. These concise and accessible accounts will bring important historical figures to life for students and general readers alike.

In the same series:

Henry VI

David Grummitt

Routledge
Taylor & Francis Group
LONDON AND NEW YORK

First published 2015
by Routledge
2 Park Square, Milton Park, Abingdon, Oxon OX14 4RN

And by Routledge
711 Third Avenue, New York, NY 10017

*Routledge is an imprint of the Taylor & Francis Group,
an informa business*

British Library Cataloguing-in-Publication Data
A catalogue record for this book is available from the British Library

Library of Congress Cataloging-in-Publication Data
Grummitt, David, 1971–
   Henry VI / David Grummitt.
      pages cm. — (Routledge historical biographies)
   Includes index.
   1. Henry VI, King of England, 1421–1471.   2. Great Britain—
Kings and rulers—Biography.   3. Great Britain—History—Henry VI,
1422–1461.   I. Title.
   DA257.G78 2015
   942.04′3092—dc23
   [B]
   2014043552

ISBN: 978-0-415-63992-7 (hbk)
ISBN: 978-0-415-63993-4 (pbk)
ISBN: 978-1-315-70835-5 (ebk)

Typeset in Garamond
by Apex CoVantage, LLC

MIX
Paper from
responsible sources
FSC   FSC® C013604
www.fsc.org

Printed and bound by CPI Group (UK) Ltd, Croydon, CR0 4YY

Contents

Acknowledgements

Medieval kings are elusive subjects for biographers and none more so perhaps than Henry VI. In this book I have tried to avoid taking sides in the perennial debate over whether Henry was a 'good' or 'bad' king. Instead, I have attempted to understand his kingship within the context of a distinctive Lancastrian identity. This identity, which I have labelled as 'Lancastrianism', was both political and cultural and it operated at both the national and international levels. Its tenets were also at times contradictory and its meaning almost always contested between the Lancastrian earl, later duke and finally king, and his servants and subjects. I believe it provides a context to explain the actions of Henry VI and the contemporary reactions to his idiosyncratic style of rule. The writing of a book like this has invariably incurred a number of debts, some academic and some personal. The work and encouragement of many scholars have proved invaluable and particular gratitude is due to Jim Bolton, Linda Clark, Sean Cunningham, Anne Curry, Michael Hicks, Chris Given-Wilson, Ralph Griffiths, Michael K. Jones, Hannes Kleineke, Malcolm Mercer, Charles Moreton, Ian Mortimer, Jenni Nuttall, Simon Payling, Ryan Perry, Carole Rawcliffe, James Ross, David Rundle, John Watts, and the wider community of fifteenth-century scholars at the annual Fifteenth Century Conference and the Institute of Historical Research's Late Medieval Seminar. Individually and as a scholarly community they have contributed to my understanding of late medieval England. The support of my family, especially my wife, Hil, and Gwen, my mother-in-law (who once again painstakingly read the manuscript from start to finish), has been invaluable, as

has been the assistance of the professional staff at Taylor &
Francis, particularly Catherine Aitken. A special note of thanks is
also due to Robert Pearce, the series editor, whose encouragement
and generous academic support has made the process of writing
a thoroughly enjoyable one. During that process we also had an
addition to the family, Lawrence, and it is to him and his sister
Cecily that this book is dedicated.

Chronology

Date	Personal	Political	General
1421	6 December: Henry VI born at Windsor		
1422	31 August: death of Henry V, Henry accedes to the throne of England 21 October: death of Charles VI, Henry accedes to the throne of France	9 November–18 December: Henry's first parliament at Westminster	
1423		20 October–28 February 1424: Parliament meets at Westminster	January: Humphrey, duke of Gloucester, marries Jacqueline of Hainault May: John, duke of Bedford, marries Anne of Burgundy 31 July: battle of Cravant
1424			17 August: battle of Verneuil
1425		30 April–14 July: Parliament meets at Westminster	
1426	19 May: Henry knighted by the duke of Bedford 31 December: death of Thomas Beaufort, duke of Exeter	18 February–1 June: Parliament meets at Westminster	
1427		13 October–25 March 1428: Parliament meets at Westminster	
1428	1 June: Richard, earl of Warwick appointed the king's guardian and tutor		12 October: English begin the siege of Orléans

Date	Personal	Political	General
1429	5 November: Henry crowned king of England at Westminster Abbey	22 September–23 February 1430: Parliament meets at Westminster	8 May: Joan of Arc raises the siege of Orléans 18 June: Battle of Patay 17 July: Charles VII crowned king of France in Reims
1430	23 April: Henry lands in Calais		
1431	16 December: Henry crowned king of France in Paris	12 January–20 March: Parliament meets at Westminster	30 May: Joan of Arc burned at the stake 14 December: council of Basel begins
1432	9 February: Henry returns to England	12 May–17 July: Parliament meets at Westminster	
1433		8 July–21 December: Parliament meets at Westminster	
1435	14 September: death of John, duke of Bedford 1 October: Henry attends his first council meeting	10 October–23 December: Parliament meets at Westminster	21 September: Franco-Burgundian treaty of Arras
1436	19 May: the earl of Warwick resigns as Henry's tutor		July: Burgundian siege of Calais
1437	3 January: death of Catherine of Valois 12 November: formal end of Henry's minority government	21 January–27 March: Parliament meets at Westminster	
1439		12 November–24 February 1440: Parliament meets at Westminster, then Reading	
1440	11 October: foundation of Eton College		2 July: decision confirmed to release the duke of Orléans
1441	2 April: Henry lays the first stone of his new college in Cambridge		July: Eleanor Cobham, duchess of Gloucester accused of witchcraft

Date	Personal	Political	General
1442		25 January–27 March: Parliament meets at Westminster	
1443			21 August: John Beaufort, duke of Somerset, leaves for France December: Somerset returns to England
1444	26 May: Henry formally betrothed to Margaret of Anjou		26 April: truce of Tours
1445	22 April: marriage to Margaret of Anjou 30 May: Margaret's coronation 22 December: Henry promises to surrender the counties of Anjou and Maine	25 February 1445–9 April 1446: Parliament meets at Westminster	
1447	23 February: mysterious death of Henry's uncle, Humphrey, duke of Gloucester, at the Bury Parliament 11 April: death of Henry Beaufort, cardinal bishop of Winchester	10 February–3 March: Parliament meets at Bury St Edmunds	
1448			11 March: treaty of Lavardin, English surrender of Anjou and Maine
1449		12 February–16 July: Parliament meets at Westminster, then Winchester 6 November–8 June 1450: Parliament meets at Westminster, then London, then Leicester	24 March: capture of Fougères 31 July: Charles VII declares himself absolved from the truce of Tours 19 October: surrender of Rouen

Date	Personal	Political	General
1450		6 November–31 May 1451: Parliament meets at Westminster 17 March: the duke of Suffolk banished from the realm for five years 30 March: Suffolk murdered aboard the *Nicholas of the Tower*	15 April: battle of Formigny May–July: Cade's Rebellion in Kent and London
1453	August: Henry becomes ill 13 October: birth of Prince Edward	6 March–18 April 1454: Parliament meets at Reading and Westminster	17 July: battle of Castillon
1454	15 March: Prince Edward created Prince of Wales c.25 December: Henry recovers from illness	27 March: Richard, duke of York, appointed protector and governor of England	
1455		9 July–12 March 1456: Parliament meets at Westminster 17 November: Richard, duke of York, appointed protector for a second time	22 May: first battle of St Albans
1456		25 February: the duke of York removed as protector	
1458			25 March: 'Loveday' in London
1459		20 November–20 December: Parliament meets at Coventry	23 September: battle of Blore Heath 12/13 October: battle of Ludford Bridge
1460		7 October–3 February 1461: Parliament meets at Westminster 25 October: the Accord names Richard, duke of York, as heir to the throne	10 July: battle of Northampton 30 December: battle of Wakefield and death of the duke of York

Date	Personal	Political	General
1461	April: Henry and his entourage arrive in Edinburgh		3 February: battle of Mortimer's Cross 17 February: second battle of St Albans 29 March: battle of Towton 26 June: Edward IV crowned king of England
1462	25 October: Henry and Margaret land at Bamburgh at the head of a Franco-Scottish army		
1463	June: Henry and Margaret resident at Bamburgh August: Margaret abandons Henry and establishes Lancastrian court in exile at Koeur		
1464			25 April: battle of Hedgley Moor 15 May: battle of Hexham
1465	July: Henry captured in Lancashire and imprisoned in the Tower of London		
1470	30 September: readeption of Henry VI 3 October: Henry released from the Tower of London	26 November–? 14 February 1471: Parliament meets at Westminster	22 July: treaty of Angers between Margaret of Anjou and the earl of Warwick 2 October: Edward IV flees to the Low Countries

(Continued)

Date	Personal	Political	General
1471	11 April: Henry returned to the Tower of London 4 May: death of Edward of Westminster at the battle of Tewkesbury 22/23 May: Henry VI murdered in the Tower of London		14 April: battle of Barnet 4 May: battle of Tewkesbury
1482	20 August: death of Margaret of Anjou		

Abbreviations

POPC   *Proceedings and Ordinances of the Privy Council of England*,
           ed. H. Nicolas (7 vols, 1834–37)
PROME   *Parliament Rolls of Medieval England, 1272–1504*, ed. Chris
           Given-Wilson (General Editor) (14 vols, Woodbridge,
           2005)
TNA   The National Archives, Kew

Place of publication is London unless stated otherwise.

Genealogies and maps

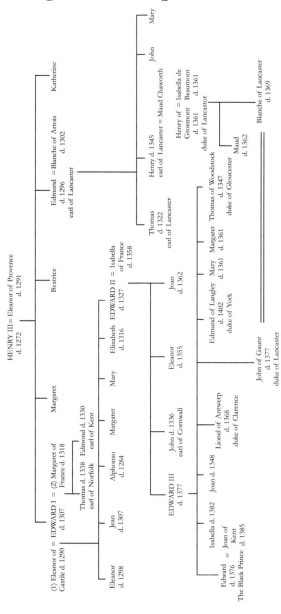

PLANTAGENET AND LANCASTER

HENRY III = Eleanor of Provence
d. 1272   d. 1291

Genealogy 1 Plantagenet and Lancaster

LANCASTER AND YORK

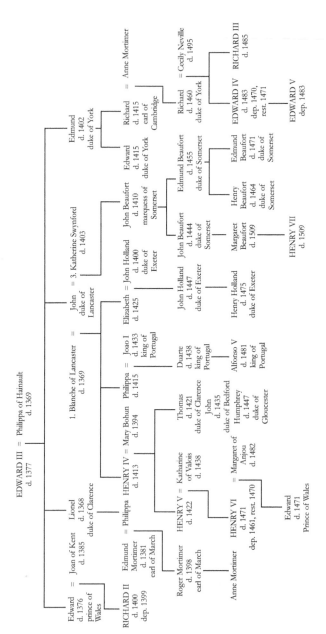

Genealogy 2 Lancaster and York

LANCASTER AND BEAUFORT

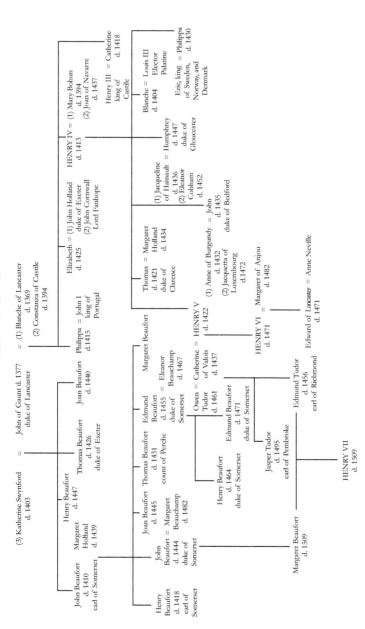

Genealogy 3 Lancaster and Beaufort

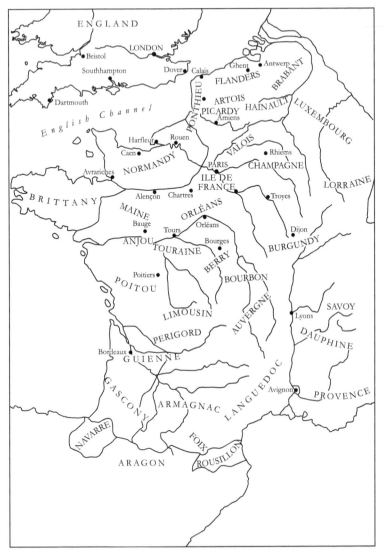

Map 1 France in the Dual Monarchy

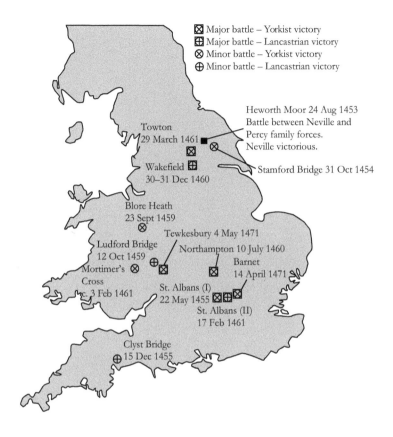

Map 2 The Wars of the Roses 1455–71. After Christopher Daniell, *Atlas of Medieval Britain 1485–1715* (Abingdon, 2011), maps 53 and 54

1   Introduction

The royal enigma

To the modern reader, Henry VI presents probably the most elusive king to have ruled medieval England. How could a man so obviously ill suited to the rigours of personal monarchy reign for thirty-nine years, commanding the loyalty of most of his subjects most of the time? How could the king, a decade after his deposition, be freed from imprisonment and placed once more, albeit for only a few months, upon the English throne? Recent historians and Henry's contemporaries alike have struggled to reconcile the various aspects of his reign and have arrived at diametrically opposed views of the nature of his kingship. Despite an explosion of detailed, archival research since World War II, which has shed light on various aspects of fifteenth-century England, and a more recent appreciation of the cultural achievements of the Lancastrian regime and its supporters, Henry himself remains an obscure figure, frequently caricatured and often two-dimensional. Medieval kings are elusive subjects for biographers, and none more so perhaps than Henry VI. In this book I have tried to avoid taking sides in the perennial debate over whether Henry was a 'good' or 'bad' king. Instead, I have attempted to understand his kingship within the context of a distinctive Lancastrian identity. This identity, which I have labelled as 'Lancastrianism', was both political and cultural and it operated at both the national and international levels. Its tenets were also at times contradictory and its meaning almost always contested between the Lancastrian earl, later duke and finally king, and his servants and subjects. I believe it provides a context to explain the actions of Henry VI and the contemporary reactions to his idiosyncratic style of rule.

Principal among the problems of gaining a rounded view of Henry VI are the contemporary sources. A great deal more ink and parchment was used during his reign to describe the life and deeds of his father, Henry V, than was used to write about the king himself. Moreover, the great Latin chroniclers of the previous generation – the monk of St Albans Thomas Walsingham, Adam Usk, and the Westminster chronicler – ended their chronicles as Henry's reign began. The London chronicle tradition and the Middle English *Brut* that dominated history writing in the mid fifteenth century simply did not relate political events in the same detail or with comparable insight. Their London bias and their sympathy with Henry's Yorkist critics in the 1450s compromised their portrayal of the king. Other chronicle sources, such as John Hardyng's vernacular verse chronicle or the Latin chronicle known to us as *Giles's Chronicle*, were completed in the knowledge that Henry's reign had led to civil war and the Lancastrian dynasty's hopes and ambitions had collapsed, due in no small part to the personal failings of its last king.[1] This tradition, of an unworldly king simply incapable of ruling competently, was embedded in the Tudor tradition of writing history and has been passed down to us today through the history plays of William Shakespeare.

Acceding to the throne at only nine months old, Henry could expect a great deal of interest in his upbringing and education. It is, therefore, no surprise that he was the recipient of an unusually large number of didactic and exhortatory tracts. Poetic works, such as John Lydgate's *Life of St Edmund* (dedicated to the young king when he visited the abbey of Bury St Edmunds in 1433) or his *Fall of Princes* (addressed to the king's uncle, Humphrey, duke of Gloucester, and written in the mid 1430s), to some extent addressed contemporary concerns over how the young Henry would adapt to the pressures of his office. Similarly, those in the so-called 'Mirror for Princes' genre have frequently been used to illustrate concern among his servants over his ability to rule effectively. Yet these texts, as literary scholars are beginning to appreciate, are far more complex and multi-vocal than mere advice manuals for princes. Although they were designed to exhort and coerce

Henry into being a 'better' king, they also spoke to a wider Lancastrian readership with its own preconceptions about the nature of effective kingship. Similarly, the material produced in the 1480s by John Blacman, one of the king's chaplains, was not simply the reminiscences of someone who knew Henry personally, but a more complex text that drew on other traditions to portray a certain view of the king and the Lancastrian political culture he represented.[2]

It is, however, the voluminous records of royal government that present the greatest obstacle to understanding the nature of Henry VI's kingship. In the fifteenth century all government was carried out in the king's name and the records of parliament, the council and other institutions of royal government are the mainstay of any historian seeking to reconstruct the king's life and reign. These bodies did not, by and large, have corporate identities that were independent of the prince in whose name they functioned. At all levels, government proceeded according to the king's will (with appropriate input, of course, from his councillors) and it was dependent upon the king's signature or his personal seals to set the wheels of government in motion. Thus there exist among the records of the king's chancery, exchequer, and other departments of government literally hundreds of documents to which Henry VI either set his personal seal or applied the royal 'RH' monogram. Occasionally, notes in the hand of his household servants appear to record direct involvement by Henry in the passage of some grant or other request: in July 1457, for instance, the chamberlain, Sir Thomas Stanley, scrawled upon a warrant granting a pension to one of the clerks of the avery 'The king has granted this.'[3] Was this evidence of Henry's personal involvement in the everyday business of kingship, of him exercising the royal grace – the most fundamental aspect of his vocation – or merely an administrative by-product of a chaotic system made worse by the 'king-shaped vacuum' at the heart of the polity?[4] It is certainly true that there is little among the administrative records that compares with Henry VII's annotations of his financial accounts or with Richard III's impassioned missives in his own hand to his supporters during Buckingham's Rebellion in 1483, yet the vagaries of archival survival are such that we should not preclude the possibility that such things once existed. Other official records, such as the Parliament

Rolls or minutes of council meetings, appear to record the king's personal intervention in matters of national importance. Yet these too, it has been argued, merely continued the fiction of royal government dependent on the proper functioning of the king as a personal monarch. On the other hand, the frequency with which he signed diplomatic documents and those related to his great educational foundations at Cambridge and Eton could be seen as testimony to his personal interest and involvement in those aspects of his rule.

The documentary record is therefore problematic, to say the least, and open to a number of possible readings. Yet, taken together and read in the context of Lancastrian kingship as a whole, it records the actions of a king who was neither mad nor uninterested in his vocation. The sources reveal a king who acted in accordance with a set of values that were recognisably Lancastrian; that is to say, Henry's actions were consistent with the political, religious, and cultural forms that had developed during the preceding century or so and had become associated with the House of Lancaster and its servants. These values, moreover, were broadly congruent with those of English political society at large. This book will reinterpret Henry's life and reign within this specifically Lancastrian context.

The verdict of history

Given the intractable and often partisan nature of the sources written during his lifetime, it is no surprise that subsequent assessments of Henry VI have differed widely. Yorkist authors writing during the reign of his usurper, Edward IV, were unsurprisingly negative in their judgement. The so-called *English Chronicle* stated simply that Henry failed in the basic requirements of effective rule; he was a king who 'held no household, nor maintained no wars', as a result of which 'the realm of England was out of all good governance'. Nevertheless, the author, like most of his contemporaries, hesitated from direct criticism of an anointed king and laid the principal blame instead on 'covetous counsel' and those self-interested courtiers and nobles who had exploited the hapless king.[5] By 1484, when Richard III arranged for Henry's body to be transferred from Chertsey Abbey to a more fitting tomb at Windsor, a picture had emerged of a king whose deep piety had made him ill suited to kingship, yet which nevertheless had left him largely guiltless in the civil wars of the 1450s and 1460s. By the time the Yorkist author of the *Crowland Chronicle* wrote his account in the mid 1480s Henry was widely revered as a saint 'by reason of the innocence of his life, his love of God and of the Church' and the many miracles performed at his tomb.[6] Henry VII tried unsuccessfully on more than one occasion to have his uncle canonised, and the image of Henry VI as a 'saintly muff' grew apace in the sixteenth century.[7] It is as such that he figured in the Tudor chronicles of Edward Hall and Raphael Holinshed and ultimately in Shakespeare's three-part history play that bears his name. In Shakespeare's work Henry was peripheral to the real action. His life was dominated by ambitious nobles, such as the duke of York, and by scheming and dangerous French women (in the persons of Joan of Arc and his queen, Margaret of Anjou), while the final part of the trilogy was designed principally to reveal the villainy of the future Richard III.

The image of the saintly Henry, the tragic victim of the Wars of the Roses, emerged virtually unscathed from the first decades of 'professional' academic history writing in the mid nineteenth century. William Stubbs, bishop of Oxford and the first Regius Professor of History at that university, considered Henry largely blameless in the catastrophe that afflicted England in the mid fifteenth century: 'he was without doubt most innocent of all the evils that befell England because of him'. The king was hard working, loyal, and, above all else, pious; only the frailties of his body and 'the germs of hereditary insanity' prevented him from carrying on 'the great Lancastrian traditions'. Yet Henry did manage to perpetuate some of the Lancastrian traditions of his ancestors: 'he was the last medieval king who attempted to rule England as a constitutional kingdom or commonwealth'.[8] Stubbs had more to say about the king than almost any of his contemporaries and Henry escaped the sort of detailed attention that saw multi-volume histories published of the reigns of his father and grandfather. It was not until 1922 that Mabel Christie published the first full-length biography of Henry VI. Christie marvelled that in the Middle Ages there should come to the throne

'a man so wholly devoid of self-seeking ambition, without a trace
of that bold and warlike spirit so much admired by his age, whose
sole aim seems to have been the practice of those virtues usually
known as the "fruits of the spirit" – charity, long-suffering,
gentleness, goodness, faith, meekness and temperance'. Henry's
fate was saintly indeed: he sacrificed himself for the good of the
country, for without his 'ruin' England would 'never have known
the strong, regenerating rule of the Tudors'.[9] A year after Christie's
biography, Cardinal Francis Gasquet, an English Benedictine and
Vatican librarian, published his *Religious Life of Henry VI*, which
drew heavily on the work of John Blacman. This was an unasham-
edly partisan account of Henry, designed more to make the case
for his canonisation than to offer any objective assessment of
his reign.[10] Whatever dubious merits these accounts had as works
of scholarship, the image of Henry VI they portrayed proved a
remarkably persistent one. Indeed, as late as the early 1970s serious attempts were still being made in English Catholic circles to
canonise the king.

In the mid twentieth century the Oxford academic K.B. McFarlane established a new orthodoxy for researching and writing on
the fifteenth century. McFarlane, and subsequent generations of
his students, transformed our understanding of late medieval
England, particularly with regard to the role of the nobility and
land-owning classes and the institutions and cultural assumptions
that conditioned their behaviour. It was McFarlane and his students
who were the first to explore systematically the copious archival
records of fifteenth-century England and to shift the focus of
their enquiries away from the king and towards the nobility. He
argued that the social and political system in late medieval England
was robust and had developed, over the centuries, into an effective
and reciprocal system of relationships between kings, their magnates, and lesser landowners. For McFarlane the crisis of the mid
fifteenth century did not arise from structural weakness, which
allowed 'overmighty subjects' to challenge the authority of the
crown, but revolved around the effectiveness of kingship as an
institution and, in particular, the inadequacies of Henry VI himself.
He brilliantly summed up this position in his 1964 lecture to the
British Academy: 'in fact only an undermighty ruler had anything
to fear from overmighty subjects, and if he was undermighty his

personal lack of fitness was the cause, not the weakness of his office and its resources'.[11]

McFarlane's legacy directly influenced the three most influential modern accounts of Henry VI's reign. In 1981 two major new studies of the king were published: Bertram Wolffe's *Henry VI* and Ralph Griffiths's *The Reign of King Henry VI*. Of the two, Griffiths (who had himself been taught by one of McFarlane's own students, Charles Ross) perhaps owed most to the 'McFarlane legacy'. At almost a thousand pages, *The Reign of King Henry VI* was a massive achievement and it placed Henry VI within the wider context of fifteenth-century government and politics, particularly the reciprocal obligations of service and patronage. For Griffiths, from at least 1437 Henry was a king who ruled as well as reigned. While happy to leave the minutiae of government to his advisors, he nevertheless took an active role in matters that concerned him: the French war, the foundation of his royal colleges at Eton and Cambridge, and, perhaps most controversially, the dispensation of patronage. From 1453, however, Henry's mental incapacity prevented him from exercising any real authority and the chaos that followed was largely due to the rival ambitions of the duke of York and Queen Margaret and her Lancastrian supporters. The portrait that emerges from Griffiths's account is of a king who essentially was 'well-meaning but lacking in judgement.'[12] Yet Griffiths also assumed that the majority of his counsellors, indeed the majority of his subjects, were self-serving and willing to exploit the opportunities for self-aggrandisement that a weak-willed king offered. Bertram Wolffe's Henry VI, on the other hand, was neither weak willed nor particularly well meaning. Wolffe identified a vindictive streak in his personality, apparent early on as he railed against the authority of his tutor, the earl of Warwick, and displayed later in his persecution of his uncle, the duke of Gloucester. He took issue with McFarlane's account of the king and instead presented Henry as being personally and actively responsible, through his ill-judged peace policy and disastrous intervention in the course of the war, for the Lancastrian defeat in France, and, ultimately, for the outbreak of civil war in the 1450s. Only after his illness of 1453–54 was Henry no longer the 'essential, unique feature of the reign'.[13] Of the two accounts of the reign, the more measured approach of Griffiths certainly met with more approval among his fellow historians; many rejected Wolffe's reading of key pieces of evidence that, he argued, demonstrated the king's personal direction of affairs, particularly during the 1440s.

McFarlane's image of Henry VI is most clearly visible in John Watts's *Henry VI and the Politics of Kingship*, published in 1996. Taking McFarlane's judgement that 'In Henry VI second childhood succeeded from the first without the usual interval', Watts considered Henry to be no king at all: he was 'inane', totally lacking the capacity for independent will, and 'a provenly useless person'.[14] The fiction that all government was made possible by the king's will was exactly that, a fiction. During the king's minority the lords cooperated in a broad council to maintain the pretence of princely rule; after 1436 this continued, largely successfully, and in the 1440s developed into a household-based system of government, maintained in large part by the efforts of William de la Pole, earl, later marquis and duke of Suffolk. Suffolk, however, was not the king and he was unable to offer the same impartial, supreme authority that was embodied in an active, ruling, adult king. Most importantly, he could not act as arbiter in the disputes between other magnates and landowners. The crisis of 1450, therefore, was principally domestic and constitutional and arose from a fracturing of the noble consensus that had maintained royal authority in the face of the king's evident and widely acknowledged inanity. Watts's account, while saying much on the political culture of late medieval England, the importance of the nobility, and an understanding of the duties of kingship based upon an extensive literature in the 'Mirror for Princes' genre, has not found general acceptance. For one, it demands that we accept every expression of the king's will found in contemporary documents to be part of an elaborate façade of royal authority. If Henry was really as non-existent as Watts would have us believe, then it surely would have been easier to depose him quickly and painlessly or maintain the fiction of a king ruling with a council than to suffer more than a decade of political strife and eventual civil war. Indeed, recent accounts of Henry's reign have attempted to establish an account of Henry that is far closer to that found in Wolffe than in Watts.[15]

Most recently, Katherine Lewis has offered a reading of the reigns of both Henry VI and his father based upon contemporary expectations of their gendered behaviour.[16] Did the success or otherwise of both kings' reigns depend on the way in which they conformed to widely understood norms of 'manly' behaviour? Lewis's work was influenced by recent studies of queenship, including some important recent work done on Henry's queen Margaret of Anjou, and a broader shift among historians towards cultural history and questions of representation.[17] She argues that Henry V exercised a 'hegemonic masculinity', exemplifying and defining contemporary notions of 'manliness' which were informed by discourses of chivalry, piety, and kingship. Henry VI, on the other hand, struggled with his masculinity, or, rather, contemporaries struggled to decide how to represent his masculinity (such as his sexual abstinence, which was at once evidence of his manly control of his urges, and problematic, as it prevented him from conceiving an heir). Because he came to the throne as a baby and was thus unable to test and prove his manhood as a youth, Henry proved impossible to fit into normative categories of contemporary masculine behaviour. While raising interesting questions about how fifteenth-century Englishmen understood concepts such as 'manliness', Lewis's work owes too much to existing interpretations of the two kings' relative effectiveness and perpetuates the idea that Henry VI was the antithesis to his father's exemplary model of kingship. The truth, as we shall see, was far more complicated than a simple 'good king/bad king' dichotomy. Henry VI's kingship can be properly understood only in the context of the peculiar nature of Lancastrian political culture.

Understanding Lancastrianism

Henry VI was the third Lancastrian king. His grandfather, Henry IV, had gained the throne in 1399 by deposing his cousin, Richard II. Henry IV (or Henry Bolingbroke as he was before his accession) claimed he had returned from exile that year to claim his recently deceased father's duchy of Lancaster and assert his position as the leading nobleman in the realm. However, his campaign to regain his duchy was quickly transformed into one to rid the realm of the tyranny of King Richard. Richard returned from campaign in Ireland to meet Bolingbroke's challenge and soon found himself imprisoned and forced to abdicate. He was subsequently starved to death in the Lancastrian stronghold of Pontefract Castle. The House of Lancaster thus came to the English throne as the self-appointed guardians of the English people against princely tyranny. The events of 1399 set a precedent that would continue to shape English politics throughout the fifteenth century.

The Lancastrian revolution created a paradox at the heart of English kingship that would have profound consequences for Henry VI and fifteenth-century England in general. The king was at once an anointed prince and, as the duke of Lancaster, a leading nobleman with estates the length and breadth of England. As the former, he represented the public authority of the crown, above and beyond the disputes of his subjects; as the latter, he was a private lord, managing estates and offering good lordship to his servants. Both Henry IV and V were determined to maintain this separation in theory and practice. The duchy of Lancaster estates were regarded as the personal property of the Lancastrian kings: in 1399 Henry IV declared that the duchy should in future be treated as 'if we had never assumed the ensign of royal dignity'.[18] Similarly, the relationship between the king/duke and servants of the duchy was a complex one. As duke, the king was expected to reward his affinity and offer them lordship, potentially advancing their suits over those of his other subjects. The Lancastrian kings were beholden to their servants in a way that was distinct from their royal predecessors; as Simon Walker observed, in the relationship between a servant and his lord, even when that lord was also king, 'one good turn deserved another'.[19] Moreover, as dukes of Lancaster the Lancastrian kings inherited a complex set of cultural values. These had emerged during the course of the fourteenth century, during which period successive earls and dukes of Lancaster had appropriated various political and religious traditions and discourses as their own.

By the time Henry VI acceded to the throne in 1422, we can identify key aspects of what we might usefully term 'Lancastrianism'. My understanding of 'Lancastrianism' is as fluid as that of the literary scholar Paul Strohm. It was certainly 'a shifting body of ambitions, grudging acceptances, and unrealized dreams; as erratically capable of imposing ideas, rallying support, and affecting historical consequences'.[20] Yet, by 1422 Lancastrianism had distilled into several distinct and relatively stable principles. These were: first, the concept of 'good government' drawing on a tradition that went back at least as far as the 1310s and Thomas of Lancaster; second, a dynastic loyalty built upon long-standing traditions of service in the households and affinity of the dukes of Lancaster and Lancastrian kings; third, a distinctive religious orthodoxy shaped by the spiritual practices of the Lancastrian kings and their closest servants; and, finally, an international ambition, realised through both war and diplomacy, that considered the House of Lancaster the equal to any princely house in Europe and, at times, made a distinction between the king/duke's personal dynastic ambitions and the policies and interests of the English crown. Thus Lancastrianism was a multi-faceted political, religious, and cultural project which could, and did, mean different things to different people. Together these ideas constituted a Lancastrian legacy that shaped and conditioned Henry VI's kingship throughout his reign.

No one aspect of Lancastrianism was distinctively novel, but the conjunction of these various positions under the Lancastrian kings at a time of political, cultural, religious, and economic upheaval resulted in a distinctively Lancastrian polity. The kings/ dukes, their servants, and, to a degree, their subjects could seize upon existing discourses and modes of representations, and appropriate and represent them in specifically Lancastrian contexts. Thus Thomas Hoccleve might have based his *Regement of Princes* (written for the future Henry V in 1411–12) on earlier Continental 'Mirrors' by Jacob de Cessolis and Giles of Rome and on the *Secreta Secretorum*, but his poem was written and, more importantly, read and understood in the specifically Lancastrian context of the political struggles between Henry IV and his son and the expectations upon Prince Henry as heir to the throne.[21] The peculiarly Lancastrian aspects of early fifteenth-century political culture, both in England and on the Continent, and how they shaped Henry VI's reign as king of England and France are the subject of the introductory chapters of this book.

Chapters 4 to 10 deal with Henry VI's life and reign. The king's early years are, of course, obscure. Very little evidence remains of his childhood and it was not until the crisis occasioned by Joan of Arc's galvanising effect on French resistance to the Lancastrian Dual Monarchy that Henry emerged centre stage. Chapter 5 deals with Henry's double coronation as king of France and England and his emergence as a ruling monarch in the wake of another military crisis in 1436. Chapters 6 and 7 deal with his majority rule from 1437 to 1450. Henry's commitment to peace and his religiosity are examined, as are the practical consequences of his rule in terms of patronage, law and order, and royal finance. Chapter 7 ends by discussing the disastrous defeat in France and the loss of Normandy in 1450 and its consequences for the regime constructed during the previous decade. Chapter 8 covers the years from 1450 to 1455, as the realm dealt with popular rebellion, the king's illness and the rise of Richard, duke of York, as the principal opponent of the regime. It ends with the first battle of St Albans, the first engagement in the conflict known as the Wars of the Roses. Chapter 9 examines the complicated events of the later 1450s, which saw successive attempts at reconciliation fail and the outbreak of war between the king and the Yorkist lords in 1459. It concludes with the battle of Towton and the deposition of Henry VI in March 1461. Chapter 10 examines the last decade of Henry's life, his exile in Scotland, imprisonment in the Tower of London, and the unlikely set of circumstances that saw his brief restoration to the throne in 1470–1, before his murder in April 1471. The final chapter deals with Henry's posthumous reputation. By the 1480s his failings as king had been largely forgotten, replaced by a popular veneration of him as a saint. His posthumous reputation reveals much about how the Lancastrian legacy survived the death of the last Lancastrian king.

There is little doubt that in all this Henry VI himself remains an elusive figure. He left no first-hand written testimony to explain his actions. His decisions, as recorded in the extensive records of royal government, were sometimes contradictory and even the extent to which they represented his own will is ambiguous. What we can be sure of, however, is that Henry operated within a cohesive set of political and cultural values and that these were shared by his closest servants and many of his subjects. By placing the reign within the context of Lancastrian norms and traditions, as they had developed over the preceding century, we can get closer to an understanding of 'perhaps the most unfortunate king who ever reigned'.[22]

Notes

1 M.A. Hicks, 'The Sources', in *The Wars of the Roses*, ed. A.J. Pollard (Basingstoke, 1995), 20–40.

2 See below, chapter 11.

3 TNA, C81/1466/40.

4 Michael Hicks, *The Wars of the Roses* (New Haven, CT, 2011), 77.

5 *An English Chronicle 1377–1461*, ed. W. Marx (Woodbridge, 2003), 79.

6 *Ingulph's Chronicle of the Abbey of Croyland with the Continuations*, ed. H.T. Riley (Rolls Series, 1854), 468.

7 Jack Lander, *Conflict and Stability in Fifteenth-Century England* (1969), 68.

8 W. Stubbs, *The Constitutional History of England* (3 vols, Oxford, 1897), iii. 134–5.

9 Mabel E. Christie, *Henry VI* (1922), 109–10.

10 Francis Gasquet, *The Religious Life of Henry VI* (1923).

11 K.B. McFarlane, 'The Wars of the Roses', in *England in the Fifteenth Century*, ed. G.L. Harriss (1981), 238–9.

12 R. Griffiths, *The Reign of King Henry VI* (1981), xxiv.

13 B.P. Wolffe, 'The Personal Rule of Henry VI', in *Fifteenth-Century England 1399–1509*, ed. S.B. Chrimes, C.D. Ross, and R.A. Griffiths (Manchester, 1972), 30; Wolffe, *Henry VI* (1981).

14 K.B. McFarlane, *The Nobility of Later Medieval England* (Oxford, 1973), 284; John Watts, *Henry VI and the Politics of Kingship* (Cambridge, 1996), 9, 135, 302.

15 Hicks, *Wars of the Roses*, 75–81.

16 Katherine J. Lewis, *Kingship and Masculinity in Late Medieval England* (2013).

17 Helen Maurer, *Margaret of Anjou: Queenship and Power in Late Medieval England* (Woodbridge, 2003); Joanna Laynesmith, *The Last Medieval Queens* (Oxford, 2004).

18 Helen Castor, *The King, the Crown and the Duchy of Lancaster; Public Authority and Private Power 1399–1461* (Cambridge, 2000), 4.

19 Simon Walker, *The Lancastrian Affinity 1361–1399* (Oxford, 1990), 9.

20 Paul Strohm, *England's Empty Throne: Usurpation and the Language of Legitimation 1399–1422* (New Haven, CT, 1998), xi–xii.

21 David Watt, 'Thomas Hoccleve's *Regiment of Princes*', in *A Companion to Fifteenth-Century English Poetry*, ed. Julia Boffey and A.S.G. Edwards (Cambridge, 2013), 47–58.

22 Stubbs, *Constitutional History*, iii. 134.

2 The Lancastrian legacy in England

Alone among post-Conquest kings of England, Henry VI had no conscious memory of anything other than being king. Unlike other child monarchs – Henry III, Edward III, Richard II, and Edward V – he had not known a time when he was merely heir apparent, a king in waiting.[1] Moreover, in very real terms (as opposed to the mere title claimed by English monarchs from 1337) Henry was also king of France; the Treaty of Troyes and the death of Charles VI in October 1422 ensured that he ruled over the dual Lancastrian monarchy before he was a year old. As king, Henry inherited a complex and contested Lancastrian legacy. His expectations, and those of his family, servants, and subjects, were conditioned not merely by generic medieval expectations of kingship, but by a jumble of sometimes contradictory legacies that were specifically Lancastrian. The reigns of Henry's father and grandfather had witnessed a rhetorical battle over the meaning of the Lancastrian political legacy, a struggle contested between the kings, their servants, and the wider realm. In an English context this revolved around two closely related issues: the nature and priorities of good government and the defence of the Church.

The Lancastrian inheritance

The domestic political legacy that Henry VI inherited had its origins more than a century earlier in the actions of Thomas, 2nd earl of Lancaster. Lancaster, eldest son of Edmund 'Crouchback' and grandson of Edward I, had emerged as the leader of the baronial opposition to Edward II. In 1310 he had presented a series of grievances to the king concerning royal finance, abuses such as purveyance (the compulsory purchase of foodstuffs for the royal household), and the reform of the king's household and council, which the following year had led to a set of Ordinances that sought to establish good government through a series of baronial restraints on royal power. After a decade-long struggle, Lancaster eventually found himself deserted by many of his followers and in open rebellion against King Edward. On 16 April 1322 he was defeated by royal forces at the battle of Boroughbridge and executed six days later at Pontefract.[2]

Even during his lifetime, Lancaster was identified with a political programme that challenged the tyranny of royal government. In 1312 the bishops had stated that the Ordinances were 'a remedy for the poor and oppressed' and Earl Thomas self-consciously pursued this agenda through parliament and through his office of steward of England. In 1321 he sponsored the writing of two tracts, one on the office of steward and, second, the famous *Modus Tenendi Parliamentum* ('The Manner of Holding a Parliament'). The *Modus* was a manifesto for parliamentary reform that would place some degree of power in the hands of the Commons, the 'middling people of the shire' who formed the bulwark of Lancaster's support.[3] This rhetoric grew in strength with Lancaster's death. Within weeks of his death, miracles were reportedly performed at his tomb in Pontefract and his cult was actively promoted from 1327 by the new king, Edward III. The hagiographical and liturgical material produced by devotees of Lancaster's cult reveals the outlines of a nascent political programme that we might term 'Lancastrianism'. Prayers for Thomas highlighted how he had died for the liberty of England's laws, for justice, and for the whole realm of England. Although Lancaster was never officially canonised by the pope, he was popularly regarded as a saint and his cult at Pontefract continued to draw pilgrims throughout the later Middle Ages.

The legacy of Thomas of Lancaster proved problematic in the last decades of the fourteenth century, both for King Richard II and for his uncle and chief councillor, John of Gaunt, 2nd duke of Lancaster. For Richard, Thomas presented a problematic figure who had challenged the rights of kings in an unpleasant echo of his own struggles against baronial opposition in the Merciless

Parliament of 1388. In this assembly the Lords Appellant, led by the king's uncle, Thomas, duke of Gloucester, and the earls of Arundel and Warwick, had presided over the execution and banishment of the king's closest advisors. It is no surprise that Richard instead championed the canonisation of Edward II. For Gaunt, however, Thomas was an ambiguous figure. While his support of his nephew's kingship at home and his own personal dynastic interests in Iberia may suggest that he had decided to ignore the domestic political legacy of his ancestor, Gaunt was too much of a politician, well aware of the devotion to Earl Thomas among his own affinity, to forgo the potential benefits that the Lancastrian legacy offered. Indeed, there is evidence that Gaunt sponsored a 'Lancastrian' version of history, circulated in manuscript as part of the widely read vernacular *Brut* chronicle, that highlighted the reforming programme of Earl Thomas.

The legacy of Thomas of Lancaster was embraced by Henry Bolingbroke, Gaunt's son and later King Henry IV. In 1387, while his father was out of the kingdom pursuing his dynastic interests in Spain, Bolingbroke joined the Lords Appellant in opposition to Richard II. This action earned the king's hatred, and in July 1397 Richard felt strong enough to move against the three senior Appellants. The remaining junior Appellants, Bolingbroke and Thomas Mowbray, earl of Nottingham, were allowed to continue at liberty (indeed Mowbray turned against his erstwhile allies and was probably responsible for the murder of Gloucester), but the following year the two men accused each other of treason. Richard's initial decision was that the matter be settled by combat, but this was later changed to banishment from the realm, Bolingbroke for ten years and Mowbray for life. Bolingbroke left England for Paris in October 1398 and in February the following year his father, Gaunt, died. On 20 March Richard revoked the letters allowing him livery of his father's lands while in exile, in effect enacting his revenge and disinheriting Bolingbroke of his Lancastrian inheritance. In exile Henry made a secret treaty with Louis, duke of Orléans (who governed France during the madness of his brother, King Charles VI), and on 4 July 1399 he landed at Ravenspur in Yorkshire while Richard was in Ireland with most of his lords and supporters. It is unclear whether initially he meant only to recover his duchy or to seize the throne, but the stress on his office of steward of England in his treaty with the French makes clear his awareness of the political legacy of Thomas of Lancaster. Richard returned to England at the end of July but found his support collapsing. On 16 August Richard received Henry at Flint castle and there, apparently with promises of his life, he appears to have submitted to his cousin. With the king safely lodged in the Tower of London, on 30 September, before the assembled Lords and Commons, it was announced that Richard had resigned the throne 'with a cheerful expression' in favour of his cousin. Henry Bolingbroke then assumed the throne, stating:

> In the name of Father, Son, and Holy Ghost, I Henry of Lancaster claim this realm of England, and the crown with all its members and its appurtenances, inasmuch as I am descended by right line of the blood from the good lord King Henry the third, and through that right that God in his grace has sent me, with the help of my kin and of my friends in recovering it; which realm was at the point of ruin for lack of governance and destruction of the good laws.[4]

Henry Percy, earl of Northumberland, and the experienced Lancastrian servant, John Norbury, now treasurer of England, then asked if parliament would accept Henry as their king, to which they unanimously gave their assent.

Henry IV's claim to the throne was tenuous at best. He had initiated searches throughout the realm's monastic archives to establish that Edmund 'Crouchback', earl of Lancaster, had been in fact the eldest son of Henry III. These had, however, confirmed that Edward I, great-great grandfather to Richard II, had indeed been the rightful heir. Henry's hereditary claim as made in parliament was thus a feeble one, based on that of his mother, Blanche of Lancaster. Nevertheless, his descent from John of Gaunt, Edward III's third son, gave him a stronger title if we accept that Edward had entailed the crown in the male line in 1376. Yet his implicit acknowledgement of descent through the female line left open the stronger claim of the Mortimer family, descended from Edward III's second son, Lionel of Clarence, and his daughter, Philippa. The weakness of Henry's dynastic claim was evident in the fact that on no fewer than four occasions in the first seven years of his reign he was forced to confirm and strengthen the Lancastrian succession by Act of Parliament. The usurpation was therefore also necessarily marked by an assertion of Lancastrian political principles. Just as Thomas of Lancaster had struggled against the misgovernment of Edward II, Henry had saved the realm of England from the misgovernment and tyranny of Richard. Richard had ruled in disregard of the laws of England (or so the Articles of Deposition claimed), and Henry's promise to respect them, while drawing on a widely known Lancastrian legacy, also masked the revolutionary and violent nature of the deposition. Indeed, Henry's statement made explicit the ambiguous nature of his claim: was he king by virtue of lineal descent from Henry III or by election, having saved the realm from tyranny? This ambiguity soon manifested itself in political crisis. Parliament, although counting many Lancastrian servants among both the Lords and the Commons, imposed financial restraints upon the crown and sought to limit Henry's freedom in matters of patronage. More seriously, within a year of his accession, Owain Glyn Dŵr, a descendant of the native thirteenth-century princes of Wales, led a major rebellion against the king. This was followed by war with Scotland in 1402, and in the next year the king's erstwhile Percy allies joined Glyn Dŵr in revolt.

The dominant theme of domestic political discourse during the ensuing two decades was therefore to establish the legitimate foundations of Lancastrian rule. How could the Lancastrians kings square the violent and illegitimate nature of the usurpation with a Lancastrian legacy that upheld law, justice, and truth? How could they assert their own view of Lancastrian kingship in the face of competing expectations, both within their own extended *familia* and within the domestic polity as a whole?

The Lancastrian legacy and the Commons

Thomas of Lancaster was, by the end of the fourteenth century, an overwhelmingly popular figure, drawing devotees from all sectors of society, but especially among those who had ties of service to the House of Lancaster. The large Lancastrian affinity was spread throughout the realm, indeed there were only seven counties in England in which the duchy of Lancaster did not own at least one manor. This affinity had served John of Gaunt in both peace and war and helped to ensure his domestic political power even when he was out of the realm. In 1399 Henry Bolingbroke had come to the throne at the head of what was, in effect, a political faction. His closest supporters were men who had served his father. On his accession, the baronial household became the royal household and took over some of the key positions of government. Henry's political debt to his father's supporters was evident in the large number of annuities granted to Lancastrian servants from royal coffers in the early years of the reign and extravagant spending on the royal household, and this led to clashes between the king and Commons in the parliaments of 1401, 1404, and 1406. Yet, despite the tensions and the well-publicised arguments, these parliaments were largely sympathetic to the king and there sat among the Commons large numbers of Lancastrian supporters. The apparently turbulent parliamentary politics of the first decade of Lancastrian rule therefore are testimony to the contested nature of Lancastrianism itself. In effect, Henry had announced the criteria of kingship upon which he would be judged – the proper administration of justice, financial prudence, and the more ambiguous concept of 'good government' – and his servants held him to account. As early as May 1402 proclamations reminded people 'that it always had been and will be the king's intention that the common profit and laws and customs of the realm shall be observed and kept'.[5] As we shall see, this popular aspect of Lancastrianism sat ill with other developing aspects of Lancastrian kingship, but the accountability of Henry IV and his successors was a defining feature of their rule that, in part, mitigated their usurpation and that emerged directly from the legacy of Thomas of Lancaster.

The accountability of Lancastrian kings to their 'public' and the extent to which they entered into dialogue about the duties and nature of government has been an important theme in recent scholarship. This dialogue was carried on in parliament, in Westminster and in the localities through formal debate, as well as through the chatter and gossip that was fuelled by official and non-official newsletters, proclamations, and other sources. It was also carried on through what we might term 'Lancastrian literature' and, especially, poetry. As Jenni Nuttall has observed, this 'Lancastrian literature reminds the Lancastrian dynasty of its linguistic origins in order to demonstrate how it has broken its promises, fallen short of expectations or changed its priorities'.[6] Rather than being apologists or propagandists for the regime, writers like Thomas Hoccleve and John Lydgate were in dialogue both with their princely patrons and with a wider Lancastrian readership, offering advice, praising successes, extolling the virtues of their kings, and reminding their readers of the moral and historical obligations of the House of Lancaster. Moreover, this dialogue was conducted in English, allowing all levels of political society to conduct debate using a lexicon of mutually understandable terms. It is no coincidence that the proceedings of Richard II's deposition in the 1399 parliament were recorded in English, nor that Henry IV patronised vernacular poets, such as John Gower, Thomas Chaucer and Thomas Hoccleve. Henry V advanced this 'Lancastrian language policy' further through the increasing use of English in government: as the Brewers' Guild of London explained, Henry V 'hath in his letters missive and divers affairs touching his own person, more willingly chosen to declare the secrets of his will, for the better understanding of the people' by his sponsorship of the English language.[7] This apparently official support for English may reflect the Lancastrian regime's continuing search for legitimacy. In the wake of Richard's deposition an appeal to the Commons both mitigated the act of usurpation itself and nullified the suspicion that Henry had come to the throne at the head of a narrow political faction. Yet it also introduced a degree of debate into the business of kingship, forcing the Lancastrian kings to submit their rule to the approbation of their servants and of the wider political nation to a far greater extent than their predecessors.

A number of Lancastrian texts from the first two decades of the fifteenth century highlight how the crown's domestic policies were subject to the scrutiny of poets and their readers. To begin with, writers such as the anonymous authors of *Richard the Redeless* and *Mom and the Soothsegger* critiqued Richard's kingship while obliquely offering advice to the current ruler. Yet these texts also offered explicit criteria with which to judge Henry IV's own practice of kingship. Thus criticisms of Richard's household had particular resonance in the mid 1400s, when Henry's lavish expenditure on his own household and the unruly behaviour of the king's servants were a cause for concern for parliament and contemporary chroniclers.[8] Equally, Thomas Hoccleve in his *Regement of Princes*, an advice poem dedicated to Prince Henry and completed between 1410 and 1411, underlined the need for princes to be both liberal in their patronage and responsible in their collection and expenditure of taxation, recognising a debate that had raged throughout the first decade of Lancastrian rule. More radically, perhaps, Hoccleve attempted to define his own version of Lancastrianism, overcoming the trauma of the usurpation by conveniently forgetting Henry IV in his list of princely exemplars and instead eulogising Prince Henry's more illustrious ancestors, Henry of Grosmont, 1st duke of Lancaster, Edward III, and John of Gaunt. Hoccleve also stressed the public nature of Lancastrian kingship, urging Prince Henry to 'win your people's voice'.[9]

There is other evidence to suggest the importance of 'your people's voice' to the politics of early Lancastrian England. In the first years of Henry IV's reign there was a widespread and cogent opposition to the Lancastrian regime that frequently used the language and ideas promoted in official discourse to question the efficiency and even legitimacy of royal government. Often this discontent took the form of expressing unease over the nature of the usurpation itself, but it also judged the government on the degree to which it had fulfilled the promises made in 1399. One such promise was Henry's commitment to 'live off his own', not to tax his subjects unnecessarily for the ordinary expenses of his household and the government. Thus demands for taxation in the first years of the reign were met with popular resistance in Chester, the South-West and in London: one London critic of the regime claimed in 1403 that the rebellious Henry Percy came 'for you and for me, in order to stop the taxes and the tallages' and reminded his listeners that on his accession Henry had promised not to levy further impositions. This sense of unease with the new Lancastrian government crystallised around rumours that Richard II was still alive and would return to reclaim his throne. Rumours of the 'hidden king', the lost ruler who would return to rescue his subjects from tyranny or oppression, were a commonplace in late medieval Europe, but the Ricardian rumours in the first decade of Lancastrian regime had a distinct character. First, they do not seem to have coalesced around an individual widely regarded as the lost king (the pretender briefly supported by the duke of Albany in Scotland appears to have convinced no one), and, second, the *ersatz* Richard had no definite political programme, merely serving as an idea around which criticism of the regime could form. The crown's initial response to popular criticism of its policies was 'wary but ultimately indulgent'. While it did occasionally respond with violence – as in 1401, when a Canterbury scrivener lost his tongue and right hand for circulating libellous bills against the king – accusations of treason were more often met with acquittals or pardons.[10] Moreover, popular dissent was part of a political discourse that in itself shaped the nature of the Lancastrian regime. Indeed, part of the appeal of the Ricardian rumour was that it allowed opposition to the crown to be voiced in a way that was potentially less dangerous than allying with actual rebels, like Thomas Percy or Owain Glyn Dŵr.

The popular opposition to and debate with the Lancastrian regime in the early years of Henry IV's reign reached a climax in 1405 with the rebellion of Richard Scrope, archbishop of York. On 26 May Archbishop Scrope, joined by the Earl Marshall of England, Thomas Mowbray, led a body of York citizens and clergy to Shipton Moor in armed rebellion against the king. They were working in concert with the rebellious earl of Northumberland, but the success of Scrope's rising was fatally compromised by the former's failure to capture the king's leading lieutenant in the north, Ralph Neville, 1st earl of Westmorland. After three days on the moor, Scrope submitted to Westmorland and on 8 June, on the direct orders of the king himself, the archbishop was beheaded. Traditionally, historians have seen Scrope's actions as linked to the selfish motivations of Northumberland in rebelling against the king; the hapless archbishop was the victim of 'the self-seeking lords with whom he misguidedly decided to make common cause'. In fact Scrope, hitherto a loyal servant of the crown, probably saw himself as interlocutor between the Commons and the king, representing the justified grievances of Henry's subjects in a language that the crown would recognise and respond to. He published, in English, a manifesto, nailed on church doors and to the gates of the city of York, calling for a freely elected parliament to discuss the burden of taxation both on the clergy and the laity, the restoration of certain lords (including Thomas Mowbray) who had been denied their lands and title by the crown, and the punishment of those individuals who had put their own advantage before the common good. In other words, Scrope's demands echoed the principles of good government that were the foundation of Lancastrian legitimacy.[11]

The crown's response to Scrope's rebellion, and to the popular opposition it experienced in the opening decade of the fifteenth century, reveals how the Lancastrian legacy was constructed through a process of negotiation between the crown and its subjects. Within weeks of Scrope's death miracles began to occur at his tomb in York Minster, and a fully fledged cult soon developed. Rather than try to fully extinguish this devotion to a traitor and rebel, the Lancastrian regime sought to control it and meld it to its own purposes. In September 1405 the king's son, John, was instructed to ensure that the temporary wooden barriers around the tomb were replaced with more permanent ones to better control the flow of pilgrims. By 1408, when Pope Gregory XII absolved those involved in the archbishop's execution, Scrope's popularity had not diminished and in the following year the crown abandoned trying to prevent offerings at his shrine. Indeed, Henry V appears to have accepted Scrope in his proffered role as petitioner to the crown, formally allowing offerings to be made to the dead archbishop, and during the episcopacy of Henry Bowet (1407–23) even Lancastrian livery collars of 'SS' were presented at the shrine.[12] As well as Archbishop Scrope, the reign of Henry V also saw a rehabilitation of Richard II. One of Henry's first acts as king was to re-inter Richard in Westminster Abbey in December 1413. The reburial rivalled the interment of the king's natural father at Canterbury cathedral in terms of cost and significance. Contemporary chroniclers noted the personal affection Henry had for the former king, in whose household he had lived briefly both before Richard became king and also for the last year or so of the reign. Yet the reburial also had symbolic importance. It sought to distance the new king from the violence of his father's usurpation and, by recognising the wrongs committed, establish a new legitimacy for the Lancastrian regime.[13] Even so, Lancastrian writers remained committed to reminding Henry V of the obligations of rule, carrying on a debate with the king and their wider community of Lancastrian readers, couched in the familiar discourse of good government.

One such text was *Crowned King*, a short, anonymous, alliterative poem probably written on the eve of Henry V's expedition to France in 1415. In it a cleric addresses the king, reminding him of his duties to rule justly, to listen to wise counsel, to value the contributions both fiscal and otherwise that the commons make, to reward his servants fairly and as promised, and, above all else, that the king should not covet his subjects' wealth. Henry, apparently, took this advice to heart. His progress of 1421, when a financially and emotionally exhausted realm was about to be asked for yet more taxes to fund the French war, demonstrated, by explicit displays of piety and the dispensation of justice, that Henry was an exemplary monarch, keeping the covenant with his people to govern justly and wisely for the common good.[14] By 1422 Lancastrian legitimacy and rule were secure. Yet it had come at a price that would have important repercussions for the reign of Henry VI. Acceptance of Lancastrian rule and submission to royal authority had been achieved through convincing political society in its widest sense that the regime had lived up to the principles and standards which it had set itself. This was achieved not through simplistic propaganda nor through oppression, but by a complex negotiation of the meaning of the Lancastrian legacy between kings, poets, chroniclers, and the public that was contested and ongoing and that continually demanded an aggressive assertion of royal authority that the king had fulfilled his obligation to rule and govern well.

The Lancastrian legacy and the Church

One way in which the Lancastrian regime continually attempted to assert its legitimacy in the first two decades of the fifteenth century was through conspicuous displays of piety and orthodoxy. The defence of the Church was one of the three main obligations of kingship, as defined in successive coronation oaths throughout the Middle Ages. Henry IV and Henry V, however, took this further, claiming for themselves a new role as the defenders of the Church and realm against the dangers of heresy. As with their political legacy, this drew on established traditions within the Lancastrian family and wider affinity, and it was subject to the same scrutiny and dialogue with their servants and the wider polity as were their more secular concerns.

Since the middle of the fourteenth century conspicuous displays of piety had been an important feature of Lancastrianism. Henry of Grosmont, 1st duke of Lancaster and John of Gaunt's father-in-law, had been explicit in his devotion to Thomas of Lancaster and in 1355 he had established a chantry chapel in St John's Priory, Pontefract, to serve as 'a shrine for the patron and protector of the Lancastrian cause'. More importantly perhaps, two years earlier he had greatly enlarged the hospital and collegiate church of St Mary Newarke in Leicester (originally founded in 1330 by his father, Earl Henry). This became the spiritual home of the Lancastrian affinity during the second half of the fourteenth century and it benefitted from the patronage of John of Gaunt and his retainers alike. The hospital and chantry were at the heart of what Simon Walker has called 'an identifiable devotional style', focused on funerary austerity, penitential rhetoric and ostentatious works of charity. A survey of Lancastrian wills in the last decades of the fourteenth century has revealed that Gaunt's retainers were some five times more likely to provide relief to the poor or the infirm than their fellow members of the gentry.[15] In eschewing the pomp of lavish funerals, in seeking to perform works of charity, and in their ownership of personal devotional material, members of the Lancastrian affinity had many similarities with developing trends in lay piety and with their radical, and heretical, contemporaries the Lollards. Yet Lancastrian devotional practice was also self-consciously public, in as much as it favoured works of charity designed to provide tangible benefits to the common good in this life as well as to benefit the souls of the departed, and through chantry chapels and prayers for the dead it gave the Lancastrian affinity a cohesion beyond the grave.

From 1399 Lancastrian piety took on a different dynamic as first Henry IV, then Henry V, sought to employ religion in the regime's search for legitimacy. From the beginning of the reign, Henry IV demonstrated his religious credentials, combining Lancastrian tradition with an astute political awareness, to assert a new, sacral character to English kingship. According to John Gower, on his landing at Ravenspur in July 1399 Bolingbroke immediately 'worshipped God on bended knee, and first prayed with devotions of sincere intent', asking for divine support for his cause.[16] His coronation in September that year was marked by his anointment with the Holy Oil of St Thomas Becket, rediscovered, so legend had it, by Henry of Grosmont. This was a ritual for which Richard II had failed conspicuously to gain papal approval. In 1401 Henry demonstrated his awareness of the symbolic importance of Lancastrian devotional practice when he presented a set of bright-blue vestments to St George's Chapel, Windsor, with an orphrey depicting the life of Thomas of Lancaster.[17] These robes reminded the Garter Knights that they, like Thomas, were knights in God's cause as well as paragons of secular chivalry. Henry appears to have taken his piety seriously. He regularly employed Carmelite friars as confessors and preachers, an order that had, through his mother and grandfather, long-standing Lancastrian connections. Indeed, the frequency with which friars, usually Carmelite, but also Dominicans and Augustinians, preached to the royal household in the early years of Henry's reign suggests a king eager to instil a degree of religious orthodoxy at the centre of political life.[18]

The religious legacy of the first two Lancastrian kings owed much, of course, to the regime's relationship with the Lollards. The Lollards were originally the followers of the Oxford theologian John Wyclif, who had been condemned as a heretic before his death in 1384. The Wycliffites (or Lollards as they were known from the early 1380s) denied the miracle of Transubstantiation, argued for the central authority of scripture in Christian life, questioned the role of priests as meditators between Christ and the laity, and, by the 1390s, called for the disendowment of church lands. On 2 March 1401, while the king was embroiled in a difficult parliament which argued over the Commons' right to redress of grievances before the granting of taxation, the relapsed heretic William Sawtre was burned at Smithfield. Eight days later, parliament passed the statute *de heretico comburendo* ('On the burning of a heretic'), which ordered the church authorities to pass the most obdurate heretics to the secular authorities to be burned. The burning of heretics was nothing new in Europe, or even in England, but the king's personal involvement should be seen as an expression of the new-found Lancastrian royal orthodoxy. Even though the petition asking that Lollards receive 'such judgment as they deserve, as an example to others of that evil sect' originated from the Commons, the king certainly took the initiative, and his writ of 26 February authorising Sawtre's execution was a clear statement of royal intent. In the 'Long Parliament' of 1406 a further statute was aimed at Lollard laymen who called for the confiscation of church lands and, by coupling them with clergy who preached that Richard II was still alive, crucially linked sedition with heresy.[19]

Despite the legislation of 1401 and 1406, the Lancastrian regime's attitude to Lollardy was ambiguous in the years before 1414. There was no concerted attempt to find and destroy Lollards and, in fact, only one other individual, John Badby, was burned for heresy in Henry IV's reign. Badby's execution in 1410 afforded another opportunity for the Lancastrian regime, on this occasion in the person of Prince Henry, to demonstrate its commitment to orthodoxy and justice. On 5 March Badby was burned at Smithfield for repeatedly denying the miracle of Transubstantiation; Prince Henry was present and may have reasoned and pleaded with the condemned man to recant his heresy and save himself from the flames. Indeed, Thomas Hoccleve in his *Regement of Princes* praised the prince for the interest he took for Badby's soul and described 'his pitous lamentacioun/ Whan that this renegat nat wolde blynne/ Of the stynkynge errour that he was ynne' (ll. 299–301). Prince Henry's willingness to engage with Lollards and his apparent attempt to reason them out of their error hints at potential sympathies between the Lollards and the wider Lancastrian affinity. It is clear that in the late fourteenth century important members of the landowning classes sympathised with the Wycliffite programme of reform. This probably extended beyond the narrow circle of 'Lollard knights' identified by contemporary chroniclers and studied by K.B. McFarlane. While there is nothing to suggest that this group was 'Lancastrian' as such, religious reform, in the shape of vernacular devotional guides, preaching, and even the translation of the Bible into English, was certainly actively supported by both laymen and clergy with connections to the Lancastrian regime in the first decade of the fifteenth century. The aim of men like Henry, Lord Fitzhugh (one of Henry IV's household knights and subsequently chamberlain to Henry V), Robert Hallum, bishop of Salisbury (1407–17), or Thomas Broun (chancellor to Archbishop Chichele) was not merely one of conservative reaction to the Lollard heresy, but aimed to shape the developing character of public worship in a way that did not threaten the stability of either the Church or government.[20] Moreover, there appears to have been support for some elements of the Lollard programme among the Commons in Henry IV's parliaments. Lollard calls for disendowment had been echoed in texts that had circulated around parliament in the 1380s and 1390s, but in the parliament of 1410 (or possibly earlier in the 1407 assembly) the so-called 'Lollard Disendowment Bill' may have been presented formally as a petition by the Commons.[21]

Any ambiguities in the Lancastrian attitude to Lollardy, however, were extinguished by Oldcastle's Revolt of 1414. Sir John Oldcastle was a Herefordshire knight who had long-standing connections to Lollardy. During Henry IV's reign he had distinguished himself in service against the Welsh rebels, sat among the Commons in the parliament of 1404, and from 1410 was summoned to parliament in the right of his wife, the Kentish heiress Joan, granddaughter of John, 3rd Lord Cobham. Prince Henry knew him personally and in 1411 he served in the expedition sent to France by the prince to assist the Burgundians against the Orléanists. Shortly after Henry V's accession Oldcastle was summoned to answer Archbishop Arundel in the king's presence at Kennington regarding his ownership of heretical books. Eventually Oldcastle was accused and found guilty of heresy and committed to the Tower of London, from where he escaped on 19 October. Oldcastle then attempted to rally support and plotted to seize the king. The authorities, however, got wind of the plot and when the rebels assembled at St Giles's Field, just outside London, on 9–10 January 1414 the king's men lay in wait for them. Over forty rebels were executed and many more, some with well-documented Lancastrian credentials, were pardoned, but Oldcastle himself escaped. He remained on the run until November 1417, when he was captured on the Welsh border before being returned to London for execution. Despite the geographical and social range of his supporters, Oldcastle's 'rebellion' was never a serious threat to the survival of the Lancastrian regime, but it did reinforce the link between Lollardy and treason.[22] Indeed, the earl of Cambridge was accused of enlisting the help of Lollards during the potentially more serious Southampton Plot of 1415. Oldcastle's fate, especially given his previous service to the crown, thus made support for

Lollardy incompatible with loyalty to the Lancastrian regime and had the effect of, implicitly at least, enlisting the political classes in the increasingly orthodox piety of the king and court. Indeed, the Leicester Parliament of April 1414 passed a statute that obliged all royal office holders to report heretics to the ecclesiastical authorities.

The remainder of Henry V's reign saw the development of a princely piety that would shape the character of Lancastrian devotional practice well into the reign of his son. Perhaps the most explicit statement of Henry's commitment to orthodoxy was his foundation in 1415 of two religious houses: a Carthusian monastery for forty monks at Sheen and a Bridgettine house at Syon. The latter foundation was innovative – it consisted of a community of nuns tended spiritually by a smaller group of monks who lived nearby – and probably owed much to the visit of Henry, Lord Fitzhugh, later the king's chamberlain, to the order's mother house at Vadstena in Sweden. The Carthusian house, on the other hand, emerged as a powerhouse of liturgical and devotional scholarship, while its inmates served as confessors for members of the Lancastrian court. The rigour and devotion that characterised the rule of both houses served as an exemplar not just for Henry V's household, but for the wider Lancastrian Church as a whole. Indeed, in 1421 the king appears to have begun plans for a wholesale reform of the monastic life in England and of the large Benedictine houses in particular. Before his death, Henry put forward thirteen proposals for the reform of monastic life (largely calling for stricter observance of existing rules). These were rejected by a committee comprising the dean of the Chapel Royal and representatives from various monastic orders, who in turn agreed upon an alternative set of recommendations.[23]

Another expression of Henry V's piety was the reform of worship within the king's own household. The Chapel Royal, the private chapel attached to the king's chamber, took on a more public, symbolic function, serving as an exemplar of Lancastrian devotional practice as well as ministering to the spiritual needs of the king and his household. One of the best-documented features of this is the importance of music in the liturgy: this was at once an expression of a growing appreciation of the 'beauty of holiness' and a means to impress visitors. In August 1415 a captured

French priest was taken to a service in the Chapel Royal near Harfleur and was 'astonished to hear such beautiful music'.[24] These practices spread out from the king and were reinforced by the Lancastrian episcopate. Archbishop Chichele's encouragement of the adoption of the Sarum Use as the standard liturgy throughout the southern province of the English Church is one example. Equally, the adoption of new national feast days, such as those for St George on 23 April and St John of Beverley (a Lancastrian patron saint of sorts through his association with Thomas of Lancaster) on 25 October, reinforced Lancastrian devotional practice, encouraged the idea of the king as *miles Christi* (Christ's knight), and made explicit the celestial intervention that had resulted in Henry's victories in France. Henry's piety and his almost messianic status were also highlighted in the triumphal procession through London to celebrate the victory at Agincourt and to welcome Queen Catherine to England in 1421.

Given the centrality of religious devotion to the self-fashioning of the House of Lancaster, it is no surprise that several contemporaries remarked upon Henry V's 'priestliness'. The French astrologer Jean Fusoris remarked that while Henry's brother, Thomas, duke of Clarence, was warrior-like, the king himself was more like a priest.[25] Significantly, the Lancastrian authors who did so much to shape the dialogue between the Lancastrian kings, their servants, and the wider public also stressed this side of his personality. Thomas Hoccleve, on the king's accession, had urged him to 'Be Holy chirches Champioun eek ay;/ Susteene hir right; souffre no thyng to be doon be/ In preiudice of hir ...' (ll. 22–24), while he exhorted the king and his Garter Knights to rally against their common enemy, not the French, but 'heresies bittir galle' (in other words, the poison of heresy).[26] The king's subjects also had the opportunity to witness Henry's piety at first hand in 1421. The royal progress undertaken between February and April that year, principally designed to raise loans for another campaign in France amidst growing murmurs of discontent, involved visits to various shrines and religious houses. Contemporary chroniclers likened the progress to a pilgrimage and carefully glossed over the financial imperative.[27] Yet the king's actions reveal a crucial aspect of the legacy he left his son: in meeting his 'public', in reinforcing the bonds of loyalty and obligation strained by the war in France,

Henry V chose to indulge in conspicuous displays of piety that were every bit as important and recognisably 'Lancastrian' to his subjects as the exemplary justice he executed, the petitions he heard, and the loans he negotiated.

Conclusion

Henry VI inherited a domestic political legacy that was conspicuously Lancastrian in character. Its two main features – a public commitment to principles of good government and an equally public piety and commitment to religious orthodoxy – had been the means by which his grandfather and father had negotiated the dangerous legacy of the revolution of 1399. Through these strategies the Lancastrian kings had, by 1422, largely won the battle for legitimacy that had dogged the first two decades of their rule. They had achieved this in part by appropriating existing political, cultural, and religious discourses and stamping them with a distinctively Lancastrian identity. Thus complaints about purveyance and systematic abuse by royal officials had been a mainstay of popular complaint throughout the later Middle Ages. The Lancastrians, both the king and his servants, also identified them as problems and collectively offered remedies. Equally, in terms of religion the Lancastrians identified themselves with popular fashions and intellectual traditions that existed with late medieval English and Continental religious practice and in so doing imbued them with an explicitly Lancastrian identity.

Moreover, the Lancastrian earls, dukes, and kings had also achieved this by skilfully deploying their own princely authority and the abilities of poets, chroniclers, and a loyal affinity of Lancastrian servants. Yet, following the revolution of 1399 the Lancastrian kings found their position as both lord and prince a problematic one. Populism and flirtations with radical religious and political positions were easier when you were simply the earl or duke of Lancaster. Thus both Henry IV and Henry V had found themselves in dialogue, often contentious, with their supporters and the wider public, often having to explain and justify their policies and actions to opponents and critics within their own affinity as well as the wider polity. The real significance of the domestic Lancastrian legacy for the infant Henry VI was that his kingship and government were open to wider and deeper scrutiny than ever before.

Notes

1 R.A. Griffiths, *The Reign of Henry VI* (2nd edn, Stroud, 1998), 1.
2 J.R. Maddicott, 'Thomas of Lancaster (c.1278–1322)', in *Oxford Dictionary of National Biography*, liv, 288–95.
3 J.R. Maddicott, *Thomas of Lancaster, 1307–1322* (Oxford, 1970), 288–92; Danna Piroyansky, *Martyrs in the Making: Political Martyrdom in Late Medieval England* (Basingstoke, 2008), 23–48.
4 *PROME*, viii. 25.
5 *Calendar of Patent Rolls, 1401–1405*, 126.
6 Jenni Nuttall, *The Creation of Lancastrian Kingship: Literature, Language and Politics in Late Medieval England* (Cambridge, 2007), 120.
7 John H. Fisher, 'A Language Policy for Lancastrian England', *Proceedings of the Modern Language Association*, 107 (1992), 1168–80.
8 Nuttall, *Lancastrian Kingship*, 17–54.
9 Paul Strohm, 'Hoccleve, Lydgate and the Lancastrian Court', in *The Cambridge History of English Medieval Literature*, ed. David Wallace (Cambridge, 2002), 640–61.
10 Simon Walker, 'Rumour, Sedition and Popular Protest in the Reign of Henry IV', *Past and Present*, 166 (2000), 31–65.
11 Simon Walker, 'The Yorkshire Risings of 1405: Texts and Contexts', in *Henry IV: The Establishment of a Regime, 1399–1406*, ed. Doug Biggs and Gwilym Dodd (Woodbridge, 2003), 161–84.
12 Piroyansky, *Martyrs in the Making*, 49–73.
13 Paul Strohm, *England's Empty Throne: Usurpation and the Language of Legitimation 1399–1422* (New Haven, CT, 1998), xi–xii.
14 Derek Pearsall, 'Crowned King: War and Peace in 1415', in *The Lancastrian Court*, ed. Jenny Stratford (Donington, 2003), 163–72; *The Piers Plowman Tradition*, ed. Helen Barr (1993), 203–10.
15 Simon Walker, *The Lancastrian Affinity 1361–1399* (Oxford, 1990), 97–101.
16 John Gower, '*Cronica Tripertita*', in *Poems on Contemporary Events: The* Visio Anglie *(1381) and* Cronica tripertita *(1400)*, ed. David R. Carlson (Toronto, 2011).
17 Piroyansky, *Martyrs in the Making*, 41.
18 Debbie Colding, 'Henry IV and Personal Piety', *History Today*, 57 (2007), 23–9.
19 Peter McNiven, *Heresy and Politics in the Reign of Henry IV* (Woodbridge, 1987), 100–4.
20 Jeremy Catto, 'Religious Change under Henry V', in *Henry V: The Practice of Kingship*, ed. Gerald Harriss (Oxford, 1985), 97–116.
21 Wendy Scase, *Literature and Complaint in England 1272–1553* (Cambridge, 2007), 87–101.
22 Maureen Jurkowski, 'Henry V's Suppression of the Oldcastle Revolt', in *Henry V: New Interpretations*, ed. Gwilym Dodd (Woodbridge, 2013), 103–30.

23 Christopher Allmand, *Henry V* (1992), 272–9.
24 Ian Mortimer, *1415: Henry V's Year of Glory* (2009), 347.
25 Ibid., 515–16.
26 Strohm, 'Hoccleve, Lydgate and the Lancastrian Court', 646–7.
27 James A. Doig, 'Propaganda and Truth: Henry V's Royal Progress in 1421', *Nottingham Medieval Studies*, 40 (1996), 167–79.

3   The Lancastrian legacy

War and diplomacy

When Henry VI acceded to the English throne in September 1422 he was not merely king of England and heir to the French throne. He was a European prince of the first rank, whose inheritance had been shaped as much by the personal dynastic ambitions of his father, grandfather and great-grandfather, as by the war and diplomacy that usually governed the interaction between the princely states of medieval Europe. Henry's great-grandfather, John of Gaunt, had claimed the kingdom of Castile and León and enjoyed independent princely status as duke of Aquitaine. His ambitions for himself and his family were truly international. Henry IV, although domestic concerns and his own ill-health dominated his reign and ultimately thwarted his foreign ambitions, maintained this view of the Lancastrian family as an international princely clan, seeking foreign marriages for both himself and his children. Henry V, of course, realised Lancastrian dynastic ambitions; his revival of the Hundred Years' War in 1415 was as much a continuation of his family's dynastic project as it was a consolidation of his domestic rule through asserting long-standing English policies in France. At times the dynastic ambitions of the House of Lancaster clashed with the largely domestic priorities of the Lancastrian affinity and public. Indeed, the negotiation of these occasionally incompatible Lancastrian priorities was a recurrent theme of the political culture the young king inherited.

John of Gaunt: the European prince

The royal court in late medieval England was a cosmopolitan place. While the mainstay of political discourse was domestic – taxation, purveyance, justice, and the issue of counsel – and the

question of England's Continental neighbours arose most frequently in English minds in the context of war, the Plantagenet
ruling elite was essentially French speaking and shared a deep-
rooted and long-standing cultural affinity with its fellow European
princely houses. The court of Edward III in the middle of the
fourteenth century, while committed to proclaiming England as
'an inviolable and independent state' and supportive of the emerging English vernacular, was still overwhelmingly Francophone,
devouring chronicles, romances, and other cultural products in
Anglo-Norman. It also provided a home to knights and esquires
from throughout Europe who shared a common aristocratic and
chivalric culture.[1] Initially because of Edward III's wider strategic
priorities in his war with France, the marriages sought and made
for the king's children confirmed the European dimension of
Plantagenet kingship.[2] The European dynastic imperative that
drove Edward's policies from the 1330s onwards found its fullest
expression in the person of his third son, John of Gaunt, duke
of Lancaster.

From an early age John of Gaunt was destined to be more than
merely duke of Lancaster and head of a domestic noble affinity.
Through his mother, Philippa of Hainault, he claimed membership
of an important princely house of the Holy Roman Empire. In
the early 1360s he was mentioned as a possible successor to the
Scottish king, David II (then a captive in England), and after this
was rejected by the Scottish parliament, Gaunt turned his attention
to Provence. However, it was his marriage in 1371 to a Castilian
princess that transformed Gaunt from an English, albeit royal,
duke to a European prince. Constanza of Castile was the exiled
daughter of the murdered Peter I (1334–69), king of Castile and
León. As part of Edward III's wider strategic purposes, the English
supported the claims of Constanza against her father's murderer,
her uncle, Henry II of Trastámara. Gaunt took his new-found
status seriously. He established a small chancery to issue documents
under a new seal as king of Castile and León and in 1385, partly
to diffuse tensions at home with his nephew, Richard II, he led
an army of 5,000 men to Iberia to claim his throne. Gaunt's cause
was furthered by a marriage alliance between his daughter, Philippa,
and King John I of Portugal in 1387. Later in the same year,
however, John came to a truce with John I of Castile and shortly
afterwards Gaunt himself came to an accommodation with his

Trastámaran rival. In return for renouncing his claim to the Castilian throne, Gaunt received a large indemnity and an annual pension. The treaty of Bayonne was ratified by another marriage alliance, this time between Gaunt's younger daughter, Katherine, and John of Castile's heir, Henry, prince of Asturias. Gaunt left Iberia for Aquitaine in September 1387 safe in the knowledge that the House of Lancaster's credentials as a European princely dynasty were secure. Indeed, Gaunt's own continuing ambitions were recognised in March 1390 when Richard II created him duke of Aquitaine for life. Crucially, the grant separated Aquitaine from the English crown and vested it in Gaunt to be held of Richard as king of France. The duke's dynastic policy did not stop there: in 1395 he tried to negotiate a marriage between Henry of Monmouth (the future Henry V) and a daughter of the duke of Brittany. If successful, this would have 'created a sphere of specifically Lancastrian influence along the western seaboard of the French kingdom'.[3] The failure of these negotiations may have resulted in a shift in Gaunt's dynastic policy, and in the final years of his life he dedicated himself to the legitimising of his Beaufort offspring with his last wife, Katherine Swynford. Nevertheless, as Simon Walker observed, Gaunt 'bears comparison with the greatest European princes' of his age and his efforts in Iberia and in France demonstrate the international princely status that was central to Lancastrian identity.[4]

This European dimension to Lancastrian identity should not be underestimated. In the 1370s and 1380s the Lancastrian household, as magnificent as any princely household, contained a large number of foreign knights and esquires, imparting 'a distinctly cosmopolitan glamour that . . . announced his real ambitions were European rather than English in scope'.[5] Lancastrian culture was equally international. While his daughters or their servants may have been responsible for the introduction and translation of such 'Lancastrian' authors as John Gower into Portugal and Spain, Iberian influences passed into England as a result of intermarriage between Gaunt's English servants and his wife's Castilian entourage.[6] Yet this international dimension was not unproblematic. 'English folk often expressed disgust at foreigners; the desire of an English magnate to become one puzzled them.'[7] Gaunt's popularity in England waxed and waned throughout the last decades of the fourteenth century, but he was particularly unpopular in the late 1370s and early 1380s, when his own ambitions in Castile at times conflicted with the priorities of the English commons, and in the mid 1390s, when his interests in Aquitaine were perceived as the determining factor in the Anglo-French peace negotiations. Even Gaunt's own affinity and the wider circle of Lancastrian supporters were ambiguous in their reaction to the duke's private, dynastic ambitions. For all of the duke's international pretensions, by the 1390s the Lancastrian affinity in England was almost exclusively English, immersed in a very different domestic Lancastrian tradition. The chronicler Thomas Walsingham was highly critical of Gaunt's actions in the 1370s, so much so that later versions of his *Chronica maiora* had the offending sections excised before 1399. He was dismissive of the expedition Gaunt sent to Portugal in 1381, which the duke stated 'was in the interests of England', but, 'though they were of very great benefit to Portugal', the force did little to weaken France's Castilian ally.[8] When Gaunt himself travelled to Iberia to claim his crown, Walsingham accused him of turning 'from a prince into a pardoner', with indulgences being sold to fund the campaign. This 'so cheapened and soiled the system in the eyes of the people that there were few who made any contribution to this latest crusade'.[9] It is tempting to suggest that at the end of his life Gaunt recognised the tension between his own princely ambitions and the expectations of his servants. He chose to be buried alongside his first wife, Blanche of Lancaster, in St Paul's cathedral, establishing a perpetual chantry to their memory. Duchess Constanza was remembered by a similar arrangement at St Mary Newarke, Leicester, perhaps designed to remind the Lancastrian affinity that Gaunt's European ambitions for the House of Lancaster survived his death.

Henry of Bolingbroke: the chivalric prince

While John of Gaunt's European adventures had been hard headed and practical, those of his son constituted another facet of the complex Lancastrian legacy. Henry Bolingbroke embodied the chivalric, martial ideal of the great European princely houses. As a ten-year-old he was elected to the Order of the Garter instead of his twenty-two-year-old uncle, Thomas of Woodstock. By the age of fourteen he had embarked on a jousting career which saw him rise to the status of one of the most accomplished knights in Europe. In 1390 he shone at the great tournament held at St Inglevert near Calais; the French champions judged him and his companions the most worthy men of the 150 or so knights that had taken part. In the same year, however, Bolingbroke decided to take his leave from domestic politics and went on crusade with the Teutonic knights against the pagan Lithuanians. Henry reached Danzig in August, accompanied by thirty-two knights and a large household. Despite a five-week siege, the crusaders failed to capture the citadel of Vilnius and had returned to Königsberg by 22 October. In July 1392 he sailed again to Prussia, but upon discovering that there was to be no campaign that year he instead travelled on pilgrimage to Jerusalem. Henry travelled through Germany, Bohemia, Austria and Italy, meeting Wenzel, King of the Romans, King Sigismund of Hungary (the future Holy Roman Emperor), and the Doge of Venice. On 23 December 1392 he departed from Venice for the Holy Land. He spent more than a week visiting the holy places before returning to England in July 1393, via Cyprus, Rhodes, and Venice.

Bolingbroke's adventures between 1390 and 1393 were central to the fashioning of the Lancastrian legacy. Henry himself was acutely conscious of his status as the scion of a major European princely house: his arrival at various places on his journey from Prussia to Venice in 1392 was announced by his heralds, while his escutcheons of arms were placed above his various lodgings. Contemporary English chroniclers celebrated Henry's deeds, extolling (and at times exaggerating) his feats of arms for the delight of their readers. Yet they also portrayed his time abroad in two distinctly Lancastrian contexts. First, they underlined the religious significance: this was chivalry for God's purpose; Bolingbroke was the epitome of the *miles Christi*. Second, and perhaps more importantly, they stressed that Bolingbroke's deeds were achieved only with the support of his servants. The author of the *Westminster Chronicle* claimed that the capture of Vilnius 'was due to the earl [of Derby] who, *together with his men*, indeed behaved in this attack with great distinction and was the very first to plant his standard on the city walls.'[10] Thomas Walsingham was even more forceful in stressing the role of Henry's servants: 'Indeed, those who belonged to his household were the first to climb the wall and to place his standard on the walls, while the others did nothing or were unaware of what was being done.' Moreover, he underlined his and his readers' common cause with Bolingbroke, writing that the 'brother of the king of Poland, who was opposing *us*, was also killed there'.[11] Walsingham, one of those authors whose texts shaped the political and cultural legacy inherited by Henry VI, was hinting here not at a common English identity with Bolingbroke, but at a specifically Lancastrian identity of chivalry and piety on a European stage. The persistence of this idea, and its importance in shaping the contribution of Henry Bolingbroke to Lancastrian identity, is evident in the work of John Capgrave. Capgrave (d 1464) was an Austin friar who had a prodigious output of biblical commentaries, a chronicle, saints' lives, and a history of famous men bearing the name Henry. His *Illustribus Henricis* put greater stress on Bolingbroke's activities as chivalric crusader and pilgrim than it did on the actual accomplishments of his reign as king. Henry, he claimed, 'esteemed no honour greater than to avenge the insults offered to the Crucified.'[12] Like Walsingham, Capgrave was careful to qualify the portrait of Bolingbroke as chivalric exemplar in specifically Lancastrian terms.

Henry V: the warrior prince

During his father's reign the future Henry V had developed into a proven soldier and military leader. Aged only seventeen, in 1403 he had fought against the Welsh rebels and the Percies at the battle of Shrewsbury, suffering an arrow wound to the face. Three years later he was charged with command of the entire Welsh campaign, and on its successful conclusion in 1410 he was appointed captain of England's largest standing garrison at Calais. As Prince of Wales, Henry was considered bellicose and aggressive. In November 1411 Henry IV put an end to his son's temporary leadership of the royal council, partly because the king objected to the prince's open support for the Burgundians in their civil war against the Armagnac faction at the French court. There is also evidence at this time for wider Lancastrian disquiet over Prince Henry's apparent enthusiasm for war. This was reflected in Thomas Hoccleve's *Regement of Princes*, presented to the prince in 1411. While the poet expected Henry to 'make many a kny₃tly rode/ And þe pride of oure foos thristen adoun', he also warned that war was too often fought 'to wynne worldly tresour and richesse'.[13] Indeed, for John Lydgate, commissioned by Prince Henry in 1412 to write a history of the siege of Troy, war might serve a still higher purpose. In uniting the thrones of England and France in a Lancastrian Dual Monarchy, Henry might yet cancel out the stain of his father's usurpation.

Within weeks of his accession in April 1413, Henry V had made clear his intentions to renew the English claim to the French throne. As early as June, preparations, in the form of the stockpiling of arms and munitions and requesting loans for the forthcoming expedition, were under way. The king also undertook a rhetorical campaign to justify his actions. In this he was careful to dispel any notion that the campaign was being fought to satisfy his own ambitions. Instead, it was presented in terms of the justice of Henry's cause and the intransigence of Charles VI. In November 1414 the chancellor, Henry Beaufort, addressed parliament, explaining that the king had exhausted all peaceful means of a resolution: 'similarly man is given a time for peace, and a time of war and of toil'. He stressed the justice of the king's cause, quoting scripture at the assembled Lords and Commons: 'unto death shalt thou strive for justice'.[14] The same message was repeated to a Great Council meeting in April 1415, but it was not until 6 July that war was formally declared. Henry also felt the need to justify his actions and the justness of his cause to his fellow princes. The outbreak of war was preceded by long and complex negotiations with the French and the king sent details of his claim to the Council of Constance, the Emperor Sigismund, and several other princes. This was done so 'that all Christendom might know what greats acts of injustice the French in their duplicity had inflicted on him, and that, as it were reluctantly and against his will, he was being compelled to raise his standards against the rebels'. Crucially, as the author of the contemporary *Gesta Henrici Quinti* makes clear, these same arguments were also made available for an English audience, suggesting the ambivalence of the domestic response to the king's decision to reopen the war.[15]

Henry V's campaign was, of course, brilliantly successful. The king set sail for France on 11 August. Just days before, at the end of July, news had broken of the so-called 'Southampton Plot', a scheme hatched by the earl of Cambridge and a few others to allegedly replace the king with Roger Mortimer, earl of March. The plot was betrayed and the ringleaders executed, but its failure was further evidence that the Lancastrian regime, and Henry especially, enjoyed divine favour.[16] Once in France, Henry's army laid siege to the town of Harfleur and on 22 September, with both sides ravaged by dysentery, the defenders surrendered. News of the town's capture was quickly conveyed back to London, probably to soothe domestic nerves, and many of the king's councillors advised a swift return to England. Henry, however, delayed in Harfleur until 8 October, when his small army of between 6,000 and 8,000 men began its march to English-held Calais. On 25 October the English were met by a much larger French force (at least 12,000 but possibly more) near the village of Agincourt. The ensuing battle resulted in a decisive victory for the English. It was the most emphatic endorsement of Henry's cause imaginable and, in no small part, was due to the king's own leadership and prowess on the battlefield.

It is easy to be carried away with the extraordinary victory at Agincourt. To the French it was an unparalleled disaster: Pierre Cochon, writing in the 1430s, captured the popular mood when he exclaimed that the battle had been 'the ugliest and most wretched event that had happened in France over the last thousand years'.[17] English writers too, such as the eye-witness author of the *Gesta Henrici Quinti*, were overflowing in their praise for Henry's achievements. Yet Lancastrian reactions to the battle of Agincourt were mixed and reveal in fact an ambiguity over the nature and possible consequences of Henry's victory.[18] Indeed, the very fact that texts such as the *Gesta* were compiled within months of the battle suggests the need to establish an official narrative of the events. Popular anxiety over the king's decision to go to war was perhaps apparent in the city of London's initial fears that the battle had ended in English defeat. Most revealing of contemporary concerns over the consequences of Agincourt was the anonymous letter written in November 1415 to the king by a member of the convocation of the clergy of the southern province (in all probability his uncle, Henry Beaufort, bishop of

Winchester). The author stressed that the victory had been achieved through the 'outstretched hand of God . . . for His own praise, the honour and glory of the English nation, and the eternal memory of the royal name'. He then warned of the dangers of over-indulgent celebrations of victory: 'let us beware lest, after such victories, the accompaniments of victory vanquish the victors – such as pride, vainglory, boasting, swelling words, cruelty, rage, and the fury of revenge'.[19] These responses reveal an uncertainty over what victory at Agincourt meant and how it was to be accommodated within the domestic and international priorities of the Lancastrian regime.

The immediate reaction to Agincourt hints at a possible divergence of views over what the battle meant to the king, his Lancastrian servants, and the wider public. The role played by the king and his demeanour during the victory pageant held in the city of London is revealing. For the citizens of London, who organised and put on the pageants, perhaps in consultation with members of the king's household, this was an opportunity for jingoistic celebration. Henry approached the city to the strains of 'Hail, flower of England, knight of Christ of the world'. At the foot of London Bridge, on the north bank of the Thames, the king was greeted by a figure of St George in full armour, while in Cornhill could be seen the arms of St George, St Edward the Confessor, and St Edmund alongside the arms of England and the Lancastrian family. At the entrance to Cheapside the figures of twelve English kings stood alongside the Twelve Apostles.[20] Alongside this exuberance, however, the king himself appears to have been anxious to portray an air of sombre and pious reflection. It has been argued that the pageant in its entirety was based upon the liturgy of the funeral office and conceived as 'a dramatically staged prayer'.[21] This, of course, reflected the king's own convictions. The later *Vita Henrici Quinti*, written around 1438, states that the king 'did not suffer this honour to be ascribed to him, but put all the praise and glory to God. Nor did he wish his helmet, with his crown which had been broken in battle, nor his armour, to be shown to the people, shunning all this popular praise.'[22] The celebrations culminated in a *Te Deum Laudamus* mass at St Paul's cathedral. The London-based author of the *Brut* chronicle, also writing in the 1430s, added that afterwards Henry went on pilgrimage to various shrines in England and ordered that St George's Day 'should be kept high and holy: and so was it never before that day.'[23] Together the London pageants stressed two mutually compatible Lancastrian ideals: first, a sense of English distinctiveness and pride, and second, the piety and orthodoxy of the king.

A third strand to the post-Agincourt celebrations, however, suggests a more contested legacy. On 1 December 1415 the king ordered the bishops and abbots to hold a solemn funeral mass for both the English and French who had fallen in the recent campaign. Part of Henry's message was a genuine feeling of remorse over a battle that had resulted in the death of so many of his lawful French subjects. Moreover, the battle had taken place on the feast day of SS. Crispin and Crispinian, two third-century French martyrs whose cult was based at Soissons. The *Vita et Gesta Henrici Quinti* states that the king himself ordered the French saints to be included in the prayers said at one of his daily masses in recognition of their intercession at the battle. French chroniclers noted the fact that the battle had taken place on their feast day and one, Thomas Basin, even suggested that their intervention resulted from the desecration of their shrine during the Armagnac/Burgundian civil war. Within a year of the victory at Agincourt, popular English poetry was also remarking on the irony of the fact that the great English victory had fallen on a French saints' feast day.[24] As Christopher Allmand observes 'the audacious and ironic annexation of two French saints . . . reflects the growing confidence of Englishmen'.[25] Yet, whatever the Lancastrian public made of the king's dedication of the victory to SS. Crispin and Crispinian, Henry's own motives may have been entirely genuine. In December 1416 Archbishop Chichele ordered the prayers for 25 October to be shared between Crispin and Crispinian and the Lancastrian saint, St John of Beverley.[26] In so doing, he reminded the English that Agincourt was not merely an English victory. It was, first and foremost, a Lancastrian victory and underlined the fact that the House of Lancaster, embodied in the person of Henry V, was an international princely house, rightfully and equally kings of England and of France.

The conquest of Normandy and the Treaty of Troyes

Henry V's legacy was defined from 1 August 1417 to 21 May 1420. In that period of less than three years Henry landed in Normandy, fought a brilliant military campaign culminating in the Treaty of Troyes when, along with Philip the Good, duke of Burgundy, and representatives of the French king, Charles VI, he sealed the Treaty and was formally betrothed to Catherine of Valois. In those months Henry confirmed his reputation as a great king, rivalling Edward III. By the Treaty of Troyes the throne of France descended to him and his rightful heirs on the death of the ailing Charles VI. It was a magnificent achievement, probably surpassing Henry's expectations when he had embarked on his invasion of Normandy less than three years before. Yet it had been achieved and was sustained by the force of the king's own personality and the support of a small, committed group of Lancastrian servants. The Lancastrian Dual Monarchy was established in the face of unease, even downright opposition, at home and hostility among many of its future French subjects.

In military terms, Henry V's conquest of Normandy was a stunning success. The city of Caen fell on 4 September 1417, after a two-week siege, and Falaise in February the following year, after a longer investment of some ten weeks. The king's ability to keep his army together over the winter was testimony to his abilities as a general. Henry was also helped by factors outside his control. In May 1418 the Burgundians captured Paris, killing their principal rival, the duke of Armagnac, and causing the Dauphin (the future Charles VII) to flee. That summer Henry V crossed the Seine and on 1 August laid siege to the Norman capital, Rouen. On 19 January 1419 the city finally capitulated and the king of England entered the symbolic and administrative capital of the duchy of Normandy. Henry's success had caused alarm among both the Dauphinists and the Burgundians, but their potential rapprochement was cut short on 10 September when John the Fearless, duke of Burgundy, was inexplicably murdered by the Dauphin's servants when the two princes met on the bridge at Montereau. From this debacle Henry emerged as the obvious candidate to rule France: Duke John's successor, Philip the Good, at twenty-four years of age, was young and inexperienced, while the Dauphin's moral authority was compromised by the events at Montereau. By December Duke Philip had agreed in principle to support a settlement whereby Henry would marry Charles VI's daughter, Catherine, and their children would succeed to the French throne. On 20 May 1420 Henry and Philip travelled together to the French court at Troyes and on the following day a solemn ceremony took place in St Peter's cathedral. The treaty was sealed by both kings (although Charles VI was too ill to attend in person) and both parties swore to maintain peace. Henry and Catherine were then formally betrothed and those present, including Duke Philip and members of both royal parties, swore to uphold the terms of the treaty. Finally, on 2 June Henry and Catherine were married.

The Treaty of Troyes did not, however, bring peace. Henry's honeymoon, as it were, consisted of him, his new bride, his father-in-law, and Philip the Good travelling to lay siege to the towns of Sens and Montereau. From there Henry (again accompanied by Philip, his brothers the dukes of Clarence and Bedford, and the Scottish king, James I, who had been a prisoner of the English since 1406) invested the town of Melun, which did not fall until November. On 1 December 1420, together in procession with Charles VI and Duke Philip, Henry entered Paris, where, five days later, the estates general of France ratified the treaty. On 1 February 1421 Henry and Catherine arrived in England. On the 23rd of that month Catherine was crowned queen of England in Westminster Abbey. The war in France, however, continued unabated and in early April the king received terrible news: his eldest brother, Thomas, duke of Clarence, had been killed during a reckless assault on superior French forces at Baugé in Anjou.[27] On 8 June, having finished his whistle-stop tour of England and presided over a parliament held at Westminster between 2 and 23 May, Henry returned to France. By now the Dauphinist forces were well established in their stronghold at Orléans, south of the River Loire, but one important northern town, Meaux, remained in their control. Situated thirty miles south of Paris on a bend in the River Marne, it was strategically important for control over the entire upper Seine region and could not be left unmolested. The town itself fell after a long and difficult siege in March 1422, but the defenders retreated to the 'Marché', a small fortress, which they finally surrendered on 10 May. The siege had been a testing one: sickness had raged among the attackers, infecting the king himself, while the Burgundians were proving fickle allies. Henry may indeed have questioned the enormity of the task facing him in enforcing the Treaty of Troyes. In any case, by the beginning of June the king's health was causing widespread concern and by the end of month he was too sick to ride. On 26 August he drew up a final codicil to his will of 1421, now including provision for his young son.[28] Five days later he was dead.

As well as its most obvious legacy – that Henry VI would inherit the throne of England and eventually France and that the Lancastrian regime would have to fight to maintain the Dual Monarchy – the conquest of Normandy and Treaty of Troyes had two consequences that would define the character of Henry VI's kingship. The first was the ambivalence (and occasionally even hostility) that Lancastrian interests in France would elicit among some of their English subjects. The Agincourt campaign, the naval campaign and defence of Harfleur the following year, and the invasion of Normandy in 1417 had been greeted with enthusiasm, demonstrated by the willingness of men to fund the campaigns and serve in person. Yet, as the war dragged on its appeal began to wane. No new retinues were recruited to leave England for France in 1419, and the calls for men to serve in 1420 and 1421 were met with widespread reluctance and excuses.[29] This unease with a long-standing commitment to the war with France and with the longer-term ramifications of Henry's policy was apparent in the parliaments of December 1420 and May 1421. In the former the king did not ask for a grant of taxation in recognition of the 'welcome conclusion of unity and peace', but in the latter assembly the king probably asked for a subsidy, which was refused on the grounds that England and France were formally at peace.[30] Some measure of the debate which surrounded this issue is suggested by the fact that the December 1421 parliament granted a subsidy even before the Commons had elected their speaker as the worsening situation in France became apparent. In December the previous year the Commons had voiced their fears regarding the long-term implications of the Treaty of Troyes. They sought confirmation from the duke of Gloucester, Henry's representative in England, of Edward III's statute of 1340, which had enacted that no Englishman or woman should be 'subject or obedient to' any future king of France. Gloucester deferred to Henry, but agreed to 'request, encourage and persuade' the king and his new queen to return to England as soon as possible.[31] It has been suggested that this merely reflected the Commons' unease over the fact that Henry had not attended parliament for over four years, but it also spoke to a wider mistrust of the Lancastrian project.

Circumstantial evidence illustrates the kind of fears that the prospect of a Lancastrian Dual Monarchy aroused among Henry V's English subjects. John Feelde, writing to Robert Frye, clerk of the king's council, in March 1419 reported that 'so now men suppose that the king will from henceforth make war in France', asking his correspondent to 'pray for ys that we may come soon, out of this unhealthy soldier's life, into the life of England'. The following year a Kentish haberdasher, Henry Gloymng, found himself imprisoned by the council back in England for questioning the king's conduct of the siege of Rouen, stating that it was only because the duke of Burgundy kept a relieving army at bay that the English were able to continue the siege.[32] More telling perhaps is the attitude of Lancastrian poets and chroniclers to the war in France. In the epilogue to his *Troy Book*, commissioned by Henry V just months before he became king in 1412 and completed some eight years later, John Lydgate celebrated the king as 'the prince of pes' and looked forward to the Treaty of Troyes bringing harmony to the kingdoms of England and France. Yet this celebration of Henry's moment of triumph was short lived and the poem itself and Lydgate's *Siege of Thebes* (1422) can be read as complex discussions of the tensions of fighting in the Lancastrian conquest of Normandy. Lydgate, for instance, warned how the Trojan prince, Hector, had compromised his military success by plundering, much as the Lancastrian armies would squander their moral advantage, had they resorted to plunder as their fourteenth-century predecessors in the Hundred Years War had done.[33] While Lydgate praised Henry V's discipline and martial prowess, other Lancastrian authors were less sure of the king's achievements. Adam Usk ended his chronicle by describing the attempts to raise men and money in 1421–22 to sustain the Dual Monarchy. 'Yet I fear, alas', he wrote, 'that both the great men and the money of this kingdom will be miserably wasted on this enterprise. No wonder, then, that the unbearable impositions being demanded from the people to this end are accompanied by dark – though private – mutterings and curses . . . and I pray that my supreme lord may not in the end . . . incur the sword of the Lord's fury.'[34]

The second consequence of the Treaty of Troyes was the antithesis of the first. There emerged during these years a group of men whose loyalty to the Lancastrian cause in France and personal dedication to Henry V himself defined their political role into the reign of Henry VI. These included his brother, John, duke of Bedford, members of the extended Lancastrian royal family (such as his uncle, Thomas Beaufort, duke of Exeter, and Sir John Cornwall, husband of Henry IV's sister, Elizabeth), churchmen (such as Archbishop Chichele, Bishop Thomas Langley of Durham, and Philip Morgan, made bishop of Worcester in 1419), and household servants (men like Sir Walter Hungerford and Henry, Lord Fitzhugh). Especially important perhaps were the 'military-minded young men' who had served Henry as Prince of Wales.[35] Yet this group also, crucially, included men whose connection to the House of Lancaster arose principally, sometimes entirely, from their participation in Henry V's French campaigns. Men such as the Sussex knight Sir Roger Fiennes and his younger brother, James, who first distinguished themselves in the Agincourt campaign, or Ralph Boteler, who first travelled to Normandy in 1418, had long careers in Lancastrian service that demonstrated a deep commitment to Henry V's legacy in France and the Dual Monarchy. Moreover, this group was not necessarily coterminous with the wider Lancastrian affinity. By 1422 the men who administered the duchy of Lancaster estates in England had developed into a large and no longer politically coherent group; those who had served alongside Henry V in the conquest of Normandy, on the other hand, shared a common devotion to what David Morgan has termed 'an ethos of public life defined as the realization of king-led war-enterprise'.[36] The strength of this ideal, sustained in part by the memory of their personal service to Henry V, was expressed in 1438 by Archbishop Chichele's foundation of All Souls' College, Oxford, whose scholars were to pray for 'the souls of the most famous king Henry V, Thomas late duke of Clarence, the dukes, earls, barons, knights, armigerous men and other noblemen and commoners who have ended their lives in the king's and his father's reign in the French war'.[37]

Conclusion

The international, dynastic legacy that Henry VI inherited was complex. In part it was defined by a narrowly Lancastrian dynastic interest that had begun with John of Gaunt's claim to the throne of Castile and León, had been perpetuated by the foreign dynastic marriages which Henry IV had made for his daughters and Henry V had made with Catherine of Valois, and which lived on in the marriage alliances that John, duke of Bedford, would make with Anne of Burgundy, sister of Philip the Good, and that Humphrey, duke of Gloucester, would make with Jacqueline of Bavaria in 1423. These marriages, and the claims to princely status and lands that they brought with them, were as much about the private dynastic ambitions of individual members of the House of Lancaster as they were about the wider strategic and political considerations of the English ruling class. Yet the international legacy was also born out of the House of Lancaster's reputation for chivalric and martial endeavour. Crucially, in the early fifteenth century this was mixed with the devotion, piety, and loyalty that came to define Lancastrian identity and that found its fullest expression in the divinely sanctioned conquest of France by Henry V. It was this aspect of the Lancastrian legacy that would, above all else, define the reign of his son.

Notes

1 Mark Ormrod, *Edward III* (New Haven, CT, 2011), 446–71; Malcolm Vale, *War and Chivalry: Warfare and Aristocratic Culture in England, France and Burgundy at the End of the Middle Ages* (1981), 14–32.
2 Ormrod, *Edward III*, 437–8.
3 Simon Walker, 'John of Gaunt', in *Oxford Dictionary of National Biography*, xxx, 174–83 (at 181).
4 Ibid.
5 Simon Walker, *The Lancastrian Affinity 1361–1399* (Oxford, 1990), 12.
6 R.F. Yeager, 'John Gower's Lancastrian Affinity: The Iberian Connection', *Viator* 35 (2004), 483–515.
7 Anthony Goodman, *John of Gaunt: The Exercise of Princely Power in Fourteenth-Century Europe* (Harlow, 1992), 49.

8 *The St Albans Chronicle, Volume 1, 1376–1394*, ed. John Taylor, Wendy R. Childs and Leslie Watkiss (Oxford, 2003), 409–10.

9 *The Chronica Maiora of Thomas Walsingham, 1376–1422*, ed. James G. Clark and David Preest (Woodbridge, 1999), 238.

10 *The Westminster Chronicle 1381–1394*, ed. L.C. Hector and Barbara Harvey (Oxford, 1982), 449 (emphasis added).

11 *St Albans Chronicle, Volume 1*, ed. Taylor, Childs, and Watkiss, 903 (emphasis added).

12 John Capgrave, *Liber de Illustribus Henricis*, ed. F.C. Hingeston (1858), 99.

13 Thomas Hoccleve, *Hoccleve's Works, III: The Regement of Princes*, ed. F.J. Furnivall (Early English Text Society, 1897), 143, 193.

14 *PROME*, ix. 66.

15 *Gesta Henrici Quinti*, ed. F. Taylor and J.S. Roskell (Oxford, 1975), 17–19.

16 T.B. Pugh, *Henry V and the Southampton Plot* (Southampton, 1988).

17 *Chronique normande de Pierre Cochon*, ed. C. de Robillard de Beaurepaire (Rouen, 1870), 276.

18 Anne Curry, *The Battle of Agincourt: Sources and Interpretations* (Woodbridge, 2000), 261–8.

19 *Letters of Queen Margaret of Anjou and Bishop Beckington and Others Written in the Reigns of Henry V and Henry VI*, ed. C. Monro (Camden Society, 1863), 4.

20 Nicola Coldstream, '"Pavilion'd in Splendour": Henry V's Agincourt Pageants', *Journal of the British Archaeological Association* 165 (2012), 153–71.

21 G. Kipling, *Enter the King: Theatre, Liturgy and Ritual in Medieval Civic Triumph* (Oxford, 1998), 201–9.

22 *Titi Livii Foro-Juliensis Vita Henrici Quinti*, ed. T. Hearne (Oxford, 1716), 21–22, translated in Curry, *Agincourt*, 268.

23 *The Brut or the Chronicles of England*, ed. F.W.D. Brie (Early English Text Society, 1908), 558.

24 Curry, *Agincourt*, 274–7.

25 Christopher Allmand, *Henry V* (1992), 100.

26 *Register of Henry Chichele, Archbishop of Canterbury, 1414–1443*, ed. E.F. Jacob (Canterbury and York Society, 4 vols, 1938–47), iii, 28–29.

27 John D. Milner, 'The Battle of Baugé, March 1421: Impact and Memory', *History* 91 (2006), 484–507.

28 Patrick and Felicity Strong, 'The Last Will and Codicils of Henry V', *English Historical Review* 116 (1981), 79–89.

29 Anthony Goodman, 'Responses to Requests in Yorkshire for Military Service under Henry V', *Northern History* 17 (1981), 240–52.

30 *PROME*, ix, 249.

31 Ibid., 254, 259.

32 *Original Letters Illustrative of English History*, ed. Henry Ellis (2nd series, 4 vols, 1827), i, 76–79.

33 Catherine Nall, *Reading and War in Fifteenth-Century England* (Woodbridge, 2012), 75–113.

34 *The Chronicle of Adam Usk 1377–1421*, ed. Chris Given-Wilson (Oxford, 1997), 270–1.

35 Gwilym Dodd, 'Henry V's Establishment: Service, Loyalty and Reward in 1413', in *Henry V: New Interpretations*, ed. Gwilym Dodd (Woodbridge, 2013), 35–74.

36 David Morgan, 'The Household Retinue of Henry V and the Ethos of English Public Life', in *Concepts and Patterns of Service in the Later Middle Ages*, ed. Anne Curry and Elizabeth Matthews (Woodbridge, 2000), 64–79 at 68.

37 E.F. Jacob, 'The Warden's Text of the Foundation Statutes of All Souls College, Oxford', *The Antiquaries Journal* 15 (1935), 420–31.

4 'Woe betide the land whose king is a child'

England and France, 1422–29

Henry of Windsor was born at Windsor castle on 6 December 1421. Catherine of Valois appears to have enjoyed a relatively trouble-free pregnancy and labour, although whether the relic of Our Lord's Foreskin, brought from the French abbey of Coulombs to Windsor to be present at the birth, had much bearing on this remains questionable. The news of the prince's birth was received amidst great celebrations throughout England and by his father, then besieging the town of Meaux. The prince was christened within days, as was the custom. His great-uncle, Henry Beaufort, bishop of Winchester, his uncle, the duke of Bedford, and the exiled daughter of William, count of Hainault, Holland and Zeeland, Jacqueline of Bavaria, acted as his godparents. When he was only five months old, his mother returned to France to join Henry V. On 31 August 1422, as we have seen, Henry V died, followed only weeks later by Charles VI of France. The first years of Henry VI's reign therefore presented two interrelated and unprecedented problems: first, how to maintain a semblance of royal authority and government for an infant king incapable of ruling himself, and second, how to enforce that authority over the newly established and fractious Lancastrian Dual Monarchy.

Arrangements for minority rule

Henry V's will, made on 10 June 1421 on the eve of his last departure for France, and the codicils, dated 26 August the following year as he lay *in extremis*, made detailed provision for his young son.[1] The arrangements for Henry VI's household and upbringing were clear enough. Thomas Beaufort, duke of Exeter, was given overall responsibility for his upbringing and named the king's guardian, while two old Lancastrian retainers, Sir Walter Hungerford and Henry, Lord Fitzhugh, were given charge of the royal household. Exeter ensured that the small household attending upon the king during his first years (spent almost entirely at Windsor) was of implacable Lancastrian credentials. The five knights who received household livery – Thomas Erpingham, John Cornwall, Louis and John Robessart, and William Phelip – had long served the king's father, both in England and in France. The four pages appointed had also previously served Henry V.[2] His nurse, Joan Asteley, who had been with him since his birth, also came from a family with long-standing Lancastrian connections. In 1423 Dame Alice Boteler (whose son, Ralph, was a close associate of Henry V and was appointed to the new king's council around the same time) joined the household as a governess. She was given charge of the king's education and, if necessary, his chastisement. Other than these details the toddler king's early years are obscure. There is no reason, however, to assume he was anything other than a normal, happy boy. Indeed, in November 1423 the young Henry was robust enough to make a personal appearance in parliament. A London chronicler recorded how, while lodged at Staines on his way from Windsor to Westminster, the king had a typical toddler tantrum: when he was carried to his mother's chair 'he shrieked and cried and sprang, and would not be carried further'; the following evening his nurse tried again, and on this occasion he 'being then glad and more cheered' happily sat with the queen.[3] Henry was, however, in good spirits when he arrived at parliament, probably sitting on his mother's knee to hear the Commons' loyal address to him, their 'tender, benign sovereign lord'.[4]

As soon as news of Henry V's demise was received in England arrangements were made to ensure the uninterrupted course of royal government. The chancellor of England, Bishop Langley of Durham, had travelled from Yorkshire, arriving at Windsor on 28 September. On that day, a small group – the duke of Gloucester, Archbishop Chichele and a handful of other bishops and peers – gathered and performed homage and fealty to the new king. Langley then surrendered the Great Seal to Simon Gauntstede, master of the rolls in Chancery. The following day Langley, Gauntstede, and the others then rode to Westminster for the first council meeting of the new reign. The key officials of the royal law courts and of the exchequer were confirmed in their offices, allowing government to be continued in as normal a manner as possible, and writs were despatched for Henry's first parliament to assemble at Westminster on Monday, 9 November. In Normandy similar arrangements were made. Bishop Kemp of London, the chancellor of Normandy, surrendered the two seals in his keeping: the seal of the duchy he delivered to the duke of Bedford, before returning to England and surrendering the Great Seal to the king himself, in the presence of Exeter and other lords, at Windsor.

Henry V's provisions for the government of England, however, were ambiguous. The parliament that met at Westminster in November was presided over by the duke of Gloucester as the most senior nobleman then in England. Crucially, Gloucester exercised this role by virtue of a commission from the new royal council, issued on 5 November, not as *custos Anglie* (keeper of England), the office he had held since May 1422 during Henry V's and Bedford's absence in France and which was deemed to have ended with the late king's death. This apparent technicality masked deep uncertainties at the heart of the Lancastrian regime over Henry V's intentions for the government of England and France, especially concerning the role that the king's uncles would play during the new reign. Gloucester himself was unhappy at the decision to prevent him from opening and closing parliament as *custos Anglie*; indeed, the controversy surrounding the council's decision was widely acknowledged and controversial, and it caused confusion: a warrant for the payment of expenses issued three days before the first parliament of the reign still mistakenly referred to Duke Humphrey as '*custos Anglie*'.[5] The codicils to Henry V's will had granted Gloucester 'the principal safekeeping and defence of our beloved son' (*tutela et defensionem nostri carissimi filii principales*), and this the duke took to give him a pre-eminence among his fellow councillors, especially when his older brother, Bedford, was exercising his duties as Regent of France. The Commons apparently shared the council's confusion. They presented a petition in parliament asking who should have the governance of the realm during the king's infancy. Ostensibly, the matter was discussed and settled in an amicable manner. On 5 December it was decided that Bedford should be appointed protector and defender of the realm and the Church and chief councillor of the king. When Bedford was in France, however, these duties were to devolve upon his younger brother. Both dukes were given extensive powers to appoint to offices and were to be assisted in governing the realm by a formally constituted council. This council comprised Archbishop Chichele, the bishops of London, Winchester, Norwich, and Worcester, the duke of Exeter, the earls of March, Warwick, Northumberland, and Westmorland, and the Earl Marshall, Lord Fitzhugh, and four knights (Sir Ralph Cromwell, Sir Walter Hungerford, Sir John Tiptoft, and Sir Walter Beauchamp). In an unprecedented step, the councillors were also bound by principles of conciliar government. These concerned the impartial appointment of sheriffs, escheators, and other royal officials; the commitment to sell wardships and other casualties to the highest bidder; that decisions could be made only by a quorum of at least four councillors; that the keys of the treasury were to be kept by the treasurer of England and chamberlains of the exchequer and that they were not 'to divulge what the king has in his treasury, save only to the lords of the council'; and, finally, that the clerk of the council was to keep an accurate register of the council's attendance and proceedings.[6]

The straightforward record of this agreement on the Parliament Roll hid what must have been a difficult and turbulent assembly. The Commons' request to know who was to have the governance of the realm may suggest their dissatisfaction with the role assigned to Gloucester by the council, but it may equally suggest their unease at the possibility of either of the royal uncles assuming regency powers in England. Bedford himself, in a letter to the city of London on 26 October, had advertised his own pretensions for pre-eminence based on the 'laws and ancient usage and custom' of England and his position as heir presumptive, and expressing his own reservations about some of the wording of Henry V's will (presumably the role envisaged for Duke Humphrey).[7] As in 1420, when news of the Treaty of Troyes reached England, the Commons' petition in the parliament of 1422 may have indicated a widely held anxiety that the good government of England might be subjugated to the ambitions of the king's uncles and their pursuit of the Lancastrian dynastic project. Bedford may have accepted the council's dismissal of his claim for quasi-regal powers quietly, but Gloucester certainly protested his belief that the title '*tutela*' granted him special powers. He cited the example of William the Marshall in the reign of Henry III, who 'was nat so nygh to the kyng as my lord is to our liege lord' but had been granted the title '*Rector Regis et Regni*' ('ruler of the king and realm'). The council, perhaps led by Bishop Beaufort of Winchester, had also searched the records and their research had found no precedent to support Gloucester's claim.[8] The decision made in parliament on 5 December rebutted the ambitions of both of the king's uncles and asserted the principle of a royal council advising and assisting the king, who was given a *persona publica*, in other words a formal and public role in the government of the realm. Yet it also crushed any possible ambition on the part of the Commons for a formal involvement in the government during the minority; the arrangements were made by the assent and advice of the Lords in parliament and only the assent of the Commons. Archbishop Chichele's sermon at parliament's opening had reaffirmed a commitment to maintain justice and ensure good government and, drawing upon the biblical precedent of Jethro's advice to Moses, the need for advice from 'honourable and discreet persons drawn from each estate of this realm'.[9] The council that governed England in the name of the young king, however, consisted of men wholly committed to the House of Lancaster, and its relatively narrow membership may have disappointed aspirations for more collective government. The conciliar government that emerged from the first parliament of the reign was indeed based upon Lancastrian principles of good and transparent government, but it also revealed an ambiguity about the Lancastrian project, the Dual Monarchy, and the personal ambitions of Bedford and Gloucester.

The effect of the arrangements made in December 1422 was to confirm the commonplace (and in this case fiction) that the king was at the apex of public life. In September 1422 Bishop Langley had handed the Great Seal directly to the infant king, who in turn, 'by the hands' of the duke of Gloucester, had passed it to Gauntstede; by July 1424, aged two-and-a-half, Henry was apparently able to pass the seal to the new chancellor unaided, merely by the 'advice and assent of the council'.[10] Thus, while

Henry was being swaddled by his nurse at Windsor, the council could write letters and issue commands as if he had written them himself. On 15 May 1423, for instance, 'the king' wrote to his 'right trusty and most beloved uncle', Bedford, assuring him he was 'in perfect health of person' and thanking him for 'the full notable service that you have done unto us in governance of our realm of France, as well of our duchy of Normandy'.[11] Equally, Henry's subjects were complicit in the fiction, recognising that ultimate authority rested in the person of the king and not the lords of the council. In June the same year, Maud, countess of Cambridge (the widow of the earl executed after the Southampton plot of 1415), petitioned for a confirmation of her annuity of £100. She addressed her request not to the council but 'Au Roy nostre soveraign seignour' ('to the king our sovereign lord').[12] As the Speaker of the Commons noted in his address to the king in November 1423, it was to the king's 'high and royal person' alone that 'recourse of right must be to have every wrong reformed'.[13] The Lancastrian regime thus embraced the theory of the king's two bodies, making a practical distinction between the infant king himself and his public *persona* (in effect, the council exercising a collective responsibility for royal government), while maintaining the fiction of an active royal presence.

Government by council, 1423–29

The government of England between 1423 and 1429 was dominated by the difficult relationship between the duke of Gloucester and Henry Beaufort, bishop of Winchester. In this the king himself, both symbolically and in a real sense, played a vital role, underlining the problem of authority which was central to the minority regime. Beaufort was the second of four illegitimate children of John of Gaunt by Katherine Swynford. In 1403 Henry IV had appointed him chancellor of England, an office he held until March 1405, and he again served as such under Henry V, between March 1413 and July 1417. During Prince Henry's ascendancy on the council between 1410 and 1411 he had been associated with the policies of 'good government' and during the French campaigns of 1415 and 1417–19 he had lent some £26,000 towards the war effort. In 1419, however, fearing that the award of the cardinal's hat meant that Beaufort would champion the rights of the pope rather than the English crown, Henry V had threatened to strip him of his lucrative see of Winchester and Beaufort had ended the reign confined to his episcopal palaces and excluded from power. Once news was received of Henry V's death, Beaufort appears to have quickly reasserted his presence at the heart of government, doubtless aided by the appointment of his elder brother, the duke of Exeter, as the new king's guardian. His position was further strengthened by a new round of lending, doubly important, given the reluctance of the parliaments of 1422 and 1423 to make significant grants of taxation. Having already partly rehabilitated himself with loans of almost £20,000 in 1421 and 1422, in March 1424 he lent a further £9,333 6s. 8d. to finance Bedford's new campaign in France. Yet it would be wrong to see these loans purely as the means by which Beaufort 'bought' his dominance of the king's council and the minority government.[14] Instead, Beaufort proved invaluable to the work of the minority government. In July 1424 he was reappointed chancellor of England and emerged as the guiding hand of a council dominated by his fellow bishops, a body which was committed to well-established Lancastrian principles of 'good government', and attempting to balance the welfare of the king and the realm with the ambitions of the duke of Gloucester.

In January 1423 Gloucester had married Jacqueline, the exiled daughter of William, count of Hainault, Holland, and Zeeland. Duke Humphrey immediately laid claim to her lands in the Low Countries and set about recovering them from her estranged husband, John of Brabant, and her uncle, John of Bavaria. In October 1424 the duke and his new wife landed in Calais and by the end of the year Gloucester had waged a successful campaign in Hainault. His successes, however, aroused the anger and intervention of Duke Philip of Burgundy, John of Brabant's cousin. As well as the undoubted strain that Gloucester's adventures put on the Anglo-Burgundian alliance, they also meant that Duke Humphrey was absent from England for six months. In the meantime Beaufort and his fellow councillors worked hard to ensure good government at home, making judicious appointments to office both centrally and locally. In February 1425 the council sent out writs summoning another parliament to meet at Westminster on the following 30 April. The unusually full writs, written in the king's name, affirmed the traditional Lancastrian values of unity and justice: 'we, in our tender years, have resolved to find out whether peace and justice are preserved among our lieges, without which no realm may prosper'.[15] The holding of the parliament also sought to remind the political nation that authority ultimately rested in the person of the young king. Henry VI, then aged three years and four months, opened proceedings. He had previously travelled with his mother from Windsor to London. At St Paul's cathedral he had been taken from his chair by Exeter and Gloucester, but had walked unaided into the church, where he had presented alms. This apparent stress on Henry's majesty suited Beaufort, who, it seems, had become a larger presence about the young king's person and in his household in the preceding months. Indeed, Henry made a number of appearances throughout the parliament. He was present, for instance, when John Mowbray, the Earl Marshall, was acknowledged as duke of Norfolk (following a long precedence dispute with the earl of Warwick).

What the 1425 parliament failed conspicuously to do, however, was to heal the growing rift between Beaufort and Gloucester. While parliament grudgingly agreed to lend Duke Humphrey 20,000 marks to further his ambitions in the Low Countries, relations continued to deteriorate between him and his fellow councillors. The lords appear to have sworn an oath before the king to keep the peace towards one another, but during the summer anti-Beaufort feeling, fuelled by Gloucester and drawing on longstanding xenophobic attitudes towards the Flemings in London, reached fever pitch. In June 1425 Gloucester was refused access to the Tower of London by the new constable, Richard Wydeville, one of Bedford's servants recently appointed to the office by the council, and this led to an increase in tension and threats made against Beaufort by the angry Londoners. By October two armed camps faced each other across London Bridge. Between the 28th and 30th of that month Gloucester was persuaded to back down (in part by the intervention of his recently arrived cousin, the Portuguese Duke Pedro of Coimbra), but on the 31st Beaufort wrote to Bedford imploring him to return to England to rein in his tempestuous brother. Duke John arrived in London in December and immediately assumed the title of Protector of the Realm, summoning a parliament to meet at Leicester on 18 February 1426.

The so-called 'Parliaments of Bats' (named in reference to the cudgels carried by MPs after they had been forbidden to carry swords) was one of the most formative of the young king's reign. Beaufort, as chancellor, gave the opening sermon, warning of the need for wise counsel and justice, urging the community of the realm to work together to support the king, and warning of the danger of Lollardy (itself a metaphor for other internal threats to unity). Beaufort and Gloucester submitted their dispute to a group of arbiters, led by Archbishop Chichele and the ailing duke of Exeter, and comprising three bishops, the duke of Norfolk, the earl of Stafford, William Alnwick, keeper of the privy seal, and Ralph, Lord Cromwell. They were reconciled in a public ceremony, in the presence of the king, on 7 March, promising to be 'good lords' to one another. Beaufort then denied he had in the past plotted against Henry V or Gloucester and the two joined hands in recognition of the 'complete and steadfast love and affection' between them.[16] Eleven days later Beaufort resigned as chancellor. Yet Gloucester's apparent victory masked contradictions at the heart of the minority government. As in Henry V's reign, Beaufort's illegitimate status had proved no match to the status enjoyed by princes of the royal blood, and thus conciliar authority had been trumped by Bedford's intervention. In contrast to the council, John Watts has suggested that the duke's power was 'personal and intrinsic, rather than delegated'.[17] At the same time, Bedford and Beaufort broadly agreed on how to best defend the Dual Monarchy. The duke's policy of siege and slow conquest was possible to maintain only with Beaufort's money, given the refusal of parliament to grant taxation, but the council's principles of collective responsibility and 'good government' had been held hostage to the ambitions of the royal dukes.

It was partly in an attempt to smooth over these difficulties and to remind the assembled lords and commons that ultimate authority lay with the young king that Henry himself was knighted by his uncle, Bedford, on 19 May 1426. The decision to stage this ceremony may have been made late in the day, when it was clear that the settlement between Beaufort and Gloucester had not entirely resolved the wider tensions in the realm. On 4 May thirty-six young men were summoned to join the king for the ceremony, and after Bedford had dubbed his nephew, Henry repeated the honour for the others.[18] Among those knighted were the heirs to several magnate families (Norfolk, Northumberland, Ormond, and Talbot), young magnates (the duke of York and the earls of Oxford and Westmorland among others), and several young men who had already distinguished themselves in France (including Edmund Hungerford, Ralph Boteler, and the younger Richard Wydeville). The aim of this ceremony was twofold: first, it reaffirmed the young king's primacy at the heart of public life for the assembled Lords and Commons; and, second, it created a body of men whose personal loyalty to Henry himself would become a defining feature of the reign in the decades to come.

The events of 1426 failed to solve the problems inherent in conciliar rule. The question remained as to what powers Gloucester would enjoy when his brother returned to France. In January 1427 matters came to a head when Bedford appeared before the council. Archbishop Kemp gave a clear defence of conciliar government during the king's minority. He outlined how 'as great authority of governance is now in our said sovereign lord's person during his said tender age as ever shall be hereafter', but as Henry was not yet able to exercise that power in person the lords of the council 'have governed and executed the said authority now being in the person of our said sovereign, the execution of which authority rests not in one singular person but in all the lords together'. Just as they had in 1422, the lords denied both Bedford and Gloucester the right to exercise any prerogative powers of the crown or claim any pre-eminence by virtue of their royal blood. Bedford, apparently moved to tears by Kemp's address, agreed at once, but Gloucester (then bed-ridden with sickness at his house in Westminster) at first refused to give way. He angrily retorted 'Let my brother govern as he will while he is in this land for after his going over into France I will govern as I see good', and stated that he would not 'answer unto any person alive, save only unto the king when he comes to his age'.[19] Under pressure from the chancellor, he finally, grudgingly, agreed, but the unresolved tension between the personal ambitions of the Lancastrian royal family and the collective responsibility for government imagined and embraced by their servants remained. In March both Bedford and Beaufort left England for France. Still Gloucester pushed his case for greater powers in England, only to be rebuffed once more by the Lords in the parliament that met at Westminster in October. On this occasion they again highlighted the king's authority, pointing out that the duke enjoyed no special powers in parliament because of his young nephew's presence there.[20]

The question of authority during the 1420s and the role of the king's uncles in the government of England (crucially no similar debate appears to have taken place over Bedford's regency of France) demonstrate the contested web of Lancastrian ideals and principles that Henry VI and his councillors inherited. Just as the establishment of the dynasty in 1399 had been achieved with the explicit approbation of the wider political nation, now in this time of acute crisis the lords of the council looked to a collective responsibility to negotiate the king's minority. This commitment to collective responsibility and notions of prudent government for 'the good public of his said realms . . . and free execution of his said laws' drew on an older Lancastrian tradition that stretched back to Thomas of Lancaster.[21] While the infant king might embody the crown of England and ultimate authority rested in his person, his councillors had a clear idea of what that authority entailed and for whose benefit it should work. The obvious ambitions of Gloucester and the potentially worrying ambitions of the heir apparent, Bedford, threatened to undermine these principles, both in the eyes of the council and, perhaps, among members of the wider Lancastrian affinity. Even their commitment to the Dual Monarchy, that most personal of Lancastrian legacies, appears ambivalent, as shown by the reluctance of the Commons in parliament to grant taxation to support the war effort in the 1420s. By 1429, however, events in France had reached a crisis and the Lancastrian regime as a whole was forced to renew its public commitment to the Dual Monarchy.

Imagining the Dual Monarchy

When Thomas Walsingham, the St Albans monk, sat down to finish his *Chronica Maiora* he was in pessimistic mood. Writing of the death of Henry V and the accession of Henry VI, he observed: 'When [Henry V's] subjects contemplated his remarkable deeds, they grew very fearful of this sudden and terrible change . . . in place of so powerful a king and wise a lord . . . they were receiving his son, not yet a year old, who was weak and without knowledge . . . Indeed, they feared the words of Solomon, "Woe betide the land whose king is a child".[22] As we have seen, in terms of the government of England, the Lancastrian establishment approached their predicament by rejecting the ambitions of the royal dukes of Bedford and Gloucester, affirming the unity of the minority council, and establishing the fiction of the *persona publica* of the infant king. Nevertheless, the actions of the aristocracy and bishops to preserve unity masked considerable problems facing the new regime in both England and France. The fear and unease that Henry VI's subjects inevitably felt at the prospect of a long minority, and the very real challenge of making real the terms of the Treaty of Troyes, demanded a concerted attempt to imagine how the Dual Monarchy might actually work in practice, represent its authority, and sell the rule of Henry VI to both his English and French subjects.

On the face of it, establishing the legitimacy of Henry VI's rule presented a larger hurdle in France than in England. Even at a most basic level, the precise basis of that authority was questionable, with ambiguities over the legal and constitutional status of the constituent parts of the Lancastrian kingdoms. The Treaty of Troyes had stipulated that the duchy of Normandy (the so-called '*pays de conquête*') be returned to the kingdom of France on the death of Charles VI. In practice, throughout the 1420s the duke of Bedford maintained a separation between the duchy and the kingdom, maintaining an administrative and judicial centre at Rouen, which led to years of jurisdictional disputes between the *Cour de Conseil* in Normandy and the *parlement* of Paris.[23] Indeed, explaining the new constitutional arrangements was not easy. The nature of Henry's kingship, and of the Dual Monarchy as a whole, was fundamentally different from the long-standing claim of the English kings to the French throne, begun by Edward III. As John Capgrave observed, as the offspring of the union between Henry V and Catherine of Valois, Henry VI 'had the titles of both kingdoms, not indeed of old, but lately, won' through the Treaty of Troyes.[24] Within weeks of his accession to the French throne, Henry's councillors in France set about the business of legitimising his rule in the eyes of his new French subjects. One of the first acts was to mint a new coinage, which signalled the inauguration of a new monarchy. Henry V's coinage minted in *le pays de conquête* from 1417 had been recognisably French in design, frequently just replacing the fleur-de-lis with the leopard. Henry VI's new coinage, issued from 1423, juxtaposed the arms of England and France, 'an heraldic representation of the dual monarchy'. The shields were topped with the legend 'HENRICUS', reinforcing the notion that these were two realms united in the person of the king. The symbolic messages contained in this new coinage were both simple and complex. The new *salute*, the chief gold coin of France, depicted an Annunciation scene, with the Virgin and an angel holding, respectively, the shields of France and England. This arrangement suggested the English angel announcing to the French Virgin the coming of a saviour, the infant Henry VI.[25]

In the same year as the new French coinage appeared, Bedford also commissioned Lawrence Calot, an Anglo-French notary, to compose verses highlighting the descent of Henry VI from the ancient royal houses of England and France. The poem complemented an elaborate pictorial genealogy showing Henry's lineage to the saintly Louis IX (1214–70), and both media were publicly displayed on the walls of major churches throughout northern France. While the image stressed the new king's ancient lineage and innate, hereditary right to rule, the poem also dwelt upon more pragmatic and immediate reasons why the French should support the Dual Monarchy. It began by rehearsing the Dauphin's part in the murder of the duke of Burgundy in 1419, went on to stress that the Treaty of Troyes was a covenant that bound all parties involved, and ended by assuring its audience that in the person of Henry VI the French crown had not passed to a foreigner.[26] It is difficult to gauge the reaction to the accession of Henry VI among the broader political society of those parts of northern France under Lancastrian rule. In 1422 the country was still in the midst of what was essentially a civil war between rival French nobles rather than a national struggle between England and France. Many Frenchmen committed themselves to defending the settlement made at Troyes, but equally, many left their estates to join the Dauphin's supporters. Furthermore, the French Church, especially the cathedral chapters of Rouen and Notre Dame, proved to be pro-Lancastrian, while the University of Paris, to a degree, also embraced the new Dual Monarchy.[27]

In England the task of legitimising the Dual Monarchy, as opposed to simply gaining acceptance of Henry VI's right to rule as king of England, was altogether more complex. The fear, expressed by the Commons in the parliament of 1420, that the Treaty of Troyes might, at some point in the future, force the subjugation of the kingdom of England to a king of France remained throughout the remainder of the decade. Such views must go some way to explaining the Commons' reluctance to grant taxation for the French wars before 1429. To allay such fears and to re-imagine the domestic Lancastrian monarchy, with all its ambiguities and the lingering questions over its legitimacy, as a true Dual Monarchy demanded a concerted rhetorical campaign on the part of the regime and its agents. In July 1426 Richard Beauchamp, earl of Warwick, one of the most stalwart defenders of the Treaty of Troyes, commissioned John Lydgate to produce an English translation of Calot's poem. The poem was accompanied, as it had been in France, by illustrated and annotated genealogies of the English and French royal families. Lydgate's explicit purpose was 'Trouble hertis to sette in quyete/ And make folkys theire language for to lette,/ Which disputen in their opynyons/ Touching the ligne of two regions' and settle all 'ambyguyté'. This prologue explicitly recognised the extent to which the very nature of the Dual Monarchy and its consequences for England were a matter that excited public debate. Yet, by translating a poem written for a French audience and stressing Henry's descent 'of the stok and blode of seint Lowys', Lydgate may have succeeded only in creating fresh anxiety about the priorities of the Lancastrian regime.[28] The same themes were also apparent in Lydgate's short verse history of the kings and queens of England, *Kings of England sithen William Conqueror*. The poem rather anxiously proclaimed Henry's 'just title, borne bi enheritaunce' to the crowns of England and France, casting the young king, like his father, as Christ's knight.[29] The broad extent to which these arguments were disseminated among the public of Lancastrian England is evident from the fact that the verse history alone survives in at least forty-six manuscripts and may have found its way into schoolboy curricula. Their success in convincing the English of the idea of the Dual Monarchy is another matter: a 1434 textbook, for example, asked students to translate the phrase 'The king of England rules the French as well, to whom he is compassionate and benevolent', suggesting a more traditional view of the relationship between the crowns of England and France.[30]

John Lydgate was the pre-eminent Lancastrian author of the 1420s and his work reveals the ambiguities and unresolved tensions that blighted the Dual Monarchy. In 1422 he penned his only prose work, *The Serpent of Division*, a history of the Roman Republic, its descent into civil war, and the death of Julius Caesar. Lydgate was explicit in his message: 'And let the wise governors of every land and region make a mirror in their mind this manly man Julius and consider in their hearts the contagious damage and importable harm of division.' In other words, only unity among the lords could save Henry's crowns. In a short verse epitaph appended to some copies of the manuscript, the text's function as a targeted warning to the dukes of Bedford and Gloucester was underlined: addressing himself to 'lords and princes of renown', Lydgate told them to 'eschewe stryf and dissencion/ Within yowreself beth not contrarious'.[31] Having given this advice, however, Lydgate seemed to accept the inevitability of the Dual Monarchy's collapse. Such a collapse, he explained, was inevitable: it was necessary, as all things are transitory, and it also followed from '*consuetudinare*' (custom), because Fortune is a fickle mistress. The poet also struggled to resolve the paradox of Humphrey, duke of Gloucester, within the Lancastrian imagination. Gloucester's 1423 marriage to Jacqueline of Bavaria was an action motivated by personal ambition that threatened to undermine Bedford's policies in France and to sow division between the king's councillors. Yet in 1423 Lydgate also wrote poetry celebrating Gloucester's impending nuptials. He praised the duke, celebrated as 'Thoroughe al þis worlde oon þe best knight,/And best purveyes of manhood and of might', and he hoped 'þat Duchye of Holand by hool affeccoun/ May beo allayed with Brutus Albyoun', even though the marriage clearly threatened the integrity of the Dual Monarchy itself.[32] Lydgate's work is thus replete with the paradoxes and ambiguities that ran through the first decade of Henry VI's rule: peace in England and France could be brought about only by prosecuting war; the union of the two realms, achieved by the 'besy peyne' of that exemplar of active kingship, Henry V, was now embodied in a small child; and, however much the regime might plan, it was 'pitous fate' that would ultimately decide the fortunes of the Dual Monarchy.

Defending the Dual Monarchy

Henry V's final instructions concerning the practical government of Lancastrian France and the overall strategy for implementing the terms of the Treaty of Troyes were also less than clear. He stressed the importance of the Burgundian alliance, the need to keep Normandy at all costs, and that none of the leading French captives taken at Agincourt was to be released until his son came of age. Initially, Philip, duke of Burgundy, was offered the regency of France, but he refused, and on 19 November 1422 John, duke of Bedford, assumed the title and responsibilities of regent before the *parlement* of Paris. Those assembled then swore to uphold the treaty of Troyes (Burgundy having previously sworn a similar oath on 7 November). On 12 December the Anglo-Burgundian alliance was cemented by the betrothal of Anne, Duke Philip's sister, to Bedford. Bedford was perfectly placed to make the Dual Monarchy a political reality. He epitomised the cosmopolitan, international princely pretensions of the House of Lancaster. He was thoroughly Francophone, patronising French monasteries, artists, and poets, and when he died in 1435 he chose to be buried in Rouen cathedral.

The challenges faced by the Lancastrian regime in France were considerable. On 30 October the Dauphin was proclaimed King Charles VII at Mehun-sur-Yèvre and set about assembling a new army to throw the English and Burgundians out of northern France with the help of his Scottish, Castilian, and Italian allies. Initially the Dauphinist forces enjoyed some successes. In January 1423 they captured the bridge over the Seine at Meulan (although this was retaken two months later) and in October they took the town of Compiègne. Nevertheless, the military initiative still lay with the Anglo-Burgundians. In March Bedford met with the dukes of Burgundy and Brittany to discuss strategy and on 17 April the three men entered into a solemn 'brotherhood-in-arms', an agreement between fellow knights to uphold the treaty of Troyes. This gave Bedford the confidence to launch a multi-pronged campaign. In Champagne, Thomas Montague, earl of Salisbury, began to reduce the Dauphinist strongholds between Paris and Chartres, while in Picardy William de la Pole, earl of Suffolk, and Sir Ralph Boteler began a siege of the strategically important castle of Le Crotoy, situated at the mouth of the Somme River. Finally, in July, Bedford instructed Sir John de la Pole, captain of Avranches, to invest the fortress-monastery of Mont-Saint-Michel in south-west Normandy. Unfortunately de la Pole decided that a raid into Anjou offered richer pickings. His folly led to defeat and his capture at La Brossinière near Angers on 26 September. This set-back was eclipsed, however, by events in Picardy. On 31 July at Cravant near Auxerre an Anglo-Burgundian army of some 3,500 men under Salisbury had defeated a Franco-Scottish army, commanded by Louis, count of Vendôme, and John Stewart, earl of Buchan, more than twice their size. The battle was a crushing defeat for the Dual Monarchy's enemies (particularly for the Scots, who were almost annihilated) and it confirmed Salisbury's credentials as an energetic and skilled commander.

Bedford maintained the military pressure on the Dauphinists in 1424. A war council, held in Paris in June, planned the conquest of Anjou and Maine (on the southern borders of Normandy) and Picardy (to the north). The Norman contingents had been reinforced by more than 2,000 men from England. The Dauphinists recognised too that the 1424 campaign would be crucial, sending a large Franco-Scottish army (with a substantial force of Lombard heavy cavalry) to win back the recently recaptured castle of Gaillon and town of Ivry in southern Normandy. On 17 August they met the Anglo-Norman army, commanded by Bedford, at Verneuil on the Normandy/Maine frontier. The result was a crushing defeat for the Dauphinists that had not only a military but also a symbolic importance. During the battle Bedford wore a surcoat combining the white cross of France with the red cross of England, embodying the Dual Monarchy, but he also wore a robe of blue velvet, similar to that he is depicted wearing in the so-called Bedford Hours, which had a symbolic connection to the Order of the Garter. By depicting himself as a chivalric knight, commanding a brotherhood of knights certain of the justice of their cause, Bedford claimed the moral high ground against the Dauphin (whose counsellors has advised him against taking the field in person). Indeed, the unjust nature of the Dauphin's cause was underlined in the battle's aftermath: the body of one of the French commanders, the viscount of Narbonne, who had been killed during the battle and who had been implicated in the murder of John the Fearless, was strung up on Bedford's orders and later quartered in front of the assembled Anglo-Norman army.[33] Militarily, the victory at Verneuil secured Normandy and the region around Paris, giving the regent the opportunity to bring peace and security to *le pays de conquête* over the coming months and to plan further advances. In the autumn an English expedition under the command of Sir John Fastolf and Lord Scales invaded Anjou and Maine.

Yet Verneuil also revealed the considerable difficulties that faced the Lancastrians in France. On the eve of the battle Bedford had dismissed the Burgundian contingent in his army, some 2,000 men commanded by L'Isle Adam. He had learnt that on 8 August representatives of Philip the Good had met with the Dauphin's servants at Dijon. Moreover, Gloucester's campaign to recover his wife's estates in Hainault had further strained the Burgundian alliance. This was not all: on 18 May a treaty of friendship between the duke of Brittany and the Dauphin had been agreed at Nantes. The solemn agreement to defend the Treaty of Troyes made the previous year by the dukes of Bedford, Brittany, and Burgundy was now in danger of unravelling. Bedford's strategy in the coming months, a strategy heralded in symbolic form by his dismissal of the Burgundian contingent at Verneuil, was to rely more and more on Englishmen and Normans to defend the Dual Monarchy. Indeed, in the next two years it was Englishmen, particularly the earls of Salisbury and Warwick, who took the war to the Dauphinists. In 1425 Salisbury laid siege to and captured Le Mans, and in September 1427, after vigorous campaigning on the Breton frontier, the duke of Brittany was forced to reaffirm his commitment to the Treaty of Troyes. In March that year Bedford returned to France and preparations were begun to complete the conquest of Anjou and Maine. Duke John crossed the Channel with 1,200 men and in June 1428 a further 2,694 men were assembled in England for service in France. The culmination of these preparations was the siege of the Dauphinist stronghold of Orléans, which began on 12 October 1428.

The siege of Orléans was to be one of the defining events of Henry VI's reign. For the Lancastrians it had a disastrous beginning: just twelve days after its start the earl of Salisbury, the most talented English commander, was killed by a cannon ball. Nevertheless, by early 1429 the campaign appeared to be progressing well. The new English commander, the earl of Suffolk, had established a ring of field fortifications around the city and on 12 February Sir John Fastolf defeated a much larger Franco-Scottish force as it attempted to intercept an English supply train bound for the siege at Rouvray. On receiving news of this set-back many French commanders deserted the city and the citizens approached the duke of Burgundy to ask Bedford for terms. On the same day as Fastolf routed the French, a young peasant girl from Domrémy in eastern France, who had experienced visions of SS. Catherine, Margaret, and Michael in which the saints had urged her to expel the English from France, met her local garrison commander, Robert de Baudricourt, and requested an interview with the Dauphin. The girl, Joan of Arc, met Charles at Chinon and, with royal and ecclesiastical approval, she joined the relief army being assembled at Blois. It arrived outside Orléans on 28 April and, after much heated discussion with the city's commander, Jean de Dunois, she joined the assault on the English-held fortress of St Loup six days later. On 6 May she led a successful assault against the city's Augustinian monastery, leaving the English garrison in Les Tourelles, a twelfth-century fortress that dominated the city's defences, isolated. The following morning, against the wishes of Dunois, who had banned unauthorised sorties, she led the assault on Les Tourelles itself, guarded by between seven and eight hundred men. Joan was wounded by an arrow in the shoulder, but by nightfall Les Tourelles had fallen. During the night the bridge over the Loire was repaired, and by the morning of 8 May the English had abandoned their remaining positions. For a short period there was a stand-off while the English, arrayed in battle positions, waited between the walls of the city and their abandoned siege lines, but before long the English turned and marched away. One group, under Lords Scales and Talbot, retreated to Meung-sur-Loire, while Suffolk led another contingent to Jargeau.

The siege of Orléans had lasted 210 days. The failure of the siege had been due in large part to the inspirational intervention of Joan of Arc, who had galvanised the cautious French captains and engendered a new enthusiasm among ordinary soldiers and citizens. Initially, the English underestimated the scale of the French revival under Joan and the energy that the victory at Orléans had given them. On 12 June, Jargeau fell and Suffolk was captured; three days later the fortified bridge at Meung fell; and on 18 June the English garrison at Beaugency surrendered. On the same day the English field army, led by Talbot and Fastolf, was routed at the battle of Patay. Joan of Arc remains a deeply mysterious figure and debate rages over her precise role in determining French strategy in these months, but the English were clearly deeply afraid of 'La Pucelle', whose intervention they variously attributed to both God and the Devil.[34] In return for the stunning victory at Orléans, the dauphin granted Joan joint command of the French army alongside the duke of Alençon. She was present throughout the series of sieges in early July which included the capture of Burgundian-held Auxerres and the town of Troyes itself. Once again, at the siege of Troyes her outspoken intervention at the war council before the dauphin was instrumental. Joan was placed in command of the siege and she led the assault on the town walls in person. On 17 July the French resurgence was confirmed when the dauphin was crowned Charles VII of France in Reims cathedral, with Joan by his side. By early September the French were outside the gates of Paris, and although 'La Pucelle' was repulsed on this occasion, the Dual Monarchy of Henry VI faced a moment of grave crisis.

Conclusion

The first six-and-half years of Henry VI's reign had given considerable hope that the Lancastrian Dual Monarchy could survive and flourish. Despite the accession of a baby to the thrones of England and France, the Lancastrians, with the help of their French allies, had consolidated and extended Henry V's conquests in Normandy. In England the political nation had accepted Henry VI as their king, quashed the personal ambitions of the king's uncles, and reaffirmed Lancastrian principles of good government. While conciliar politics and parliamentary arguments had revealed an undercurrent of ambiguity and unresolved tensions at the heart of the minority government, the overwhelming feeling among the king's English subjects was one of unity and a sense of responsibility to defend the achievements of Henry V both at home and abroad until his son came of age. The appearance of Joan of Arc outside Orléans in April 1429, her stunning victory, and the coronation of Charles VII at Reims demanded that the Lancastrian establishment rethink its strategy and forced upon the young Henry VI a far more prominent role in the government of both realms.

Notes

1 Patrick and Felicity Strong, 'The Last Will and Codicils of Henry V', *English Historical Review* 116 (1981), 79–102.
2 TNA, E101/407/13.
3 *A Chronicle of London, from 1089 to 1483*, ed. N.H. Nicolas (1827), 112.
4 *Chronicles of London*, ed. Charles Lethbridge Kingsford (Oxford, 1905), 279–81.
5 TNA, E101/407/13, f. 23.
6 *PROME*, x, 26–27.
7 R.H. Sharpe, *London and the Kingdom*, iii, 367.
8 S.B. Chrimes, 'The Pretensions of the Duke of Gloucester in 1422', *English Historical Review*, 45 (1930), 101–3.
9 *PROME*, x, 13.
10 *Calendar of Close Rolls, 1422–29*, 46, 154.
11 *POPC*, iii, 86–87.
12 Ibid., 107.
13 Kingsford, *Chronicles of London*, 281.
14 G.L. Harriss, *Cardinal Beaufort: A Study of Lancastrian Ascendancy and Decline* (Oxford, 1988), 149.
15 *PROME*, x, 205.
16 Ibid., 287–92.
17 John Watts, *Henry VI and the Politics of Kingship* (Cambridge, 1996), 116.
18 TNA, E101/408/1, f. 6.
19 *POPC*, iii, 237–42.
20 *PROME*, x, 347–9.
21 *POPC*, iii, 239.
22 *The St Albans Chronicle, Volume 2, 1394–1422*, ed. John Taylor, Wendy R. Childs and Leslie Watkiss (Oxford, 2011), 774–5.
23 Christopher Allmand, *Lancastrian Normandy 1415–1450* (Oxford, 1983), 121–51.
24 John Capgrave, *Liber de Illustribus Henricis*, ed. F.C. Hingeston (1858), 124.
25 J.W. McKenna, 'Henry VI of England and the Dual Monarchy: Aspects of Royal Political Propaganda, 1422–1432', *Journal of the Warburg and Courtauld Institutes* 28 (1965), 145–62.

26 B.J.H. Rowe, 'King Henry VI's Claim to France: In Picture and Poem', *The Library*, 4th series, 13 (1933), 77–88.

27 Allmand, *Lancastrian Normandy,* 211–40.

28 *The Minor Poems of John Lydgate*, ed. H.N. MacCraken (Early English Text Society, 1911), ii, 613–22.

29 Ibid., 716.

30 *English School Exercises, 1420–1530*, ed. Nicholas Orme (Turnhout, 2013), 77.

31 John Lydgate, *The Serpent of Division*, ed. H.N. MacCracken (Early English Text Society, 1910), 65–68.

32 *Minor Poems*, ed. H.N. MacCracken, ii. 601–8.

33 M.K. Jones, 'The Battle of Verneuil (17 August 1424): Towards a History of Courage', *War in History* 9 (2002), 375–411.

34 Malcolm Vale, *The Ancient Enemy: England, France and Europe from the Angevins to the Tudors* (2007), 89–100; Kelly de Vries, *Joan of Arc: A Military Leader* (Stroud, 1999), 31–53.

5 Coronations and counsel, 1429–37

In 1429 Henry VI's slow and reasonably uneventful passage through childhood was rudely interrupted. During the first seven years of the minority, while his uncles and the other lords, sometimes acrimoniously, dealt with the business of war and government in both England and France, the king enjoyed an apparently tranquil childhood spent mainly at Windsor. The advent of Joan of Arc, a series of defeats in France, and the coronation of the Dauphin as Charles VII at Reims in July transformed the situation. By the end of 1431 Henry had been hastily crowned king both in England and France, and his counsellors had set about in earnest preparing him for the rigours of kingship. Within another six years he had been declared of age and the formal minority had come to an end. In some ways these years witnessed the high points of Henry's reign. Beset by financial crisis and continuing squabbles within the Lancastrian royal family, faced with a resurgent French monarchy, and, in 1435, betrayed by their ally, the duke of Burgundy, the English political nation responded by rallying behind their king. By 1437 Henry and the Lancastrian regime had weathered the storm and, so it must have seemed to many, survived the perils of the long minority to approach the future with confidence.

Two coronations

The impetus behind the decision to bring forward Henry's coronations came from France. Despite the opinion of many English chroniclers, who claimed the decision had been made in the parliament that assembled at Westminster on 22 September 1429, it was the duke of Bedford and his council in Paris and Rouen who pushed for a speedy coronation in direct response to that of Charles VII at Reims the previous July. The plan involved a rather hastily arranged ceremony at Westminster, before the launch of a major military expedition to France, led by the king himself, to secure his coronation as king of France. Bedford had been pressing for a coronation in France to counter the French resurgence under Joan of Arc since at least April, but the English council seems to have been initially reluctant to commit to an expensive expedition overseas. On 18 October, however, the council in England wrote to the burghers of Ghent informing them that the decision to go ahead with the two coronations had been made; similar letters were also despatched to Paris, Rouen, and other French towns. The message was clear: Henry's coronation at Westminster was a direct response to events at Reims and a prelude to an assertion of his own right as king of France. Preparations for the expedition to France, clearly the most important part of the double coronation in the eyes of Bedford, began in earnest in the autumn of 1429. On 13 October Bedford assigned the government of Paris and the English-held territories outside Normandy to the duke of Burgundy, allowing him to concentrate on the duchy and the preparations for his nephew's arrival.

On 5 November, with the king just a month shy of his eighth birthday, the English coronation ceremony began. That evening thirty-two Knights of the Bath, including the young earl of Devon and the earl of Warwick's son, Henry, were dubbed and the king lodged in the Tower of London. On the following morning Henry was escorted to Westminster. He sat in state in Westminster Hall before being carried to the abbey by his tutor, the earl of Warwick. There he first received the acclamation of his subjects. Then the young king endured a long and gruelling series of prostrations while various bishops sang mass and said prayers over him, ritual clothing and unclothing, the swearing of the coronation oath, and the taking of the regalia. The most important parts of the ceremony were the coronation with St Edward the Confessor's crown by Archbishop Chichele and the anointing. The latter was of special significance. Like his father and grandfather, Henry was anointed with the holy oil of St Thomas Becket (miraculously given to the saint by the Virgin): 'first his breast and his two teats, and the middle of his back, and his head, all across his two shoulders, his two elbows, his palms of his hands; and then they laid a certain soft thing, as cotton, to all the places anointed; and on his head they put a white coif of silk'. This was kept in situ for eight days before being removed and the king's head washed 'with white wine warmed lukewarm', although the lice that had greeted those that removed his grandfather's cap were thankfully absent on this occasion. The anointing with the Becket oil was doubly significant, as Henry was not anointed also by the traditional English oils of catechumens and chrism. This brought Lancastrian practice into line with that of the Most Christian Kings of France, who were anointed only with the sacred oil of Clovis. Contemporaries remarked on the king's stamina and bearing throughout the ceremony, but one noted that St Edward's crown proved 'over heavy for him, for he was of a tender age', and later in the ceremony he wore a lighter crown that had been made for Richard II.[1] The party then made its way back to Westminster Hall for the coronation banquet, where Henry sat in state, flanked by Cardinal Beaufort and his mother.

The coronation banquet was an opportunity to stress the symbolic importance of the day's events through a series of elaborate pastry sculptures. The first course included figures of St Edward the Confessor and St Louis bearing a figure of the young king 'inheritor to the *Fleur-de-Lis*.' The second stressed the Lancastrian image of Christ's Knight, 'cherishing the Church' and alluding to the imperial nature of Henry's kingship. The third 'subtlety' was a vignette of St George and St Denis presenting Henry to the Virgin and Christ child with the verse, 'Shecythe youre grace on hym,/ Thys tendyr and whythe vertu hym avaunce,/ Borne by dyscent and tytylle of right/ Justely to raygne in Ingelonde and yn Fraunce.'[2] The commitment of those present to the Dual Monarchy was clear, as were their expectations and the obligations of the king himself. Henry's English coronation also had important repercussions for the government of the realm. The king's presence was visible at the parliament that had met in September. He was there on its opening day, again on 12 December, when the Commons made their first grant of a lay subsidy since December 1421, and also eight days later, when parliament was prorogued and a second grant made. Parliament noted that the king had taken the traditional coronation oath and thus on 15 November the duke of Gloucester formally relinquished the title of Protector of the Realm granted seven years previously. Cardinal Beaufort was also readmitted to the council, despite his being a cardinal and the potential for his loyalties to be divided between Rome and England. These actions signalled the beginning of the long process of ending the king's minority.

Attention now shifted to the task of preparing for Henry's coronation as king of France. The first challenge facing those tasked with organising the coronation expedition was recruiting and paying for the army. The expedition would be expensive not only because of the simple fact that it would involve transporting the king and his household to France and maintaining them there for a prolonged period of time, but because the military situation demanded that it should also have the strength to operate effectively as a field army. The parliamentary grants of December 1429 were a recognition of this fact, but it was not until the end of the assembly, on 23 February the following year, that sufficient funds were secured in the form of an extension of the wool subsidy. The council had clearly anticipated the Commons' generosity and between 18 and 20 February indentures had been sealed with the captains who were to lead the expeditionary forces. Already in January 3,199 men had been sent to France with the Bastard of Clarence, and the agreements made in February assembled another 1,196 men-at-arms and 3,596 archers for service in France. This was the largest single force assembled for service in France during the reign and in only one other year (1436) did the number of English soldiers crossing the Channel exceed this number. The core of the army, as it had been for his father's first venture to France in 1415, was the royal household. Seventy of the 114 captains were esquires and named officers of the household; their principal task was to guard the king's person. The remaining captains, bringing the great bulk of the men-at-arms and archers, were the nobility and knights. No fewer than twenty-one peers agreed to serve in person, underlining the commitment of the political nation both to the idea of the Lancastrian Dual Monarchy and to Henry VI personally.[3] Cardinal Beaufort, now firmly established as the leading figure on the council, also accompanied the king to France. On 24 February, the day after he had presided over the closure of parliament, Henry and his entourage began their leisurely progress through Kent, arriving in the English-held town of Calais on St George's Day (23 April) 1430.

The situation that greeted them in France was a difficult one. Initially much was expected of the duke of Burgundy. Cardinal Beaufort prepared to negotiate in person with Duke Philip and it is probable that the duke's new bride, Isabel of Portugal (Beaufort's niece and Henry's half cousin), who stayed at the English court en route to her wedding in Flanders on 30 January, was also expected to lobby on behalf of the English. On 12 February Duke Philip agreed to serve Henry with 1,500 men in return for 12,500 marks, and on 8 March he was granted the county of Champagne, indicative of the expectation that he was to capture the city of Reims, its capital, in preparation for the coronation. In the event no Burgundian troops ever entered Reims and it soon became apparent to the king's councillors that Henry's coronation would have to be secured by English arms alone. In the last week of July Henry travelled from Calais to Rouen, where he would remain until November 1431. At least one important obstacle to Lancastrian designs had been removed in May 1430, when the Burgundians had captured Joan of Arc. She was transferred to Rouen, where she was tried and eventually burned at the stake in May 1431. Her death was probably seen as a vital precursor to Henry's coronation. Henry kept a splendid court while at Rouen. He was accompanied by Bedford (whose regency had ended with the king's arrival in France) until January 1431 and attended by the duke of Brittany throughout the summer and autumn of that year, while his presence also witnessed a spate of artistic production, such as the celebrated Bedford Book of Hours, a sumptuous manuscript presented to the king by his aunt, Duchess Anne. During 1431 more troops were sent from England, over 3,500 men in three separate contingents commanded by the young earl of Salisbury, Lord Clinton, and Beaufort's nephews, Thomas, count of Perche, and Edmund, count of Mortain. By the autumn they had secured the king's passage from Rouen to St Denis and then to Paris.

On Sunday, 16 December 1431 Henry left his lodgings and progressed on foot from the Hôtel des Tournelles to Notre Dame for his coronation. Parisian observers would comment unfavourably on what, to them at least, seemed a very English affair. Comments on the poor quality of the food served at the coronation banquet and on how the English stole alms given at the ceremony may reflect entrenched national rivalries, but the fact that Cardinal Beaufort presided (and crowned Henry with a brand new crown purchased especially for the occasion) and the notable absence of the duke of Burgundy from the ceremony underlined the fact that Lancastrian kingship in France was contested and that Henry was only one of two individuals claiming to be the rightful king of France. Another oddly English custom was the acclamation, which echoed throughout the cathedral and which had not been seen at a French coronation for more than a century and a half. The post-coronation festivities were also dominated by Englishmen: Walter, Lord Hungerford, acted as the king's carver during the banquet, while the following day the earl of Arundel was prominent in the jousts. On 21 December the king attended a meeting of the Paris *parlement*, where the traditional oaths of kingship were recited. Interestingly, it seems the young king was unable to speak publicly in French, with the earl of Warwick making such pronouncement as necessary on his behalf. His contact with his French family seems to have been restricted to his doffing his hat towards his grandmother, Queen Isabeau, as he passed by her window at the Hôtel de St Pol during his entry to Paris. Indeed, he did not remain long in the capital of his French kingdom: he remained in Paris until 26 or 27 December, returning to Rouen, which he left on 12 January 1432, before heading to Calais, via Abbeville, arriving there two weeks later. On 9 February he landed at Dover, reaching Eltham by Valentine's Day. He would never again set foot in his realm of France.[4]

Henry's English subjects were clearly relieved to have him back. The king's presence in France had not notably advanced the Lancastrian cause and just days before his coronation in Paris the duke of Burgundy had concluded a six-year truce with Charles VII on the pretext that the English had not paid him the sums agreed in 1430. On 21 February the king made a solemn entry into London, affording his English subjects an opportunity to demonstrate their loyalty and happiness at his return, but the various tableaux that greeted Henry also underlined his English subjects' expectations of him as he moved slowly towards adulthood. At London Bridge the king was welcomed to the city by three empresses, Nature, Grace, and Fortune, who presented him with gifts representing strength, knowledge, and prosperity. At Cornhill there was a tabernacle of wisdom, attended by the seven sciences: grammar, logic, rhetoric, music, arithmetic, geometry, and astronomy. There was also a boy, seated as a king, with Mercy, Truth, and Clemency to govern him and attended by the officers of the royal law courts. At the Great Conduit between Poultry and Cheapside three virgins, Mercy, Grace, and Pity, poured wines of temperance, good governance, and consolation. At Cheap Cross the king was confronted with a more familiar piece of Lancastrian propaganda, a royal genealogy stressing his descent from St Edward and St Louis, while finally at the Little Conduit at Cheapside there stood a vignette of the Trinity accompanied by a multitude of angels. After a solemn service of thanksgiving, the king reacquainted himself with the royal regalia in a service at Westminster Abbey (contemporaries noted how well Henry had acquitted himself in carrying the heavy sceptre of St Edward), before he finally retired to Westminster Palace.[5]

In tangible terms the coronations at Westminster and Notre Dame had achieved little. The English position in France was not greatly improved nor diminished, although the actions of the duke of Burgundy confirmed that the Lancastrian Dual Monarchy was essentially an English undertaking. Symbolically, however, the coronations were of great importance. At a stroke they ended Gloucester's claim for pre-eminence among the king's counsellors by virtue of his birth and Bedford's regency in France (although not, as we shall see, the prominent and controversial role of the king's uncles in the government of both realms). They also prepared the way for the king to take a more active role in government and made even more urgent the necessity to prepare him for the rigours of kingship. Henry himself appears to have coped with the demands placed upon him in these years remarkably well. He was clearly well coached and advised and responded admirably. Certainly the actions of the young king gave no hint of the problems that were to come.

From boy to man: educating the prince

As the vignettes that greeted Henry on his return to London made abundantly clear, kings were not merely born but were also made through education and training. By the beginning of the fifteenth century there was a long-established tradition of educating princes through a combination of limited formal learning, the consumption of didactic literature within the wider household environment, and practical experience and instruction. The future Edward III, for example, had been taught etiquette and manners, as well as singing, dancing, and equestrian skills, by his aristocratic tutor, Sir Richard Damory. Formal works of instruction included vernacular translations of Vegetius's *Epitoma Rei Militaris*, Giles of Rome's *De Regimine Principum*, and an assorted collection of liturgical and historical works, as well as romances, legends, and biblical stories. As a boy Henry V had received similar instruction in the practical accomplishments – riding, hunting, music, swordplay – of the aristocracy, as well as a formal education in Latin. In 1395/96 ten Latin grammar books were purchased in London for his use. As Prince of Wales he was expected to heed 'the learned counsel of his elders', and his uncle, the bishop of Winchester, prepared him for the intellectual challenges of kingship, probably introducing him to the Continental 'Mirrors for Princes' genre.[6] This body of didactic writing, of which the best known was probably the pseudo-Aristotelian *Secreta Secretorum*, sought to educate princes by reference to a series of biblical, classical, and historical exemplars of good and bad kingship. They were also a means to explore the reciprocal obligations of kings and their subjects, the importance of counsel, and the cardinal virtues of Prudence, Justice, Temperance, and Fortitude. Significantly, these texts were designed for consumption not only by the prince, but also by his wider household and, in the early fifteenth century at least, the broader political nation. Thomas Hoccleve based his *Regement of Princes* (written for Henry, Prince of Wales, in 1411–12) on earlier Continental 'Mirrors' by James of Cessolis and Giles of Rome and on the *Secreta Secretorum*. The 'Mirrors' were rewritten, as we have seen, with a specifically Lancastrian audience in mind and were, to judge by the forty-six surviving manuscript copies, distributed widely.

For the first few years of Henry VI's life, however, such things lay in the future. At Windsor and in the handful of other royal residences he frequented during these years, his upbringing was in the hands of his mother, Queen Catherine, and his nurse, Dame Alice Boteler. Yet even as a toddler Henry was exposed to didactic messages about the nature and duties of kingship. In 1425 the keeper of the Great Wardrobe purchased from Henry V's executors a series of tapestries to decorate Windsor and other royal residences. They included Old Testament stories, romances, and histories depicting kings both real and mythic. It is impossible now to know the extent to which, if at all, the infant king engaged with the tapestries' depictions of giants, mythical beasts, and knights, but the stories they told shared many features in common with the 'Mirrors' with which Henry would later become familiar.[7] Dame Alice also no doubt introduced him to proper aristocratic codes of conduct and to the religious ritual of the Lancastrian chapel royal, which would figure so prominently in later years. In May 1427 a Latin primer and a set of organs were purchased for him, perhaps evidence of an early fascination with church ceremony. Indeed, in March 1428 Archbishop Kemp wrote to the bishop of Dax in southwest France that the young king was precocious enough to have learnt some of the liturgy off by heart. Yet Kemp's eagerness to show the king as learned and devout should be contrasted with other evidence suggesting that Henry's concerns were those more typical of a small boy. In the same year two sets of coat armour and a long-bladed sword, 'for to learn the king to play in his tender age', were purchased for him, while early in 1427 a gilt model of a ship, mounted on four wheels so it could be pulled along, was bought from the duke of Exeter's executors. At times the king's behaviour caused embarrassment at court: in February 1428 he snatched a gold collar recently presented to the earl of Oxford and gave it to a visiting Polish knight. The unfortunate councillors were forced to issue a warrant ordering the exchequer to reimburse Oxford 20 marks for the lost collar. Other evidence points to a happy child, taking an interest in the world around him: when he made his ceremonial entry to Rouen in July 1430 he was unsurprisingly captivated by a mechanical figure that gushed wine and milk from its breasts![8]

On 1 June 1428 the council appointed Richard Beauchamp, earl of Warwick, to have responsibility for the king's upbringing and the transition from boyhood to adolescence. Henry was then six-and-a-half years old, six months shy of the traditional age at which a young nobleman's care was transferred from a female to a male environment. In some ways Henry had already been prepared for this change by the introduction of older, noble-born boys into the royal household. In June 1425 the council had decreed that the noble heirs in the king's wardship should reside there, the most notable of whom was Richard, duke of York, who lived in the royal household following the death of his guardian, the earl of Westmorland, in that year. Warwick was explicitly charged with regard to his duties in educating the young king and reiterated the familiar contemporary patterns of princely education. The earl was to teach the king to love God, eschew vice, and embrace virtue, 'laying before him mirrors and examples of times passed of the good grace and sure prosperity and wealth that have fallen to virtuous kings . . . and of the contrary fortune that hath ensued to kings . . . of the contrary disposition'. He was to ensure Henry learnt 'nurture' (manners), writing, and languages (French and Latin) and the earl was given authority to chastise the king should he misbehave or fall behind in his studies. The day-to-day responsibility for the king's education and his general well-being was entrusted to Master John Somerset, a Cambridge academic and cleric who had served at court since 1427 as a physician and scholar. Warwick's role also had a political purpose: he was granted the power to remove, in consultation with the king's uncles and the council, 'any person suspect of misgovernment' within the royal household, except the great officers or those appointed specially by the royal dukes or council.[9]

Indeed, the council's concern with the composition of the king's expanding household was evident in the appointment of his closest body servants. Warwick's influence was evident in the choice of several of his servants and relatives to serve in the king's chamber. Just days after the earl's own appointment as guardian, four knights and four esquires were named to attend upon the king, dressing him, serving him at table, and being constantly at his side. These men had long traditions of service to the House of Lancaster, both in England and France. Sir Walter Beauchamp, for example, a relative of the earl of Warwick, had probably been associated with the House of Lancaster since 1399. He had been Speaker of the Commons in the parliament of 1416, had served the king's father in France, and had been a member of the minority council since 1422. Probably at least in his fifties when appointed to attend upon the young king (he died in 1430), he demonstrated Warwick's and the council's determination to surround Henry with men who embodied Lancastrian principles of service and dynastic loyalty. The great officers of the king's household also represented this commitment to upholding the legacy and achievements of the king's father and grandfather. The steward, the man responsible for the 'household-below-stairs' and the king's domestic needs, was John, Lord Tiptoft, who had served as both Speaker of the Commons and treasurer of England during the reign of Henry IV. The king's chamberlain, with overall responsibility for the household-above-stairs, was the Hainaulter Sir Louis Robessart. He had served as standard-bearer to Henry V and had been elected one of the Knights of the Garter. In 1422 he was one of five knights appointed to the new king's household. His commitment to the Lancastrian cause was absolute, and he was killed in a skirmish near Amiens in November 1431.

Precise details of Henry's education and personality in the years between 1428 and 1437 are elusive. His earlier, relatively secluded life spent mainly at Windsor and Eltham gave way to a more varied itinerary, including, of course, months spent at Calais, Rouen, and Paris for his French coronation, and which involved a larger and formal household establishment. Despite this, the king's day-to-day life remained constrained by the ritual of the royal court, which was governed in turn by the liturgical routine of the chapel royal. The chapel, headed by the dean with a staff of almost fifty priests, clerks, and choristers, had responsibility for the spiritual and liturgical life of the court. Its ceremonies dominated the everyday life of the king's household, beginning with matins at seven in the morning, followed by a high mass at ten, vespers at four o'clock in the afternoon, immediately followed by compline, and ending (at least by the 1440s) with prayers for the Virgin, St George, and the Holy Trinity, and a prayer invoking divine help for the king. Each week formal processions were held, involving the entire household-above-stairs and usually attended by the king.

The chapel royal also supervised from 1429 the formal crown-wearing ceremonies. To the traditional occasions of Christmas, Easter, and Whitsun, by the early fifteenth century further ceremonies had been added at Epiphany, All Saints, and the two feasts of St Edward the Confessor.[10] All this took place within a chapel that had developed under Henry V as a cultural powerhouse, famed throughout western Europe for the excellence of its music. It proclaimed the sacral nature of Lancastrian kingship, while advancing the splendour and magnificence of the royal house.

Opportunities for the king to see and be seen by his subjects were few and far between, limited to a few appearances at parliament and such formal events as his entry to London in February 1432. Yet there are glimpses of a boy growing in confidence and stature and becoming increasingly aware of his own exalted position. In November of that year Warwick approached the council seeking a clarification and extension of his powers regarding his governance of the king and of his intimate household servants. The earl explained that his task had become more difficult recently, considering how 'the king is grown in years, in stature of his person, and also in conceit and knowledge of his high and royal authority and estate'. This, naturally enough, had led him 'more and more to grudge with chastising and to loathe it', and Warwick feared he would earn the king's lasting enmity if his powers were not affirmed by the council. He wanted an assurance from the duke of Gloucester and his fellow councillors that 'if the king at any time will conceive for that cause indignation against the said earl' they would 'do all their true diligence and power to remove the king there from'. Here Henry was probably merely developing the growing self-awareness and wilfulness that comes with age, but his behaviour could also have political significance. Warwick was aware that the king's conversations were not always monitored by himself or one of the four knights appointed in 1428 and that Henry 'has been stirred by some from his learning and spoken to of divers matters not behoveful'. The council agreed that Warwick or one of the four knights should constantly be at Henry's side, except for 'such persons as for the nearness of blood and for their estate ought of reason to be suffered to speak with the king'. Finally, Warwick demanded that the councillors tell the king in person their decision that he should accept his governor's chastisement 'and intend the more busily to virtue and to learning'. This they agreed to do the next time Henry came to London.[11] As we shall see, Warwick's concerns in 1432 were linked to a wider struggle at court and within the council to dominate the government of the young king, but they also illustrate the simple difficulty of attempting to control the behaviour of a ten-year-old who was also the anointed king of England and France. As the end of the official minority loomed, his councillors would have to find ever more subtle ways of educating Henry and preparing him for personal kingship.

It is against this backdrop of a king approaching adolescence that the various exemplary texts presented to Henry during the 1430s should be considered. These volumes, while ostensibly having much in common with the genre 'Mirrors for Princes' and directed at the young king himself, had equally important messages for the wider Lancastrian household and thus contributed in different ways to the task of preparing Henry for majority rule. One of the best-known of these texts is John Lydgate's *Lives of SS. Edmund and Fremund*. This was presented to the king on the occasion of his visit to the monastery of Bury St Edmunds in the winter and early spring of 1433–34. The lavish, illustrated manuscript has traditionally been seen as an effort by Lydgate to combine the genres of hagiography and 'Mirrors for Princes' in a long poem which offered Henry possible, if sometimes contradictory, exemplars for kingly behaviour. Lydgate appears to praise the pacifism and idealised Christian life of St Edmund, while Fremund offers an alternative model of martial, Christian kingship. It is tempting to think, however, that the young Henry was more engaged with the graphic descriptions of battle and death and of ghostly appearances by the martyred Edmund than he was by the commentary the text offered on the dilemma of the Lancastrian legacy in France and Lydgate's attempt to curry royal favour for his monastery and the Benedictine order in general. Yet the complex and occasionally contradictory text could still fulfil a didactic function. Lydgate spoke to a wider Lancastrian household audience, drawing parallels between the young king's riding household and those men who accompanied St Edmund into East Anglia. He drew attention to the three crowns borne on Edmund's banner, signifying kingship, virginity, and martyrdom, linking them to the two crowns of England and France worn by Henry and how 'afterward in heuene/ The thrydde crowne to receyue, in certeyne/ Ffor his meritis a boue the sterrys seuene'. As such, the text, produced for a Lancastrian household audience, may have stimulated debate over the future of the Dual Monarchy, the nature of Henry's kingship, and suitable exemplars for princely rule.[12]

A series of texts produced in the late 1430s reveal that this debate over the nature of Henry's kingship and process of educating the prince did not stop with the end of his formal minority. It was the context for the production of two lives of the king's father around 1437: the *Vita et Gesta Henrici Quinti* ('Life and Deeds of Henry V'), addressed to Walter, Lord Hungerford (a councillor and former steward of the king's household), and Titus Frulovisi's *Vita Henrici Quinti* ('Life of Henry V'), dedicated to Humphrey, duke of Gloucester. The latter text drew on the former, and both were designed to advance Henry V as an exemplar for the young king. They also reminded the king's household and closest advisors of Henry V's legacy and the traditions of military service, piety, orthodoxy and good government which underscored Lancastrian legitimacy. Above all else, however, the lives of Henry V stressed that the strength and legitimacy of his kingship arose primarily from the king's own prowess and personal example. Yet few didactic texts were as unambiguous as this. John Lydgate's mammoth poem *The Fall of Princes*, commissioned by Gloucester in 1431 and completed by 1439, presented 500 examples of men drawn from history and mythology who had fallen from great wealth and power to poverty and obscurity, to illustrate the vagaries of fortune. This was one of Lydgate's most widely copied texts, extant in over thirty manuscripts, and it demonstrated how established literary forms – in this case Giovanni Boccaccio's *De Casibus Virorum Illustrium* ('On the Fates of Famous Men'), a fourteenth-century text that gave short biographies of various victims of fortune from Adam to the present day – could be recycled and employed as a didactic tool for the king and his counsellors. Another text, offered ostensibly as an advice manual for the young king but which also contributed to the wider debate on the nature of Lancastrian kingship, was the anonymous *Tractatus de Regimine Principum ad Regem Henricum Sextum*, probably compiled in the late 1430s by a cleric close to the king. It largely consists of quotations from various classical and patristic sources (Aristotle and his medieval commentators, Thomas Aquinas and Giles of Rome, as well as Augustine of Hippo and Gregory of Tours), but it also included Cistercian and other monastic commentaries. The tract differed from others in 'Mirrors' genre by stressing the importance of prayer and a style of kingship modelled on the mercy, charity, and perseverance of Christ. Importantly, the author saw peace with France as the ultimate measure of effective rule; good and wise rulers, after all, hate war.[13] What these texts demonstrate is that the nature and character of Henry's kingship was still in flux as he entered his majority. Different parts of Lancastrian political society could offer different, and at times mutually exclusive, models of kingship. Yet all of these differing views were reconcilable with one of the many strands of political thought found within Lancastrianism. By the late 1430s the good Lancastrian prince could variously be a warmongering conqueror, a pious man removed from the everyday business of government, or an assiduous governor carefully listening to counsel and responding to the concerns of his subjects. These competing priorities crystallised around the defining issue of Lancastrian kingship: the future of the Dual Monarchy and the resolution of the war with France.

From boy to man: politics and counsel 1432–37

Historians have traditionally seen the period between the king's return from France in February 1432 and the formal assertion of majority rule in November 1437 as years of 'indecision and inactivity, even of helpless waiting'.[14] These years witnessed disputes over the best course of action in France (was the defence of Calais or Normandy the priority, or should peace be given a chance?) and continued squabbles between the king's uncles and Cardinal Beaufort over domestic policy and the personnel of the royal council and household. Yet they also revealed the inherent strength and stability of the Lancastrian polity in the face of internal difficulties and external threats. This stability was made possible by the ecumenical nature of Lancastrianism itself and an innate optimism that Henry would eventually come of age and develop into a king able to reconcile the different constituencies within his twin realms.

Henry's return to England in February 1432 afforded the duke of Gloucester the opportunity to reassert his domestic political authority. Bedford remained in France, while Cardinal Beaufort, who had attended the 1431 parliament at Westminster before returning to France, accompanied the king only as far as Calais. Beginning in February 1432, changes were made in both the government and the king's household. In part this was designed to merge the two administrations that had previously existed, with Henry himself in France and to serve Gloucester as the king's lieutenant in England, but they also reflected the temporary ascendancy of Duke Humphrey over his rivals. John Stafford, bishop of Bath and Wells, replaced Archbishop Kemp as chancellor, while Walter, Lord Hungerford, was replaced by John, Lord Scrope, a known partisan of Gloucester, as treasurer of England. In the royal household Gloucester's dominance was assured by wholesale changes among the chief officers and staff of the chapel royal. Ralph, Lord Cromwell (who had only been in office for three weeks), was replaced as chamberlain by Sir William Phelip, while Sir Robert Babthorp was named steward in place of the aged John, Lord Tiptoft. All four men had implacable credentials as servants of the House of Lancaster, and both Phelip and Babthorp had recently served the king in France. Cromwell, at least, saw Gloucester's hand behind these changes and took his dismissal as a personal affront. He demanded that parliament make a 'declaration of his innocence and good name and reputation', exonerating him from any suggestion he had displeased the king.[15] Gloucester was also keen to control the daily routine of Henry's spiritual life: at the end of February Dr John Walden was dismissed as the king's confessor and John Lowe named in his place; on 1 March the king received a new almoner, while Master Robert Gilbert, who had served as dean of the chapel royal for fifteen years, was replaced by another royal chaplain, Robert Praty. All the new officials were to appear before Gloucester in person to receive their commissions. These appointments, along with the appointment of another clerk who had accompanied Henry to France, William Lyndwood, as keeper of the privy seal, may also represent the duke's desire to assert traditional Lancastrian values of religious orthodoxy in the household. Lyndwood, Praty, Lowe, and Robert Felton, the new almoner, were all men noted for their opposition to and persecution of heretics. In May 1431 Duke Humphrey had established his own credentials as a champion of orthodoxy by defeating a dangerous Lollard conspiracy in London, Oxfordshire, and the Midlands.

These changes, and the political controversy that accompanied them, underlined both the importance of the royal household as an institution of government and its importance in shaping the character of the young king. The relative autonomy of the chief household officers and the influence of the knights and esquires who made up Henry's chamber staff were evident in the concerns, noted above, that the king's tutor, the earl of Warwick, expressed to the royal council in November 1432. Indeed, Warwick's complaint that Henry was being distracted from his studies by the activities of his household companions reveals that the men of the household were not simply the creatures of Gloucester, Bedford, or Beaufort. They were aware that their proximity and intimacy to the king gave them a political importance that rivalled that of the royal dukes and other lords. This need not be seen as being driven by selfish ends, the desire to exploit their position for personal aggrandisement, but by a belief that, as the king's closest and most frequent companions and servants, they were best placed to interpret and implement his developing will. Warwick had drawn attention to Henry's developing self-awareness in November 1432, and again in 1434 the council noted that the king had as 'great understanding and feeling, as ever they saw or knew in any prince, or other person of his age', although they were keen to point out that he was not yet able to make decisions independently.[16] The king's growing independence from his uncles was demonstrated in the parliament of 1432 when Gloucester attempted to move against Beaufort. The cardinal was accused of potentially treasonable dealings with the papacy and of attempting to illegally export bullion from the realm (some £6,000 worth of his jewels had recently been seized in the Kentish port of Sandwich). In June Beaufort appeared before Henry and the Lords in parliament to declare his fidelity to the king, challenging any who wished to accuse of him of treason to do so openly. The Lords, including Gloucester, debated this, but on the command of the king himself Beaufort was declared a loyal and true subject. Henry's intervention here was crucial: he appears to have been personally close to his great-uncle, who had been such a constant presence while the king had been in France, and it was the king himself who ultimately thwarted Gloucester's ambitions once more.

It was in this context, of the king slowly emerging as an independent political focus, that the appointment of William de la Pole, earl of Suffolk, as the steward of the household was so important. Taking office in August 1433, Suffolk was already an important figure in the government of the realm. He had been sworn to the council in November 1431, possibly at the instigation of the duke of Gloucester, and through his wife, Alice Chaucer, granddaughter of the poet Geoffrey Chaucer, he was closely related to the Beauforts. Yet, like many of the men who surrounded the young king, he owed his position not to the patronage of Gloucester or Beaufort, but to his long history of service to the House of Lancaster. Suffolk was born in 1396, and in 1415 he, his father, Michael, and elder brother (also Michael) accompanied the king to France. His father died of dysentery at the siege of Harfleur, while his brother was killed at Agincourt, so, aged just nineteen, William found himself earl of Suffolk. From 1422 Suffolk was one of Bedford's leading captains in France, but in 1429 he was defeated and captured at the hands of Joan of Arc's army at Jargeau. He was released in the spring of 1430 after the payment of a large ransom. His captor, Jean, count of Dunois, the Bastard of Orléans, was half-brother to the duke of Orléans and count of Angoulême, the two most important prisoners taken by the English at Agincourt. A condition of Suffolk's release, it seems, was that he agreed to work towards the release of the French captives, something that would have grave consequences both for Suffolk and the House of Lancaster as a whole. From 1431 Suffolk was an assiduous attendee of the royal council (he claimed to have missed only fifty meetings between his appointment and February 1436), and he was handsomely rewarded for his services. Furthermore, his position as steward of the royal household made him ideally placed to develop his own personal relationship with the young king, unmediated by the royal uncles and the council.

In 1433, however, Henry was still only eleven years old and real political power still lay elsewhere. John, duke of Bedford, as the heir apparent, potentially wielded the most influence, but his relationship with his brother, the duke of Gloucester, was strained over the future conduct of the war. Indeed, as Henry grew older and the time when he could make decisions on his own drew nearer, it became ever more difficult to plan strategy in France. In the spring of 1433 Bedford, Gloucester, Beaufort, and the other members of both the English and Lancastrian French councils met at Calais. Partly this was designed to celebrate Bedford's recent marriage to Jacquetta of Luxemburg (following the death of Duchess Anne the previous year), but the meeting was also convened in the hope that the English would meet with representatives of both Charles VII and Philip, duke of Burgundy. These hopes came to nothing, but in June Duke Philip sent his ambassador, Hugh de Lannoy, to London to treat directly with the young king. Lannoy met Henry on 26 June at his Guildford hunting lodge, reporting to his master that the king was a good-looking, healthy child who had spoken in French to the Burgundian ambassadors. Lannoy returned to the Low Countries convinced of the intransigence of both the French and English positions, but the meeting's real significance lay in how the Burgundians had bypassed the king's councillors in Calais and decided to approach Henry in person. Just eight days before Lannoy met the king, Bedford and the other councillors had returned to England and a parliament had been summoned to meet at Westminster on 8 July to discuss, among other things, the future course of events in France. Bedford wanted more money, as the military situation had worsened since the king's departure the previous year, but he was also keen to defend himself against rumours that this was due to 'the negligence and carelessness of the duke himself'. He challenged his accusers to confront him openly in parliament. None did, and the king thanked Bedford personally for his 'good, laudable and fruitful services'. In November, during the parliament's second session, the Commons asked if Bedford would remain in England. They praised his personal prowess in defending the king's rights in France, his own achievement at the battle of Verneuil ('which was the greatest deed undertaken by Englishmen in our time, save for the battle of Agincourt'), his financial probity, and his exercise of justice. They asked that he remain not only on account of his 'birth and consanguinity to the king', but 'all the more so for his said good governance', which would ensure 'the good and restful governance and keeping' of the two realms, as well as 'the welfare of the king's noble person'. The lords supported their request and Bedford agreed, receiving a guarantee that his principal charge of defending the king's interests in France (which Duke John believed had been Henry V's abiding wish for him) would be maintained. He was also granted extensive powers to summon and prorogue parliament and appoint all the great officers of state.[17]

The restatement of Bedford's pre-eminence in the government of both England and France was highly significant. It confirmed the arrangements implicit in Henry V's deathbed wishes, but it also sought to regulate the stages of the king's final transition to manhood. The Commons sought confirmation of Bedford's situation, not only because he was the heir apparent and Henry's most senior blood relative, but because he best embodied the Lancastrian ideals of martial prowess and, crucially, good government. Alone among the king's relatives, Duke John had demonstrated the credentials necessary to counsel and advise the king as he neared the years of discretion. Bedford remained in England until June 1434. By this time he had secured more money for the war in France, in terms of taxation and a diversion of funds from that part of the duchy of Lancaster held for the performance of Henry V's will, and reaffirmed the principle of broad, conciliar government until Henry reached full maturity. Yet, with Bedford's departure, the tension between the growing political importance of the king and conciliar government inevitably resurfaced. The council met with the king on 12 November 1434 to restate its powers and obligations. Though the councillors recognised Henry's precocious abilities, 'nevertheless to acquit themselves truly to God, to the king, and to his people they dare not take upon themselves to put him in conceit or opinion that he is as yet endowed with so great feeling, knowledge and wisdom that must in great part grow of experience, nor with so great foresight and discretion to depart and choose, namely in matters of great weight and difficulty'. In other words, their response suggests that Henry was beginning to flex his political muscles, but that they considered him to be still a child and that decisions would continue to be taken by the council in his name. It was also designed to thwart any who might seek to bypass the council and govern through the king himself. It was significant that the councillors on this occasion were led by Cardinal Beaufort and accompanied by the chief officers of his household, Suffolk and Sir William Phelip. The one notable absentee was the duke of Gloucester.[18]

If the years since 1432 had witnessed a steady realisation that Henry was slowly moving towards maturity and a time when he could play a full role in the government of the realm, the years 1435 and 1436 were ones of political and military crisis that thrust the young king to the forefront of events and brought about an inevitable, yet perhaps premature, end to the years of minority rule. On 14 September 1435 John, duke of Bedford, died (aged just 46) in Rouen. Just a week later the Burgundians entered into a separate treaty with the French at Arras, whereby they renounced the Treaty of Troyes and recognised Charles VII as the rightful king of France. The English ambassadors had been hoodwinked by the French and Burgundians, unaware of separate negotiations between the two sides that had been in progress since February 1434. The effect on Henry VI was immediate. He took Duke Philip's defection as a personal affront, bursting into tears on receipt of the news. Twenty years later he recalled the treachery of his 'good uncle' to the duke of Alençon, stating that, if he lived long enough, he wished to make war on the duke of Burgundy 'because he abandoned me in my boyhood, despite all his oaths to me, when I had never done him any wrong'.[19] The Franco-Burgundian treaty of Arras heralded a renewed French offensive against the Lancastrian possessions in France. The departure of the English representatives from Arras on 6 September had coincided with a renewed French offensive in Normandy, and in December Dieppe fell to a surprise attack. On 3 December the council in England informed the estates of Normandy of their plans to send reinforcements to the duchy under the duke of York and the earls of Suffolk, Salisbury, and Mortain. Nevertheless, more French successes followed in the early months of 1436, and not only in Normandy. On 8 March Duke Philip announced his intention to lead an army against the English town of Calais, and on 17 April the English garrison in Paris surrendered to the French.

Henry's assumption of full regal powers thus took place against the backdrop of the most serious crisis to confront the Lancastrian regime since the death of Henry V thirteen years previously, and one that threatened the very existence of the Dual Monarchy. On 1 October 1435 the council travelled to Eltham Palace to meet, for the first time, in the presence of the king. Their purpose was to appoint Richard Wydeville as an interim lieutenant of Calais following Bedford's death. Thereafter Henry appears to have regularly attended council meetings, the main focus of which was to organise expeditions for the defence of Normandy and the Calais Pale. These meetings, however, did not only deal with matters of defence, and before long Henry was involving himself personally in the day-to-day business of kingship. On 10 April 1436, in response to a petition from William Aiscough, Henry authorised a presentation to the parish church of Ditton in Cambridgeshire. The previous month the council had written to Cardinal Giordano Orsini in Rome announcing that the king would soon be taking up the reins of power, while in the same month a letter to the Norman estates had stated that from his fourteenth birthday (6 December 1435) the king had been attending constantly to his affairs.

The context and importance of these changes was made clear in the spring of 1436. In February commissioners were appointed to collect loans in each English county and on 26 March the council despatched further letters to towns, the heads of religious houses, and probably prominent individuals requesting men and money for the relief of Calais. In both cases the requests were phrased as coming directly from the king; the loan commissioners, for instance, were to 'say the king greets them heartily well and trusts verily that according to the truth and love that they owe to bear to him and the wealth of this realm', the audience would contribute appropriately towards the planned expeditions.[20] A further letter to the heads of religious houses, moreover, written on 16 June, revealed that the council planned for Henry himself, 'with God's mercy, to give rescue thereto in our person'.[21] In other words, the emergence of the king as an active and participating ruler was a direct response to the military crisis occasioned by the Treaty of Arras. At fourteen, Henry was the youngest monarch since the Norman Conquest to begin his majority rule, a realisation not of his precocious tendencies but of the reality that only the ultimate authority of the king could unite his subjects and defend his realms effectively against external threats. In the end, any plans for Henry to lead the expedition were short lived. While the duke of Gloucester negotiated with the king and council at Canterbury over the financial terms of the relief expedition to

Calais in late June and early July 1436, the army under Edmund Beaufort, earl of Mortain, originally destined for France, had been diverted to Calais and it was this force, rather than any led by Gloucester or the king, that finally broke the Burgundian siege on 29 July.

The decision to place Henry at the head of the regime's response to the crisis of 1435/36 had irreversible consequences. On 19 May 1436 Warwick had formally resigned as the king's tutor, and Henry's personal involvement in all aspects of royal government continued to develop apace. Yet the king's burgeoning role in government was carefully managed and each new development appears to have been approved by a meeting of a great council, a broad and inclusive gathering of lords and other leading members of the political nation. In the autumn of 1436 the great council approved the king's ability to make time-limited grants of office, lands, and other royal favours; in April 1437 this developed into a formal recognition of his ability to dispense patronage in the form of life grants. While precedents for each of these different forms of exercising the royal grace had occurred before the formal approval by the great council, it was still significant and indicative of the regime's commitment to Lancastrian principles of conciliar and consultative good government. This process was finalised at a meeting of the king's council held at Clerkenwell on 12 November 1437. In the presence of Gloucester, Beaufort, Archbishop Kemp, and the other councillors, four new members were admitted to its ranks (Richard Neville, earl of Salisbury, the bishop of St David's and two household officials, Sir John Stourton, the treasurer of Henry's household, and Robert Rolleston, keeper of the Great Wardrobe) and Henry ordered that the council should have the same powers as Henry IV had granted to his councillors in 1406. In the parliament of that year the council had initially been given a certain freedom to make decisions independently for the good of the realm, in the context of the king's debilitating illness, while later in the year the dispensation of patronage was largely made the preserve of the council. In 1437 the king's freedom to make grants was not so fully curtailed, but the reference to conciliar government and the memory of Lancastrian 'constitutionalism' in the context of a king on the threshold of adulthood was significant. Nevertheless, the royal minority was at an end and the councillors swore to 'make faith unto the king to counsel him well and truly in such matters as shall be opened unto him by way of the king's council'.[22] Just days shy of his sixteenth birthday, Henry VI now ruled personally as well as reigned over his subjects.

Conclusion

The years 1429–37 had seen events in England driven primarily by the course of the war in France. The emergence of Joan of Arc and the coronation of Charles VII had forced the Lancastrian council to bring forward Henry's own coronations as king of England and France. The treaty of Arras and the Burgundian attack on Calais had thrust the king to the centre of government and scuppered the council's plans for a slow and measured transition to full princely authority. Yet Henry's emergence as a ruling, adult king was not, as John Watts has suggested, 'so elaborate, so publicly managed, and so frequently thwarted' because of any incapacity or shortcoming in the king himself.[23] Henry's acquisition of the full responsibilities and powers of kingship was public because transparent, conciliar government lay at the heart of the domestic political legacy of the Lancastrian kings. That this occurred so early in his life was a measure of the crisis of 1435/36, but it was also testimony to the robust nature of Lancastrian principles and the existence of a general consensus among the political elite about how to best protect and preserve the Dual Monarchy. Henry was expected to defend the Lancastrian legacy both at home and abroad, to lead his subjects in war (perhaps a little optimistic for any fourteen-year-old), and to listen and respond, and to be seen to listen and respond, to his council in the exercise of his grace. The dominant theme in English politics over the next decade or so was the extent to which Henry listened to counsel and exercised discretion in making his royal will felt.

Notes

1 *The Historical Collections of a Citizen of London in the Fifteenth Century*, ed. James Gairdner (Camden Society, 1876), 164–8.

2 Ibid., 169–70.

3 Anne Curry, 'The "Coronation Expedition" and Henry VI's Court in France, 1430 to 1432', in *The Lancastrian Court* (Stratford, 2003), 29–52.

4   B.P. Wolffe, *Henry VI* (1981), 59–63.

5   *Chronicles of London*, ed. Charles Lethbridge Kingsford (Oxford, 1905), 97–116.

6   John Matusiak, *Henry V* (Abingdon, 2013), 34–37.

7   TNA, E159/202, *Recorda* 4 Hen. VI, Easter rot. 3; E101/408/2.

8   *Chronique de Pierre Cochon*, ed. C. Robillard de Beaurepaire (Societé de l'Histoire de Normandie, 1870), 312–13.

9   *POPC*, iii, 296–300.

10 *Liber Regie Capelle*, ed. Walter Ullman (Henry Bradshaw Society, 1959), 14–22.

11 *POPC*, iv, 133–7.

12 John Lydgate, *The Life of St Edmund, King and Martyr*, ed. A.S.G. Edwards (2004).

13 *Four English Political Tracts of the Later Middle Ages*, ed. Jean-Philippe Genet (Camden Society, 1977), 40–173.

14 Wolffe, *Henry VI*, 65.

15 *PROME*, xi, 17–18.

16 *POPC*, iv, 287.

17 *PROME*, xi, 77–78.

18 *POPC*, iv, 287–9.

19 Gaston du Fresne de Beaucourt, *Histoire de Charles VII* (6 vols, Paris, 1881–91), vi, 137.

20 *POPC*, iv, 352b.

21 James A. Doig, 'A New Source for the Siege of Calais in 1436', *English Historical Review* 110 (1995), 404–16.

22 *POPC*, v, 72.

23 John Watts, *Henry VI and the Politics of Kingship* (Cambridge,1996), 124.

6 Majority rule (I)

Patronage and piety, 1437–50

K.B. McFarlane's damning conclusion continues to dominate the scholarly debate over the personal rule of Henry VI. In the years after 1437, McFarlane pronounced, 'second childhood succeeded first without the usual interval and under him the medieval kingship was in abeyance'.[1] The extent to which the king was actively involved in the day-to-day government of the realm and therefore the extent to which he was to blame personally for the clear breakdown of public authority during the 1440s, leading to the crisis of 1449–50, are questions that have animated most historians of fifteenth-century England. Some, following McFarlane, contend that he was no king at all, a man simply incapable of exercising any real authority, while even those who do see a more active monarch have to admit that Henry falls into that group of 'bad kings' who punctuate the history of medieval England. Yet Henry's kingship should be judged not only against such relatively straight-forward criteria. By the time he formally came of age and assumed the mantle of personal rule, Henry's actions and the expectations of those who served him were conditioned by a complex set of distinctly Lancastrian political and cultural values. At times, such as the periods of tension between conciliar government and the king's personal authority, these values were at odds with one another. On other occasions, such as the peculiarly Lancastrian relationship between spirituality and kingship, they encouraged kingly behaviour that was neither conventional nor easily compat-ible with the longer-term structures of English government. Hen-ry's adult rule was also mediated through and conditioned by his household, a body of men whose loyalty was at once to him as an individual, as duke of Lancaster, and as ruler of the Dual Monarchy, as well as, in an impersonal sense, to the crown of England.

Patronage, counsel and the royal household

The later Middle Ages have been dubbed the 'age of the house-hold', and in this regard Lancastrian England followed more general trends emerging in Europe during the fourteenth and fifteenth centuries.[2] We have already seen the important role the royal household fulfilled under Henry IV and Henry V, combining the existing governmental, ceremonial, and symbolic functions of the later Planatagent household with the practical, political and military functions of the household of the duke of Lancaster. During Henry VI's minority the royal household's role remained important: it met the everyday corporal and spiritual needs of the king and his entourage; it served as a military establishment during the coronation expedition to France; and it operated to educate the young king and involve him and his servants in a wide-ranging discourse about the nature of princely government. In the period of Henry's adult rule between 1437 and 1450 the household also emerged as the administrative and political centre of the kingdom. Historians of Henry's reign have generally followed the criticisms made by some contemporaries and dismissed the royal household as corrupt, faction ridden, and responsible in no small part for the eventual demise of Lancastrian kingship.[3] More recent work, however, has suggested an alternative account of its role during the 1440s. Faced with the manifest shortcomings of the king himself, his leading household servants, most importantly William de la Pole, earl, later duke of Suffolk, worked hard to maintain an edifice of public, royal authority through the institutions and structures of household government. In John Watts's account of the 1440s, it was Suffolk, rather than Henry, who actually ruled, exploiting the opportunities (for both the public good and his own private profit) afforded him by his proximity to and intimacy with the king. This attempt to conceal Henry's inadequacy was doomed to failure as royal authority could only really be derived from the royal *persona publica* exercised by the king himself, and the unfortunate Suffolk became the scapegoat for Henry's failure.[4]

Yet household government, that is, rule through the men and institutions of the essentially private networks and authority of the king's personal following, was a defining feature of Lancastrian political culture. Indeed, the forms of household government that developed during the reign of Henry VI would come to define the English polity during the reign of an adult male king for the next two hundred years. The problems of the 1440s were not a result of household government per se, nor principally because of tensions between public and private forms of princely authority, but emerged because the ambitions and methods of the household became increasingly at odds with other, equally Lancastrian principles, aspirations, and theories of governance.

In many ways the Lancastrian household of the 1440s remained recognisably that which had attended upon the king during his minority. It remained itinerant, spending long periods (including the major religious feast days) at Windsor, Sheen, Kennington, and Eltham, but also perambulating around the various royal hunting lodges and smaller royal houses in the Thames Valley. The household also travelled widely throughout England, usually spending three or four months each year riding through Kent (particularly Canterbury to visit his grandfather's tomb and the shrine of St Thomas), the Midlands, East Anglia, the West Country, and even, in 1448, Yorkshire and Durham. In this Henry was not unusual and followed the pattern set by previous medieval English kings, but during the 1440s the financial situation may have added extra urgency to the household's need to find lodgings and food outside the Thames Valley region. In terms of the size of its membership, the household grew inexorably during Henry's majority rule: a complement of 120 esquires of the king's chamber during the late 1430s, for example, had risen to 278 between 1448 and 1452. By 1449 it has been estimated that no fewer than 1,200 souls were dependent on the royal household for their livelihood. For many, membership of the household was nominal; the right to wear royal livery marked someone out as the king's man and bestowed, all being well, a degree of status in their locality. Indeed, membership of the royal household became increasingly synonymous with membership of the wider Lancastrian affinity, and the interaction and cross-over between office-holding at court and on the duchy of Lancaster's estates became increasingly marked during Henry's majority. In part, this was also a money-saving expedient – fees met by the duchy estates did not need to be paid by the treasurer of the household – but it also underlined the centrality of the household, and the personal connections of lordship it implied, to the Lancastrian project. Remarkably, given its expansion and the complaints of contemporaries, Henry VI's household actually cost less than those of his immediate predecessors. Between 1395 and 1396 Richard II's household expenses ran at c. £27,000–£32,000 per annum, while Henry IV's household cost some £20,000 per annum, prompting numerous complaints in parliament. Yet Henry VI's household expenditure remained constant at around £10,000 per annum between 1437 and 1453.[5]

The personnel of Henry's household during the period 1437 to 1450 also showed a remarkable consistency and sense of continuity with that of the minority and his father's reign. The credentials of the chief officers of the household remained as before: men like Suffolk (steward of the household throughout the period), Sir William Phelip, later Lord Bardolf (chamberlain until 1441), Ralph Boteler, Lord Sudeley (Phelip's successor as chamberlain), and Sir Thomas Stanley (controller of the household from 1441) were all men with implacable and long-standing Lancastrian credentials, serving both in England and on the Continent. They were also members of the formally constituted royal council, blurring the distinction between the world of the 'court' and that of the 'council'. Below this level, the knights of the king's chamber also exhibited continuity between the majority and minority households. Sir John and Sir William Beauchamp, Sir Robert Roos, and Sir Edmund Hungerford, the king's carvers at the beginning of the majority, remained in place throughout the period, ensuring a degree of continuity into adulthood among the king's most intimate servants. Equally, the staff of the chapel royal remained largely unchanged. However, below this level, the expansion of the household and the new opportunities offered by a king eager to assert his own independence allowed new men to prosper. For example, the Staffordshire esquire John Hampton, an usher of the chamber since 1425, became, in July 1437, one of the esquires of the king's body, a role that involved actually dressing the king. Hampton's promotion marked the beginning of a startling accumulation of grants, offices, and money for himself, his family, and friends. By

1450 he had become the target of popular disquiet over the way in which certain household men had enriched themselves at the expense of the commonwealth. Yet Hampton was also a committed, personal servant of the king. He was intimately involved with the royal foundations at Eton and Cambridge, he was instrumental in the arrangements for Margaret of Anjou's journey to England in 1445 (and became her Master of Horse), and in 1449–50, as a resurgent French crown conquered Lancastrian Normandy, he was entrusted with the safeguard of key fortresses in the Calais Pale. Hampton's career was by no means unique during the 1440s and several household men such as James Fiennes, Thomas Daniel, John Norris, Edward Hull, John Penycoke, and others, profited greatly from the king's largesse, to a greater or lesser degree of public notoriety. These men highlight one of the main issues of the period 1437 to 1450: the dispensation of royal patronage and the inherent tension between the public authority of the council and the essentially private nature of the king's household. Both forms of government were, in their own way, equally Lancastrian, and the failure of Henry VI and his servants to negotiate successfully the balance between the two would contribute greatly to the political crisis of 1449–50.

Following the formal end of the minority government in November 1437, Henry's new role in the government was most acutely felt in matters of patronage. Late medieval kings had an obligation to be 'good lords' to their servants. As well as the less obvious benefits of status that royal service conveyed, servants also expected tangible rewards, in the form of land, money, and office, for their hard work. Kings had to balance this need for largesse against the requirement not to alienate large portions of the royal patrimony or bankrupt their exchequer by burdening it with annuities and fees. Servants sought patronage simply by petitioning the crown for vacant offices or other grants; it was the responsibility of a prudent king to assess these requests, seek counsel when necessary, and reward his servants in a way deemed acceptable by the rest of the political nation. Very soon Henry VI was found wanting in this crucial aspect of kingship. As early as February 1438 his councillors were concerned that his liberality was hurting the royal purse: he had, for example, pardoned a customs collector of his debts, costing the crown some £1,666, while throughout the spring of that year a number of grants to leading nobles, some endorsed by the council, saw the alienation of substantial portions of the crown lands. In May the following year the king sold the lordship and castle of Chirk in Wales and other properties in the West Country, purchased for the crown by Henry V in 1418, to his great-uncle Cardinal Beaufort for a bargain price. Later the duke of Gloucester claimed that when he heard of this sale he stated that 'whoever laboured, moved, or stirred this matter first unto your lordship counselled you neither for your worship nor profit'.[6] Around this time efforts appear to have been made to regulate, but importantly not control, the king's dispensation of patronage. The king's chamberlain began to note on some bills the king's answer, while a secretary was appointed to handle the work of the signet, the king's personal seal which, when appended to a petition, could serve as a warrant to the Great Seal, thus turning a petition into a grant. Most importantly, Adam Moleyns, clerk of the council, began to routinely annotate bills with the names of those councillors present when they were granted. Before long a division began to appear in the process of counsel and the dispensation of patronage. While day-to-day matters of government and administration continued to be dealt with by the council, matters of policy and patronage were increasingly decided by the king with or without his councillors present.

On occasion the king's new-found enthusiasm for exercising his royal powers could prove disastrous. In 1440, for example, the council were involved in easing the regional rivalry between Thomas Courtenay, earl of Devon and Sir William Bonville, steward of the duchy of Cornwall. In the spring of 1441, however, the council's efforts at peace making were undermined when Henry granted the office of steward of the duchy to the earl, perhaps unaware of the rivalry between the two men and the existing grant to Bonville. The council had to try to rescue the situation, convening a meeting with the king and securing a royal letter to the earl instructing him to not to attempt to exercise the office until the council had decided what to do next. Eventually the two sides submitted to an arbitration award in the presence of the king. Nevertheless, Henry's ill-considered grant of the stewardship had worsened rather than healed the rift between two of his leading subjects. While the king's dispensation of patronage may sometimes have been ill advised and over-generous, it does not follow that it was without principle or direction. The surviving files of petitions signed by the king or sealed with the signet between 1438 and 1441 reveal a certain consistency in the matters that caught Henry's attention. First, petitions from members of the clergy or concerning religious houses appear to have found a ready ear in the king. Second, those petitions presented by or on behalf of his household servants often show evidence of the king's personal scrutiny. In these cases Henry was operating within the accepted norms of Lancastrian political culture: he was rewarding personal loyalty and exercising good lordship to his servants, while his concern for the religious demonstrated the piety and commitment to the Church that was a hallmark of Lancastrian kingship. Occasionally annotations on the petitions reveal something of the process of obtaining the king's grace and of Henry's own role. In October 1440, for example, one of the king's chaplains, Edmund Port, petitioned over his disputed appointment as abbot at the Irish abbey of St Mary in Trim. Henry initialled the bill and Moleyns noted 'the king wills the supplication be sped by my Lord Chancellor'.[7] Similarly, in January 1441 John Penycoke, one of the yeomen of the king's robes, petitioned for a life grant of the office. Again, it was warranted by the king's signature and endorsed to the effect that 'the king wills that his chancellor make out letters patent upon this his grant'. The bill was signed in the hunting lodge in Windsor Park in the presence of Sir Ralph Boteler.[8] It is difficult not to imagine that his grant, and many similar ones initialled by the king, represented Henry's will, albeit at times mediated through the intervention of his intimate household servants, and that, on the level of the individual petition, the king was acting in a fashion that would have been deemed appropriate by many of his servants. Thus it was the king's generosity and the sheer number of suitors making their way to him in the early 1440s, not his willingness to rewards his servants as such, that threatened to undermine royal authority.

By the early 1440s it was clear that Henry's willingness to make grants, and the apparent lack of control over access to the king, were raising serious concerns. The influence of the king's household servants was not out of place in itself, but Henry's apparent ability to exercise discretion and, in John Watts's words, his failure 'to maintain the public quality of [his] rule even in [his] most private surroundings' was problematic.[9] It was in response to this situation that the councillors reasserted their formal role in the dispensation of patronage in November 1441. The records of the council were kept with a renewed rigour, carefully recording the names of those present when decisions were taken, and formal sessions appear to have been convened once more. Around this time (although the precise date is uncertain) moves were made to institute a formal system of scrutinising petitions in council before passing them to the king. This new ordinance was approved and signed by the king, and certainly by the autumn of 1444 new arrangements were in place to regulate the flow of petitions for grace.[10] On 7 November that year, however, the king issued letters patent reaffirming the validity of all grants made under the sign manual, signet, or endorsed by the chamberlain or clerk of the council.[11] By early 1445 the number of warrants authorised solely by the king was increasing again, and there was a corresponding decline in the activity of and attendance at formal meetings of the council. These changes, as we will see, probably had much to do with the reassertion of personal, royal authority that accompanied the king's marriage, but they also underlined the simple fact that, in an age of personal monarchy, real power was inextricably bound up with the person and personality of the king himself.

Indeed, the five years between the king's marriage in April 1445 and the outbreak of popular unrest in the summer of 1450 mark the high point of Lancastrian household government. Henry's counsel was dominated by a small group of intimate companions. Principal among these, of course, was the earl of Suffolk (promoted to duke on 2 June 1448), but he was joined by William Aiscough, the king's confessor and bishop of Salisbury, John, Lord (later Viscount) Beaumont, Adam Moleyns, bishop of Chichester from 1445, James Fiennes, created Lord Saye and Sele in 1447, John Sutton, Lord Dudley, and Reginald Boulers, abbot of Gloucester. The extant council records show that these individuals dominated the process of counselling Henry, while their influence was recognised by contemporaries and increasingly seen as malign. Alongside these men, grants and other acts of government were also routinely witnessed by a small group of a dozen or so household knights and esquires, as well as Thomas Clerk, clerk of the privy seal, and John Blakeney, the signet office clerk. These men worked together, promoting each other's suits and, occasionally, using their proximity to the king to thwart the designs of others. Historians have traditionally seen their acquisition of offices and other grants as indicative of a willingness to subvert the public good for their own private profit and of their manipulation of a weak king. Intimacy with the king clearly enabled certain individuals to profit, sometimes at the expenses of proper process. In 1447, for instance, as the duke of Exeter lay on his deathbed, Sir Edmund Hungerford and one of the esquires of the body, Gilbert Parr, rushed to petition the king for a lease of Exeter's manor of Berkhamsted. The grant was duly made by signet warrant, bypassing the privy seal. The king explained how Hungerford and Parr had informed him 'that our cousin John duke of Exeter was either dead, or in point to die'.[12] Similarly, the local influence of household men (such as that of Suffolk in East Anglia or Fiennes in Kent) has been considered an extension of their corrupting influence at the centre of government. In reality, as we shall see, their actions in the localities were often made in response to particular local crises and designed to mitigate the effects of Henry's failure to exercise royal leadership at both a national and a local level. Throughout the 1440s these men showed themselves conspicuously loyal servants to the crown, making the best of royal failures at a local level, while dedicating themselves to the fulfilment of the king's overriding concerns: peace with France and the establishment of his two great educational and religious projects at Eton and Cambridge.

Royal piety and the king's foundations

Henry VI's most enduring legacy was, without doubt, his foundation of Eton College and King's College, Cambridge. It was also, in many ways, the fullest statement of his commitment to a particular version of the Lancastrian legacy. In devoting so much energy to Eton and King's, Henry was acting in accordance with the ideals and aspirations of many of his closest servants and counsellors and, in a peculiar way, providing the royal leadership that was so conspicuously absent in many others aspects of his rule. It has been argued that in the foundations, as in so much of his reign, the king was merely a cypher, that the impetus and energy needed to begin and sustain so ambitious a project came from others, and that in some ways the illusion of a group of household men working together under the king to establish the new colleges acted as a substitute for the type of martial endeavour that more often, and ideally, marked the beginning of adult rule. Although the evidence for the king's role in the foundations is as ambiguous as that of Henry's involvement in other areas of policy and government during the 1440s, two factors point to the central role Henry played. First, the foundations were suitably magnificent projects that placed the king's ambitions at the apex of other similar projects undertaken by his family and servants. Second, the surviving documentary evidence is unusual enough in format to suggest a level of personal involvement on his part.

Education within a religious context was, as we have seen, central to the Lancastrian project in the fifteenth century. From proper education grew wisdom, and the wisdom of kings and their servants was vital to the proper functioning of the kingdom. Out of wisdom grew the ability to govern properly, dispense justice, uphold orthodox religion, and defend the realm. In their petition to the Commons in 1445 the provost and scholars of the king's new college in Cambridge explained that 'where the study of knowledge and wisdom prevailed more, a more eminent secular knighthood prospered'.[13] This was a belief shared and put into practice by leading Lancastrians throughout the early years of Henry's reign. It resulted in the foundation of religious houses, which functioned as centres both of prayer and of education. His father's foundations of the two religious houses at Sheen and Syon were remarkable displays of princely piety, but Henry V's actions were mirrored by other Lancastrians. Walter, Lord Hungerford, founded Heytesbury and several chantries between 1415 and his death in 1449, while in 1439 Archbishop Kemp founded Wye College, Suffolk founded Ewelme and Ralph, Lord Cromwell, established his collegiate church at Tattershall. Perhaps the clearest expression of the inclusive Lancastrian identity central to these foundations was at Archbishop Chichele's college of All Souls, Oxford, where the scholars studied and prayed for those who had lost their lives in the Lancastrian wars in France. In Lancastrian France too, Henry's early reign was notable for the establishment of universities at Caen (established in 1432 by the Lancastrian Norman council in the presence of the young king himself) and Bordeaux (1448). Besides the foundation of Eton and King's, there is other evidence of Henry's personal commitment to education within this specifically Lancastrian context. It may lie behind his special devotion to the 'bookish saints' Dunstan and Anselm, Anglo-Saxon archbishops of Canterbury, and his attempt in 1442 to canonise King Alfred, a king noted for his wisdom and law giving and popularly identified as the founder of Oxford University. The Lancastrian commitment to education also had more tangible expression. In June 1440 a warrant under the king's signet ordered the delivery of twenty-seven books from the royal library to furnish the library of All Soul's, Oxford. This came a year after the donation of 129 books to Oxford by the king's uncle, the duke of Gloucester. Duke Humphrey's donation was followed by a further 134 volumes five years later. In 1445 the king continued this tradition by endowing a new library at Salisbury cathedral.

In August 1440 moves began in earnest to establish a college dedicated to the Virgin Mary at Eton, a short distance from Henry's birthplace and favourite residence at Windsor. In that month the rector of the parish church, the recently installed John Kette, a former canon at Windsor, sold the advowson to the king. In September the king appointed Archbishop Chichele, the bishops of Bath and Wells, St Asaph, and Salisbury, the earl of Suffolk, John Somerset, Thomas Beckington, John Hampton, James Fiennes, Adam Moleyns, William Tresham, and Richard Andrewes (warden of All Souls, Oxford) to receive the revenues of the alien priories in England (seized by Henry V in 1414). These lands were to fund the establishment of a college for priests and twenty-five poor scholars. The college was officially founded on 11 October. The language of the foundation charter contains a clear and personal statement of the king's intentions in establishing the college:

> Wherefore we, who, by the will of the same king of kings by whom all kings reign, have now taken into our hands the governance of both our kingdoms, from the beginning of our

majority, have considered in zealous contemplation, in what manner, how, or by what kind of royal gift, according to our devotion and the custom of our elders, we can make suitable honour to the same lady and our most holy mother, to the satisfaction of her spouse; and finally, having contemplated such things in intimate meditation, it was settled in our heart that, in honour and support of such and so great a holy mother, we will found a college in the parish church of Eton near Windsor, which is not far from our place of birth.[14]

The following months witnessed a concerted effort at the papal *curia* to secure for Eton the granting of indulgences designed to draw pilgrims to it and further boost its income. Building work began on the college in the summer of 1441 and the first mass was celebrated there by Beckington in October 1443. From the beginning, Eton was a project accomplished by Henry's closest servants in fulfilment of their master's wishes. While the presence of Archbishop Chichele among the college's feoffees underlined how the project chimed with Lancastrian sentiments more generally, the presence of men like Suffolk, Somerset, Aiscough, Moleyns, and Hampton spoke of the king's personal commitment to it.

Around the same time as the king's plans for Eton were beginning to bear fruit, moves were afoot for a new college in Cambridge. In September 1440 three commissioners, including the king's physician John Somerset, were appointed to acquire land there worth £200 *per annum*. The Royal College of St Nicholas, as it was initially known in honour of the king's birth saint, was to be devoted to the education of the clergy and the extirpation of heresy. On 2 April 1441 Henry himself laid the first stone of the new college building. At first it seems the two foundations were conceived of as separate entities. Henry does not seem to have made a connection between Eton and Cambridge, and in February 1441 he had granted revenues from the alien priory of Ogbourne to support five Eton scholars at Oxford. By 1443, however, the king appears to have had one of his characteristic changes of mind. In July he dismissed the team, led by William Alnwick, bishop of Lincoln, charged with drafting new statutes for his Cambridge college and took the responsibility into his own hands. The next month a new site was acquired for a much larger college. On 1 July the following year a quadripartite agreement of mutual assistance was made between Winchester College and New College, Oxford (both founded by William Wykeham, bishop of Winchester until his death in 1404) and Eton and King's. Henry had intended to lay the foundation stone of this new building, but a dangerous outbreak of plague in the town prevented him from travelling and, on 29 September 1444, it was Suffolk who laid the first stone of the chapel of the new Royal College of the Blessed Virgin and St Nicholas. The new statutes, when they finally appeared in 1447, were more-or-less verbatim copies of those Wykeham had written for Winchester and New College. Eton was designed as a 'feeder school' for King's, and by 1446 its size had been increased to seventy scholars. Its patron's perhaps surprising choice of Cambridge over Oxford was probably influenced by the energetic lobbying of John Langton, chancellor of the university and bishop of St David's, and William Bingham, rector of St John Zachary in London and founder of God's House college in Cambridge. Despite not being a graduate and having no obvious ties to the town or university, in the mid-1430s Bingham had set about establishing his own college there. In 1439 he petitioned the king, claiming that there was a serious shortage of grammar schools and lack of Latin throughout the realm and, as a result, 'the wisdom, cunning and governance of the kingdom', not to mention the king's subjects' souls, were in danger.[15] In 1448 when the college of God's House was formally established, Bingham was careful to credit the king with its foundation. Langton's support of Henry's foundation at King's may, in part, have been designed to thwart Bingham's ambitious plans for his own college in the town.

There is little consensus among historians about with whom the real credit for the foundation of Eton and King's should lie. John Watts and Katherine Selway have both argued that the real impetus came from the king's servants, principally Suffolk, but also from clerics, such as Beckington and William Waynflete, a master at Winchester who became the king's confessor. The foundations were thus not the personal acts of a pious king but 'on the contrary public acts of the Lancastrian monarchy, owing their motivation to the needs of the government rather than to Henry VI's personal will'.[16] While the foundations were certainly a public statement of the regime's commitment to Lancastrian values, and the involvement of the king's household and councillors underlined the corporate nature of the regime, it need not negate the king's own commitment to Eton and King's. While Henry needed the involvement and commitment of men like Suffolk, Somerset, Waynflete, and Hampton to actually achieve his ambitions, the idea and driving force behind the foundations could equally have been the king's desire to realise his own vision of the Lancastrian legacy. In 1446 Henry boasted of his pride at Eton: 'it surpasses all other such schools whatsoever of our kingdom . . . it ought in prerogative of its name, and be named henceforth the king's general school, and be called lady mother and mistress of all other grammar schools'.[17] During the course of the next year or so Henry evidently decided that his existing plans on the two sites did not match the grandeur of his ambitions, and plans were drawn up specifying exactly the appearance and design of the new buildings.

It was to set down his new plans for Eton and King's that Henry drew up his 'will and intent' on 12 March 1448 for his two colleges. It is difficult to believe that this document, in the form of a tripartite indenture of which one copy remains at Eton and another at King's, represented anything other than a clear statement of the king's idiosyncratic wishes regarding his two foundations. Throughout the early part of the year Henry appears to have been involved in discussing the minutiae of the building to be done at the two sites with his councillors. These detailed instructions were headed 'the appointment made by the king' and at several points throughout the document Henry added his initials or his full royal signature 'R Henricus'. The will was witnessed by Suffolk and Waynflete. The preamble to the will echoed but also expanded upon the sentiments expressed in the October 1440 foundation charter of Eton:

> for as much as it has liked unto our Lord for to suffer and grant me grace for the principal notable work purposed by me after that I, by his blessed sufferance, took unto myself the rule of my said realms for to erect, found and establish unto the honour and worship of his name especially, and of the blessed Virgin our lady saint Marie, increase of virtues,

and cunning in delectation, and establishment of the Christian faith, my two colleges . . .

The will provided £666 13s. 4d. a year to each of the colleges from the revenues of the duchy of Lancaster until the works were complete. The schedule of works was ambitious in the extreme. At King's a magnificent quadrangle cloister, chapel, and ante-chapel dwarfed the other Cambridge colleges, while at Eton Henry was keen to specify that the new minster choir would exceed Wykeham's foundation at New College, Oxford in size. The king also specified the statues of saints and of the Virgin that the scholars would see in their church. The king entrusted the oversight of the projects to Waynflete, now bishop of Winchester, warning those involved in the foundations that they would answer at the Day of Judgement for any failures to achieve his intent. It was an intensely personal project. Henry called not upon the public authority of the crown to realise his ambitions, but on personal ties of friendship and loyalty and on the ultimate authority of divine retribution: he asked that his heirs and successors be 'willing, faithful and tender lovers of my desire', but reminded them of the 'terrible consequences and full fearful implications of Holy Scripture against the breakers of the law of God, and the letters of good and holy works'. The king's anxiety that his foundation projects be seen through to completion, and the melding of royal and personal authority which it entailed, can be seen in the fact that no fewer than six seals were affixed to the indenture: the Great Seal, the great seal of the duchy of Lancaster, the seal of those duchy lands enfeoffed for the upkeep of the two colleges, the duchy signet of the eagle, and the king's signet of arms. The document was then to be closed by the privy seal.[18]

Building at King's continued along the lines laid out in the 'will and intent' into the 1450s, before the money ran out, but at Eton Henry's initial plans were soon overtaken by even more ambitious designs. By the end of 1448 it seems the king had decided to demolish the previous seven years' work in favour of even grander buildings. In January 1449 the clerk of the works at Eton led a nine-day tour to measure the dimensions of Salisbury and Winchester cathedrals, which resulted in plans to extend both the nave and the choir. The resulting design, if it had been completed to

Henry's plan, would have resulted in a building that would have been as large as any of the great English gothic cathedrals. Again, it is difficult to imagine that the initiative for this sudden and destructive change of plan came from anyone other than the king himself. The period 1447–48 marked the high-water mark of household government. As we shall see, peace with France had been achieved, the troublesome duke of Gloucester had been removed, and household men were in the ascendancy in many parts of England. The regime appeared secure and the realm well governed (despite a continuing shortage of money and some notorious incidents of local disorder); Henry was now free to govern in the way he wanted and the new building at Eton was an unambiguous statement of royal intent. Naturally, his loyal servants were ready to facilitate his wishes. Building at Eton, as at King's, continued in fits and starts throughout the 1450s, but the college fell on hard times with its patron's deposition in 1461. The building that now stands at Eton is only the choir of this proposed monument to Henry's priorities as king.

Justice, finance, and the government of England

One of the defining features of medieval kingship was the principle of 'good government'. The coronation oath outlined the king's obligations in this regard: he was to provide justice, defend the realm, and defend the Church. These commonplaces had been refined since 1399 and the Lancastrian notion of good government was more specific. The commitment to provide impartial justice and maintain order at a local level by a close cooperation between the royal government and landowners remained a paramount concern, but the ideas of fiscal responsibility and the proper shepherding of the crown's resources (which would alleviate the need for excessive and unnecessary taxation) were also increasingly urgent concerns voiced by the Commons in parliament. During the minority of Henry VI these issues became more pressing, but their solution was problematic while the king was a child. Once he had come of age the public became ever more vocal in their demand for good government, and the regime's response to the twin challenges of justice and royal finance became touchstones by which to judge the success or failure of Henry's kingship.

Even before the Lancastrian revolution of 1399, royal finance had been one of the main ways in which the relationship between the king and his subjects had been negotiated. During the four-teenth century there developed a system of public finance in which the political nation, represented by the Commons in parliament, acknowledged their obligation to provide the king with the means to defend the realm and maintain his estate through grants of taxation; in return, the king recognised his duty to offer redress of grievances and his commitment to good government. From the accession of Henry IV this reciprocity was given more force, first, by a worsening fiscal situation which saw the king demand more of his subjects' wealth in taxation to meet the everyday costs of government, and second, by the very public Lancastrian com-mitment to fiscal responsibility. This situation resulted in the Commons' demand in 1404 for the resumption of crown lands, returning to royal possession all the lands held by the king or his predecessors since 1366; and demands by parliament to know the true wealth of the crown continued to be made throughout Henry IV's reign. In Henry V's reign initial enthusiasm for his French wars calmed the Commons' complaints about the excessive cost of royal government and the household, but, as we have seen, by the end of the reign the scale of taxation was again causing mur-murings in parliament. The relative poverty of the crown and an awareness of its dwindling resources greeted Henry VI's council on his accession in 1422. It was agreed that all grants of royal land were to be provisional until the king came of age. Indeed, the minority witnessed a suspension of the usual debate between the king and his subjects over their respective financial responsi-bilities. Parliament was reluctant to grant extraordinary taxation and, while grants both of the subsidy on wool and customs of tonnage and poundage made during Henry V's reign were extended, it was not until 1428 that the Commons approved a lay subsidy and not until January 1430, in anticipation of the king's coronation in France, that the first fifteenth and tenth, the most reliable form of lay taxation, was paid into the exchequer.

The dire financial situation of the minority government was revealed in 1433 when the treasurer of England, Ralph, Lord Cromwell, presented an estimate of royal revenue and expenditure to parliament. Cromwell's purpose was simple: he wanted conciliar authority to prioritise funds for the royal household and the upkeep of the king's palaces over the payment of fees and annuities. To constantly juggle the competing demands of government and powerful individuals was proving too much for the embattled treasurer. Cromwell estimated the crown's annual income at some £65,000 per annum, while its expenditure ran at almost £81,000. This was no short-term crisis and annual deficits of this nature throughout the minority had resulted in a total royal debt of over £168,000.[19] The immediate reasons for this shortfall were clear. First, the cost of the royal household, while reduced from previous reigns, still represented the single largest item of expenditure. Second, no sustainable arrangement had been found to meet the costs of the English garrison at Calais (almost £12,000 per annum), and in 1433 the 'old debts' owed to successive treasurers of the town totalled over £45,000. Finally, while the lucrative subsidy on exported wool had been extended, this was at a lower rate than that granted to Henry V, resulting in an annual shortfall of some £12,000 during the minority. Moreover, the peculiar circumstances of the minority added to the government's financial woes. Since 1422 some £5,000 per annum from the lands of the duchy of Lancaster had been set aside for the performance of Henry V's will. This revealed the tension between the private lordship of the king as duke of Lancaster and the wider responsibilities of the crown. Similarly, the king's personal estate in Wales, Cornwall, and the lordship of Richmond in Yorkshire and the Midlands were not available to meet the general costs of government through the exchequer. While the feoffees of the duchy of Lancaster were important crown creditors throughout the first half of the reign (lending some £114,000 between 1422 and 1441, all of which was promptly repaid), the notion that the duchy of Lancaster was separate from the crown's estates persisted. In 1441, on the termination of Henry V's enfeoffment, the duchy revenues were not employed for the defence of the realm and the war in France, but appropriated for the maintenance of the royal foundations at Eton and Cambridge. For various reasons, then, the reign of Henry VI witnessed a sustained fiscal crisis, with average annual income some 40 per cent lower than that enjoyed by his father. There can be little doubt that this contributed to a wider sense of crisis that developed as the king's majority progressed.

The 1433 statement of royal income and expenditure also reveals another defining, and vitally important, feature of Lancastrian fiscal culture. While budget statements and 'views' of the exchequer had been drawn up in the fourteenth century for scrutiny in parliament, such statements had probably been examined only by the lords of the king's council. In 1404, 1421, and 1426 (and probably on other occasions) such declarations had been compiled to be declared to the Lords in parliament, but had not been enrolled on the Parliament Roll. Nevertheless, as the Commons' concerns about royal finance in the parliaments of 1404, 1406, and 1421 and the extra-parliamentary discourse contained in poems such as *Crowned King* show, the debate over fiscal responsibility was one carried on at all levels of political society. Henry VI's minority, and the resulting ambiguity around royal authority, made this discussion impossible to contain. In this respect Cromwell's statement in 1433 marked an important watershed: it was made before the Lords and the Commons and recorded officially among the records of that assembly. Moreover, the 1433 statement established a precedent that continued into the majority: while such declarations were, as previously, routinely read to the Lords, on some occasions the Commons were also involved in the scrutiny of royal finance.[20] This distinctively inclusive Lancastrian discourse of fiscal responsibility was also carried on through informal channels, such as poetry. By the 1440s there was an apparently widely held view that, although the crown was impoverished, the commons had shouldered more than their fair share of the burden, while certain individuals had enriched themselves at the expense of the commonwealth. The anonymous poem *A Warning to King Henry*, written during the 1440s, attacked his household men: 'Ffor ye have made the kyng so pore/ That now he beggeth fro dore to dore.'[21] As we shall see, these sentiments played a large part in fomenting the crisis of 1449–50.

Yet the financial problems of the 1430s and 1440s did not only result from decisions made in the council chamber and in parliament. These decades witnessed the beginnings of the one of the most sustained economic and agrarian crises to hit pre-modern Europe. The so-called 'Great Slump' began in renewed outbreaks of plague and a serious agrarian crisis during the 1430s and grew in severity, due to a general contraction of trade and credit throughout Europe, in the next decade. The effects of these economic changes impacted upon different parts of the realm and different sectors of society in a variety of ways. While some benefitted from reduced rents and relatively stable grain prices, others felt acutely the shortage of bullion that resulted in a contraction of overseas trade. A sense of economic uncertainty, however, appears to have contributed to a more general feeling of unease during Henry VI's majority. The crown's poverty contributed to this, with familiar complaints about such issues as the royal right of purveyance (the ability to purchase food for the royal household at less than market value) resurfacing during the 1440s. In 1439, 1442, and 1445 the Commons attempted to curb abuses of purveyance and it was one of the factors identified by the rebels in 1450 that contributed to the commons' economic hardship. More importantly perhaps, as Richard Britnell has reminded us, economic conditions provided a means by 'which fifteenth-century people evaluated the governments under which they lived'.[22] As such, the 'Great Slump' of the mid-fifteenth century played an important role in the collapse of Lancastrian royal authority.

We have very little evidence of Henry VI's own attitudes towards the crown's financial position in the 1430s and 1440s. His profligacy with royal grants, his agreement to the sale and leasing of crown property on unfavourable terms, and his willingness to pardon royal debtors all suggest a cavalier attitude to notions of fiscal responsibility. Henry too seemed eager to carry on his family's differentiation between the public resources of the crown and his own private resources as duke of Lancaster. Yet there is evidence that Henry was aware of contemporary concerns about the costs of the Lancastrian project, and particularly the long-term implications of Henry V's conquests in France and the Dual Monarchy. In November 1440, in one of the most significant actions of the majority regime, Henry agreed to the release of Charles, duke of Orléans, the most prominent French prisoner taken at the battle of Agincourt. In the following year the council made 'a plain declaration' of the factors that moved Henry to agree to the duke's release, to counter a general 'noise and grudging' among his subjects and to assure them that the decision had not been made 'of simpleness, nor of self will, nor without notable causes' on the king's part. Both contemporaries and later historians have disagreed over the extent to which Henry was behind the decision to free Orléans: to some, such as the aggrieved duke of Gloucester, the declaration merely gave voice to a peace policy driven by Cardinal Beaufort; to Ralph Griffiths, the document was 'the clearest revelation of the king's feelings' and evidence of 'a sincere, Christian revulsion at the further shedding of blood'; to John Watts, it was another expression of public policy made by the council, rather than any statement of the king's own wishes.[23] Nevertheless, the sentiments it ascribes to the king are consistent with other ostensible expressions of his will and, crucially, show that Henry's attitudes to the war in France were wholly consistent with certain themes recurrent in Lancastrian political discourse. In terms of the crown's financial position, the declaration echoes widely held Lancastrian concerns over the cost of the war and fiscal responsibility. It gave the example of Edward III, who, despite winning notable battles and employing the knighthood of England in pursuit of his French ambitions, still sought an honourable peace. During the course of his wars he had 'expended in two years and a half, five hundred thousand marks' (£366,666), yet, due to the size and strength of the kingdom of France, Edward had recognised that outright military victory was impossible. He thus listened to counsel to ease 'the grievous and importable labour' the war put upon his subjects. Similarly, Henry pointed to his own father, who had also recognised the heavy burden of taxation 'which caused weariness in the great part of those that had long borne it'. The futility of the present war was underlined in terms not only of the unnecessary shedding of blood, but also of the 'great and notable sums of money and goods' that his subjects were being forced to pay.[24] The arguments for peace made in the declaration therefore were part of a discourse of fiscal responsibility which had been prominent in the parliaments of Henry IV and V and which would continue to form an important part of the debate over Henry's kingship throughout the 1440s and 1450s.

Closely connected to notions of fiscal responsibility was the crown's obligation to offer impartial justice and maintain law and order. The relationship between the domestic duties of the king and his foreign ambitions was a complex one: on the one hand, the burden of taxation could cause poverty and lead to an upsurge in related crime, while unruly soldiers returning from the wars were a constant source of concern for local communities; on the other hand, war offered a 'pressure-release valve', allowing restless men opportunities in royal service and harnessing the energies of the aristocracy in a king-led martial endeavour. Henry's father had offered a rare example of a king who, albeit for a short period of time, appeared to have reached the perfect balance between war abroad and peace at home.[25] At the heart of Henry V's success, however, had been his own character and personal involvement in the dispensation of justice. It was the king alone who could act as the impartial arbiter of his subjects' disputes and offer the kind of supreme, personal authority that his nobles would respect. It is perhaps in this crucial aspect of kingship that Henry VI failed most spectacularly between 1437 and 1450. Traditionally it has been argued that these years saw the rise to local prominence of self-serving courtiers, who used their access to the king to challenge and usurp existing local power structures and subvert law and justice. It was a period notable for several notorious personal disputes involving some of the king's greatest subjects, disputes which Henry did nothing to settle and even aggravated through his ill-judged interventions. More recent accounts, such as that of Helen Castor, have stressed the complexity of local politics and how the king's servants often struggled to represent royal authority in the absence of proper leadership from the king himself.[26] Rather than being seen as the villains of traditional historiography, men such as the duke of Suffolk have emerged as the valiant champions of Lancastrian rule, attempting to maintain some semblance of public authority in the face of Henry VI's shortcomings.

There can be little doubt that Henry spectacularly failed to exercise the obligations of kingship with regard to the maintenance of justice and local law and order. His disastrous intervention in the Courtenay/Bonville feud in the West Country has already been noted, but it was not an isolated incident. As the king's majority began, a similar dispute was brewing in Bedfordshire, where the established dominance of Reynold, Lord Grey of Ruthin, was being challenged by the newly ennobled Lancastrian retainer John Cornwall, Lord Fanhope. Fanhope was able to use his influence with the king and council to secure a special commission which undermined the commission of the peace, headed by Lord Grey. In 1439 events reached a head when Lord Fanhope prevented the justices from holding their sessions in Bedford town hall, causing a riot which resulted in eighteen people losing their lives. As a result, both sides were brought before the council, but both Lords Fanhope and Grey were able to secure the king's pardon without punishment. The king's generosity had again undermined the rule of law and the public authority of the crown. Henry's ill-considered interventions were also felt in the Midlands in 1444 when he decided to advance his boyhood companion, the young Henry Beauchamp (the son of his former tutor, the earl of Warwick), creating him England's premier earl and granting him the duchy of Lancaster lordship of Tutbury in Staffordshire. Warwick's promotion threatened to undermine local power structures both in the Midlands, where his elevation to premier earl, then to duke, challenged the authority and standing of Humphrey Stafford, earl of Buckingham, and in the household, where his friendship with Lords Sudeley and Beauchamp threatened to undermine the network created by the earl of Suffolk. In the parliament of 1445 Buckingham (now himself a duke) challenged Warwick's precedence and this ongoing feud was prevented from escalating further only by Warwick's untimely death in June 1446. Once again, Henry's failure to appreciate the dynamics of local politics ensured that the crown was a destabilising factor in the government of England during the 1440s.

It is, however, in Kent and East Anglia that Henry's failures were most notorious. In East Anglia it is commonly supposed that a group of household men, notably Thomas Daniel, John Heydon, and Thomas Tuddenham, used the protection of the duke of Suffolk, the steward of the duchy of Lancaster's lands there, to undermine the authority of existing landholders, such as the duke of Norfolk, and enrich themselves at the expense of local men. The evidence for this comes primarily from the voluminous and colourful correspondence of the Paston family. Nevertheless, as Helen Castor has shown, the duchy of Lancaster connection in East Anglia was an established and long-standing one. The disputes of the mid 1440s were part and parcel of the usual cut-and-thrust of local politics, particularly when acquisitive newcomers, like the Pastons or Sir John Fastolf, were involved. The problem was not Suffolk's malign influence in local affairs, rather his inability to represent both the public authority of the crown and the private power of the duchy of Lancaster; this was something only the king could combine successfully. Yet only from 1448 was there a serious breakdown in local order. Robert Hungerford, Lord Moleyns, a Wiltshire man with no East Anglian connection, made a violent attempt to wrest control of the Paston manor of Gresham, with the apparent backing of the royal household, while household men were also involved in attempts to dispossess Fastolf of property in the region.[27] This apparent collapse of law and order from 1448 was, as we shall see, indicative of a more general crisis that affected the Lancastrian realms in the late 1440s and may represent Suffolk's failure to maintain the illusion of effective royal lordship. In Kent the 1440s were notable for the rise to prominence of James Fiennes. Fiennes, one of the king's leading household men, was the younger son of a Sussex family who acquired property in the county in the early 1420s, but by 1440 he was already an established figure, having served as sheriff and represented the county among the Commons. By the mid 1440s he had gathered around him a group of lawyers from the west of the county, and especially from the area around his own seat at Knole near Sevenoaks, who dominated the major county offices of sheriff, escheator, justice of the peace, and MP. To Cade's rebels in 1450 (and many subsequent historians), Fiennes and his circle were the epitome of the covetous household servants who had subverted royal government to their own ends, but there is very little evidence of any wrong-doing on their part before 1447. In fact, the mid 1440s in Kent were noteworthy for the deaths of many of the powerful individuals who had dominated the county's government for most of the fifteenth century and for a shift in the location of political power in the county from east to west. These local factors combined with other national and international concerns in the late 1440s to produce a sense of acute unease in the county, a feeling only made worse by the evident lack of effective lordship offered by the king.[28]

Conclusion

It would be foolish to argue that Henry VI was anything other than a failure as king during the 1440s. In England he failed in two key aspects of kingship. First, he failed to show proper judgement in the dispensation of patronage, allowing the regime to fall victim to accusations of corruption and cronyism. Second, he failed to exercise effective lordship over his greatest subjects, failing to offer the kind of princely authority that could dispense impartial and effective justice. Yet it is simplistic to argue that Henry was merely a bad king, a wilful meddler or incompetent who made bad decisions at the wrong time. Similarly, it seems mistaken to argue that here was no king at all, a princely vacuum at the centre which others struggled, and failed, to fill. The simple problem was that during the 1440s Henry's kingship developed into a product of the various and at times contradictory strands of thought and behaviour that constituted Lancastrianism.

First, it should come as no surprise that the king relied primarily on his household rather than his nobles for support and counsel. In some ways this was the inevitable outcome of a reign that had started while the king was still an infant, yet it also reflected the personal ties of loyalty and lordship that had sustained the House of Lancaster throughout the fourteenth century, had enabled the revolution of 1399 to succeed, and had helped Henry V to establish the Dual Monarchy. The private, baronial roots of Lancastrianism had not disappeared by 1437, and the Lancastrian household strengthened those features throughout the 1440s to mitigate the king's obvious shortcomings. Henry's eagerness to reward his servants might have had unfortunate consequences, but it was explicable in terms of the good service they undoubtedly rendered him. Second, the apparently idiosyncratic nature of Henry's kingship was consistent with certain strands of Lancastrian identity. We need not try to explain the foundation of Eton and King's as the desperate attempts of the king's councillors to find a project that could draw together his subjects in the absence of a royal martial endeavour. The foundations were Henry's own expression of Lancastrian piety, similar to that practised by many of his leading subjects. While the attention and energy they demanded from all concerned might have been better employed elsewhere during the 1440s, they were nevertheless a statement of kingly intent consistent with a shared set of broadly Lancastrian values.

Henry's kingship was not solely a product of his own will and ambitions. It was also shaped by his subjects' response to his rule, a response that was in turn conditioned both by distinctly

Lancastrian concerns and by more general expectations of princely government. Thus Lancastrian notions of fiscal responsibility, voiced by the commons both in and out of parliament throughout the early fifteenth century and apparently shared on one occasion at least by Henry himself, clashed with more general expectations that the king would lead armies in person and distinguish himself in war. Similarly, subjects struggled to reconcile abstract notions of impartial royal justice with the complex vagaries of local politics and the need to reward the growing Lancastrian affinity for its service in the localities. As we shall see in the next chapter, throughout the 1440s there was a growing public debate over the nature of kingship and the personality of the king himself. This in itself was a distinctly Lancastrian feature of political life, a result of the regime's need for public approbation since the revolution of 1399, but one that would have far-reaching consequences. From 1447 a combination of factors – a deepening economic and fiscal crisis, the regime's failure to keep the lid on violent tensions both at court and in the localities, and a swift decline in the English position in France – conspired to fatally undermine Henry's kingship.

Notes

1 K.B. McFarlane, *The Nobility of Later Medieval England* (Oxford, 1973), 284.
2 David Starkey, 'The Age of the Household: Politics, Society and the Arts c.1350–1500', in *The Later Middle Ages*, ed. S. Medcalf (1981), 225–90.
3 See B.P. Wolffe, *Henry VI* (1981), 106–34 and R.Griffiths. *The Reign of Henry VI* (1981), 295–362.
4 K.B. McFarlane, *The Nobility of Later Medieval England* (Oxford, 1973), 284; John Watts, *Henry VI and the Politics of Kingship* (Cambridge, 1996), 216–36.
5 G.L. Harriss, 'The Court of the Lancastrian Kings', in *The Lancastrian Court*, ed. Jenny Stratford (Donington, 2003), 7–9.
6 *Letters and Papers Illustrative of the English Wars in France during the Reign of Henry VI*, ed. J. Stevenson (2 vols in 3, Rolls Series, 1861–4), ii(2), 448.
7 TNA, C81/1425/55.
8 Ibid., C81/1426/28.
9 Watts, *Politics of Kingship*, 143.
10 *POPC*, vi, 316–20.
11 *Calendar of Patent Rolls, 1441–46*, 312–13.
12 TNA, C81/1370/50.
13 *PROME*, xi, 440.
14 Ibid., 345.
15 A.H. Lloyd, *The Early History of Christ's College, Cambridge* (Cambridge, 1934), 356.

16 Barrie Dobson, 'Henry VI and the University of Cambridge', in *The Lancastrian Court, The Lancastrian Court*, ed. Jenny Stratford (Donington, 2003), 58.
17 *English Historical Documents Vol. IV 1327–1485*, ed. A.R. Myers (1969), 918.
18 Robert Wills, *The Architectural History of the University of Cambridge and of the Colleges of Cambridge and Eton* (Cambridge, 1886), i, 350–80.
19 *PROME*, xi, 102–13.
20 TNA E403/779, m. 4; 798, m. 13.
21 *Political Poems and Songs*, ed. Thomas Wright (2 vols, Rolls Series, 1859–61), ii, 229.
22 Richard Britnell, 'The Economic Context', in *The Wars of the Roses*, ed. A.J. Pollard (Basingstoke, 1995), 64.
23 Griffiths, *Reign of Henry VI*, 443; Watts, *Politics of Kingship*, 106–7, 143–4.
24 *Letters and Papers Illustrative of the English Wars in France*, ed. Stevenson, ii(2), 451–60.
25 E. Powell, *Kingship, Law and Society: Criminal Justice in the Reign of Henry V* (Oxford, 1989).
26 Helen Castor, *The King, the Crown and the Duchy of Lancaster* (Oxford, 2000).
27 Ibid., 82–155.
28 David Grummitt, 'Kent and National Politics, c.1399–1461', in *Later Medieval Kent, 1220–1540*, ed. Sheila Sweetinburgh (Woodbridge, 2010), 234–50.

7 Majority rule (II)

The collapse of the Dual
Monarchy 1437–50

At the heart of the Lancastrian project stood the Dual Monarchy. Henry V's great achievement was to succeed where his predecessors as kings of England had failed in realising their claim to the French throne. The Treaty of Troyes had a distinctly Lancastrian flavour: by the marriage of Henry V and Catherine of Valois, it also fulfilled the ambition, begun by John of Gaunt, to elevate the House of Lancaster to the status of a European princely dynasty. Henry, of course, could not have foreseen the circumstances in which his son would accede to the thrones of England and France, and the fifteen years of minority rule witnessed an increasingly desperate attempt to assert Henry VI's authority in his French kingdom. There is little doubt that the nature of the Lancastrian legacy in France and the future of the Dual Monarchy were the defining features of the first three decades of Henry's reign. The future of the Dual Monarchy set members of the Lancastrian royal family against one another and divided Henry's subjects. It also provided one of the few arenas of public life in which the king himself expressed a definite and consistent preference. That his preference was for peace rather than war, albeit at the cost of dismantling many of the achievements of his father, was in many ways logical and explicable within the framework of Lancastrian kingship. Yet it also undermined royal authority and fatally compromised the reputation of those men who had executed the king's policies during the 1440s. In 1449–50 Henry and his councillors were outwitted by the French king Charles VII, losing Normandy in a military campaign even more audacious and successful than that carried out by Henry V thirty years previously.

Defeat in France and the collapse of the Dual Monarchy was a grievous blow to the kingship of Henry VI and one from which he never fully recovered.

War and peace, 1437–45

If Henry VI's subjects hoped that the beginning of his majority rule would signal a firm and decisive policy on the war in France they were to be disappointed. The years between 1437 and 1445 saw policy vacillate between overtures for peace and new military expeditions. The latter were usually small, limited in their objectives, and, crucially, none was led by the king in person. Henry's preference, and one apparently shared by many leading members of his household and council, was for peace. The reasons for this were several: first, by the late 1430s it was clear that outright military victory over the House of Valois would be impossible to achieve; second, the financial strains of the war, both in England and in Lancastrian France, were unbearable; and, finally, it seems the king had a genuine aversion to war and the shedding of Christian blood. The search for peace and the prosecution of limited military campaigns were not, however, mutually incompatible. Advantage on the battlefield easily translated into advantage at the negotiating table. Indeed, in 1416 Henry Beaufort, bishop of Winchester, had told parliament 'bella faciamus ut pacem habeamus' ('Let us make wars so we might have peace').[1] The trouble was that by the late 1430s Charles VII and his supporters were becoming increasingly confident that there was little need to compromise in their dealings with the Lancastrians; the half-hearted and incompetent manner of the English military operations in the early 1440s served only to reinforce this impression. Paradoxically, without success in war the long-lasting peace that Henry and his servants looked for would prove impossible to achieve.

The beginning of Henry's formal majority rule was marked by the arrival in Normandy of a new lieutenant-general, the king's former tutor, the earl of Warwick. Warwick was an experienced and capable soldier and his presence in the duchy consolidated the Lancastrian position there. The earl, however, was already ailing when he arrived in France, and he died in Rouen in April 1439. The late 1430s were notable also for the rise to prominence of the Beaufort brothers, John, earl of Somerset, and Edmund, earl of Dorset. They were the nephews of Cardinal Beaufort, and, while their uncle's influence (and money) had much to do with their advancement, the king's own involvement in their careers should not be ignored. Earl John had been released from eighteen years of captivity in France in the summer of 1439 and in December that year he indented for six months' service in Normandy, receiving royal grants to help pay his ransom in return for 'better service to the king in this expedition'.[2] The cardinal's efforts to secure the lieutenancy of Normandy for his nephew, however, failed amidst opposition from the duke of Gloucester. They were also not helped by Somerset's demands regarding the conditions under which he was willing to serve. Eventually, in July 1440 the duke of York reluctantly agreed to a second term as lieutenant-general, although it would be almost a year before he arrived in the duchy. More significantly perhaps, in March 1438 Earl Edmund had been made captain-general and governor of Maine, a command separate from Warwick's in Normandy and the *pays de conquête*. His army of 1,700 men arrived in France in June that year, but they did not assist in the defence of Normandy, instead campaigning in Maine before the arrival of a large French army, led by Charles VII in person, forced their return to Normandy. Dorset's expedition highlighted the confused nature of English military operations during the late 1430s and this in turn reflected the king's growing interest in the conduct of affairs in France. Edmund, in particular, was the recipient of Henry's personal favour: in 1442 the confirmation of his earldom of Dorset explicitly recognised the service he had rendered eight years previously in the relief of Calais. The promotion of the Beaufort brothers, as we shall see, would have important consequences for the future of the Dual Monarchy.

In 1439 the military imperative in Normandy took second place, however, to the efforts to secure a lasting peace. In June and July an English delegation, led by Cardinal Beaufort and Archbishop Kemp, met their French counterparts in a meeting brokered by the Burgundians (and especially Duchess Isabel, the grand-daughter of John of Gaunt) near Oye in the Calais Pale. The Burgundians, driven by the need to re-establish commercial relations, had reassessed the cost of their unilateral peace with Charles VII in 1435 and had made overtures to the English the year before. They now hoped to broker a more general settlement. On 21 May Henry had presented Kemp with formal instructions at Kennington, but four days later the king also gave Beaufort secret, oral instructions regarding 'all the king's mind and intent as regards the crown', and powers to conclude a binding agreement.[3] The English position was one that smacked of weakness and a willingness, almost desperation, to conclude a peace: in return for abandoning his title as king of France, Henry would receive Normandy and Gascony in full sovereignty. Moreover, the duke of Orléans, the most prominent French prisoner taken at Agincourt, whom Henry V had stated should not be released until his son came of age, was to be set free in order to work for peace on Henry's behalf. In August Kemp returned to England with a deal that offered a truce of up to thirty years in return for Henry's abandoning his French title. The English council, led by the duke of Gloucester, unambiguously rejected the proposal, fearful that it would allow a slow reconquest by the French under the pretence of the truce and an unacceptable diminution of Henry's honour. They argued that it would show 'too great a simpleness and lack of foresight in him that accepts it'. The council's summary of their arguments captured the Lancastrian dilemma perfectly: to abandon the Treaty of Troyes now would be tantamount to recognising some 'lack of might or of right or of courage' on the king's behalf and accepting as pointless the sacrifice of men, money, and materials that had been made to date.[4] On this occasion the council's will prevailed, but Henry registered his feelings by insisting on the release of Orléans, who was finally set free the following year.

The release of the duke of Orléans was an event of huge symbolic and real importance. Throughout the early summer of 1440 debate raged in the council over the duke's release. Both the French and the Burgundians saw his release as an essential precursor to a lasting settlement, while some among the English council hoped that Orléans' presence would strengthen the noble revolt against Charles VII (known as the *Praguerie*) led by the dukes of Alençon and Bourbon. Gloucester, almost alone among the king's council, steadfastly opposed Orléans' release, arguing that he would not be bound by any oaths made while a prisoner. Nevertheless, on 2 July Henry confirmed his determination to release the duke and on 28 October at the high altar of Westminster Orléans publicly swore to abide by the conditions of his release and never to take up arms against Henry VI. The symbolism of this piece of political theatre was underlined when Gloucester ostentatiously stormed out of the abbey as the duke made his solemn vow. Orléans' release clearly caused public unease: as one of John Paston's correspondents remarked, 'God give grace the said lord of Orléans be true.'[5] It was to counter these fears that the council released its justification of the king's decision in early November. This document made very practical arguments for peace, but it also underlined the fact that Henry's desire to end the war was motivated by his genuine desire to heal the divisions in Christendom. In 1417 at the council of Constance, Pope Martin V had been forced to agree to summon regular general councils of the Church. In 1431 he had summoned such a meeting to deal with the Hussite heresy in Bohemia. By 1439 relations between the new pope, Eugenius IV, and the council had reached a nadir and in June the council had declared the pontiff a heretic for his close contact with the Orthodox Church in Byzantium and deposed him in favour of an anti-pope, Amadeus, duke of Savoy, whom they elected Pope Felix V. This schism clearly troubled the young king. In the declaration he condemned the council of Basel and stressed the obligation of Christian princes to strive for peace, 'the which peace had and made, were like to be one of the greatest earthly means to the appeasing of the said trouble of the Church, and generally of the support of God's Church, and of the Christian faith and belief'.[6]

During the early 1440s, then, competing and contradictory factors shaped Lancastrian policy in France. First, Henry's 'Christian pacifism' and his desire to heal the rifts in the Church provided an important impetus to the peace negotiations.[7] The move towards peace was given greater urgency by the worsening financial situation both in England and in Normandy. Second, there was the emotional attachment to Henry V's achievements and a commitment to the terms of the Treaty of Troyes, explicit in the duke of Gloucester's opposition to the release of Orléans, but also implicit in the foundation of All Souls' College, Oxford and in the memorials to those who had given their lives in the Lancastrian cause. Related to this was the very practical question of how to compensate those who had benefitted materially by the Lancastrian land settlement in Normandy, should land be returned to the French. Moreover, as we shall see, Lancastrian France still provided an important source of patronage and the means of fulfilling the ambitions of important individuals. Yet in reality the single most important factor in determining the future of the Dual Monarchy was not the struggle between the 'war' and the 'peace' party in England, but the attitude of Charles VII. Lancastrian hopes of Orléans' role in securing a peace were initially dashed not because the duke reneged on his promises, but because the French king simply refused to receive him. It was not until September 1442 that the two were eventually reconciled. During the early 1440s there was a growing confidence at the Valois court and a realisation that the Lancastrian position was untenable. It was evident in the hostility that Charles demonstrated to his erstwhile Burgundian allies and the vigour with which the French king met the challenge of his rebellious nobles and his enemies on his eastern border with the Empire. By 1443, when peace negotiations with the English began in earnest again, the House of Valois was in a much stronger position.

The initial English response to the failure of the 1439/40 initiatives for peace was to plan another round of military campaigning. The duke of York's army enjoyed limited success in 1441, failing to bring the French king to battle on the Seine and Oise rivers, and further reinforcements crossed to Normandy the following year, allowing Lord Talbot to begin the siege of Dieppe in October 1442. Meanwhile Charles VII began a campaign against English-held Gascony that eventually foundered in the cold winter of 1442. In February the following year the English council began to debate whether armies should be sent to Normandy, Gascony, or both. Since the previous summer the council had been in negotiation with John Beaufort, earl of Somerset, about the conditions under which he would lead an army to France. By March 1443 these had been agreed: Somerset would cross the channel with an army of some 4,500 men and hold a command completely independent of York in his capacity as lieutenant-general of Normandy. Although Somerset would begin operations from the duchy, his intention would be to cross over 'into ground occupied by the enemy and there use most cruel and mortal war'.[8] The desire to bring the French to battle was an implicit criticism of York's conduct two years previously and on 5 April Henry wrote to his lieutenant-general explaining the terms and objectives of Somerset's service. The king had also granted Somerset's request that he be appointed captain-general and governor of Anjou and Maine on the expiry of his brother Dorset's term of office. The decision to send Somerset marked an important departure in English war policy: it revived the plans put forward by Sir John Fastolf in 1435 to keep a separate field army to take the war to the French, and it promised the earl the spoils of any victories. His indenture contained a clause granting him 'such countries, lands, towns, castles, fortresses and places as he shall get within the said realm and duchy or elsewhere which he shall reduce to the king's obedience'.[9] Finally, on 8 August, as Somerset and his army began their march through Normandy, he was elevated to the title of duke in recognition of the importance of the expedition.

Historians have struggled to explain the appointment of Somerset, an ailing and relatively inexperienced commander, to command so vital an endeavour. Some have seen the hand of Cardinal Beaufort, keen to carve out a patrimony for his nephews and ensure the status of the Beauforts 'as the principal nobility of Lancastrian France', behind the expedition.[10] Yet few on the council, the cardinal included, could have had any confidence in Somerset's abilities and it is notable that his more capable younger brother, Dorset, was conspicuously ignored. The decision to appoint Somerset and to accede to his demands for wide-ranging powers and an independent military command is most likely to have been the king's. Henry's desire to appoint a 'lord of our blood and lineage' flew in the face of common sense but spoke of the king's attitude to the Dual Monarchy as the personal concern of the Lancastrian royal family. Henry's confidence in Somerset was entirely misplaced. Problems in recruiting the army were testimony to the doubts that the wider military community had over the earl's competence, while Somerset's own failure to appear at the muster set for Portsmouth on 17 June 1443, whether for reasons of ill-health or neglect, underlined his unsuitability for the task in hand. On 9 July the council drew up a strongly worded criticism of his behaviour in the king's name, ordering him to muster his army immediately, 'all excuses ceasing', and depart for

Normandy by 17 July.[11] Somerset eventually departed for France four days later and by the third week in August he was ready to cross into enemy territory. His campaign was a predictable disaster. He first laid siege to and captured the town of La Guerche belonging to the duke of Brittany, officially at least still an ally of Henry VI. His army then wandered aimlessly around Anjou, failing to take the stronghold of Pouancé. By December the money had run out, and Somerset returned to England early in the new year to a uniformly hostile reception. Henry's anger towards his 'cousin' was well documented by English chroniclers and when the duke died in May 1444 rumours soon started that he had taken his own life, unable to live with the shame of his failure. It is most likely that he died of natural causes, but the failure of the 1443 expedition appears to have compromised Cardinal Beaufort's influence and may have confirmed Henry's desire for a peaceful settlement of the French war.

While the council in England negotiated with Somerset over the 1443 campaign, diplomacy had continued both in England and in France. In April the duke of York concluded a perpetual peace with Isabel, duchess of Burgundy, and in June an English delegation, led by Suffolk (whose presence had been specifically requested by Charles VII), travelled to France. The aim of this new French initiative was nothing less than a marriage between Henry VI and Margaret, daughter of King René of Anjou, Charles VII's brother-in-law. A match between Henry and the thirteen-year-old niece of the French king was an enticing one. For Charles VII it offered the possibility of an advocate for peace at the heart of the English polity; for Henry VI it was a compelling gesture of his earnest desire for peace; for the English council it offered the opportunity to secure the Lancastrian dynasty through the birth of a son; while for René of Anjou it secured his place within the French king's counsels and promised the opportunity to regain the counties of Anjou and Maine from the English. The debacle of Somerset's 1443 expedition strengthened the case for peace and in February the following year a new mission, again led by Suffolk, assembled to meet the French at Tours. The importance of the next few weeks for the future of the Dual Monarchy was recognised by all concerned and Suffolk was keen to establish that this new policy represented the king's will approved by the whole council, including the duke of Gloucester. The earl was aware that rumours abounded in London of his sympathy for the French, a result of his captivity there in 1429–30 and his personal friendship with the duke of Orléans. The council's declaration, made on 1 February, thus made explicit that Suffolk had his fellow councillors' support and that in travelling to France he was executing the king's will.[12] Indeed, the matter of the king's marriage was something that the council had consistently refused to be drawn on. In 1430, 1438, and in the early 1440s they had rejected proposals for marriage from Spanish, Austrian, and Portuguese ambassadors. In 1442 the king and his council briefly entertained the idea of a marriage alliance with the French count of Armagnac, one of the leaders of the *Praguerie* rebellion. Commissioners were sent to Gascony to negotiate a match, armed with instructions signed by the king. As Henry explained, the matter of his marriage was one of the utmost personal importance, a fact underlined by his addition of his signature, 'the which, as you know well, we be not much accustomed for to do in other cases'.[13] There is thus no reason to suspect that in 1444 the apparent enthusiasm for an Anjou match represented anything other than the king's personal wish.

The English ambassadors, escorted by the duke of Orléans, arrived at Tours on 26 April 1444. They presented a signet letter from the king addressed to Charles VII as our 'dear uncle of France'. It represented a significant shift in the English position: unlike in 1439/40, the council were now willing to countenance Henry's surrender of his French title in return for a lasting peace and possession of Normandy and Gascony in full sovereignty. This formed the basis of a twenty-one-month truce that was confirmed by the betrothal of Margaret to Henry on 26 May, with Suffolk standing as the king's proxy. Margaret came with no dowry except a paltry 20,000 francs. She also renounced all interests in her father's property and titles (including the prestigious but ultimately worthless kingdom of Jerusalem). Crucially, the marriage also came with the unwritten assumption, at least on the part of the French, that the English would surrender the county of Maine. While Suffolk made no such promises at Tours, despite allegations later laid against him, this was the quid pro quo accepted by Henry, who on 10 October the following year made that promise verbally to the French ambassadors in England. The agreement made at Tours demonstrated how the advantage had shifted decisively to Charles VII. The contemporary recognition of the new situation was underlined by the fact that the duke of Brittany, ostensibly still a vassal of the Lancastrian king, ratified the treaty on behalf of Henry's Valois rival.

In November 1444 an English delegation, again led by Suffolk (now promoted to the rank of marquis), left to collect Henry's bride. Early in March the two were married by proxy in Nancy and on 9 April Margaret arrived in Porchester, near Southampton. On 22 April she and Henry celebrated their nuptials at Titchfield Abbey in front of the king's confessor, Bishop Aiscough of Salisbury. Towards the end of 1444 royal commissioners had been sent out to solicit loans to meet the costs of the wedding and Margaret's new household. Their instructions ironically spelt out the disadvantages of the Anjou match: Henry thanked Suffolk and the other councillors for providing him with a queen 'of a high and noble birth, greatly endowed with gifts of grace and of nature', but who brought little else in terms of tangible benefits. The commissioners were to stress the king's 'special rejoicing and comfort, that he stands in right good trust and hope of a peace finally to be concluded and had between him and his uncle of France'.[14] The facts that a match to the 'French queen's dowerless niece' was disparaging to the English,[15] that the truce allowed Charles VII to reorganise and equip his armies while the Lancastrian garrisons in Normandy were run down, and that the tacit agreement to surrender Maine fatally compromised the Lancastrian position were all conveniently forgotten to satisfy the king's naïve desire for peace.

The peaceful king: contemporary views of Henry VI

Few, if any, medieval kings have had so much written about their character by both contemporaries and later scholars as has Henry VI. The king's personality and aptitude to meet the challenges that confronted him troubled his servants and subjects, fascinated foreign observers, and have caused long debate among historians. As J.W. McKenna and others have observed, there was little to choose 'between the fool evoked by Henry's detractors and the monk evoked by his friends'.[16] Yet the image of the 'saintly muff' (as J.R. Lander dubbed him) emerged largely in the years after 1450 in the context of hostile Yorkist explanations for the outbreak of the Wars of the Roses and later attempts to rehabilitate the king's reputation.[17] For those writing or talking about the king's personality during the period 1437–50 the sense of confusion was much more acute. Their assessments of the king reveal a sense of apprehension about Henry and his style of rule, and a struggle to reconcile their observations and opinions with specifically Lancastrian and more general views of kingship.

The appearance and demeanour of the young king clearly intrigued visitors to the Lancastrian court. When the papal tax collector Piero da Monte visited Henry in 1437 he found the fifteen-year-old king punctilious in his observance of the daily liturgical rituals of the court. Da Monte concluded: 'I judge him not to be a king or worldly prince . . . but a monk or a religious man, more religious than a man of religion.' Yet he also observed the king to be 'mild, gentle and calm', to have 'an old man's sense, prudence and gravity', and to have answered questions 'wisely'.[18] Da Monte's observations of a prince who was accessible to his servants and counsellors, abstemious in nature, and who spoke only briefly were not out of line with contemporary manuals on kingly behaviour (such as the *Secreta Secretorum*, which spoke of the virtue of brevity), but one wonders how much the description of the king as monk-like owed to briefings from Henry's courtiers and councillors. Archbishop Kemp, of course, had previously praised the six-year-old king for learning parts of the liturgy by heart. Other foreign commentators were, however, less positive about the king's attributes. In 1448 Henry wrote to Pope Eugenius IV recommending his chaplain, Thomas Kemp, for the vacant bishopric of London. The papacy approved the request, but within a year the king had changed his mind, instead writing in support of Marmaduke Lumley, bishop of Carlisle. Eugenius refused to undo his previous decision, despite the claim that William Grey, the English proctor in Rome, had misrepresented the king's original intention. The pope returned Henry's original letter recommending Kemp and reminding the king of the need for gravity in taking advice, chastising him for changing his mind and thinking ill of his servants.[19] Such inconstancy was a feature of Henry's character and, as we have seen, had already caused problems with the distribution of royal patronage in England.

Even more damning, perhaps, was the report made by the French ambassadors who met the king in 1445. Henry, it is alleged, did little more 'than stand about in a variety of opulent costumes, grinning broadly and crying "Saint Jehan, grant mercis!" whenever Charles VII's name was mentioned.'[20] A closer reading of their report, however, suggests a king who, while clearly guided by his more experienced councillors, dictated the course of events and fulfilled certain important aspects of kingship. First, his dress ('a rich robe down to the ground, of cloth of gold' and 'a robe of black velvet down to the ground') and the surroundings of the palace expressed the magnificence of Lancastrian kingship. Second, the ambassadors were aware of divisions within the English council, and especially a perception that the marquis of Suffolk was championing peace in the face of opposition from the duke of Gloucester. They also believed that the desire to end the war came principally from Henry, motivated by the close familial ties and a genuine abhorrence of bloodshed. The ambassadors noted how the king was flanked by Gloucester and Suffolk and how he turned to each in turn while Archbishop Kemp outlined the English position. Once Kemp had finished his speech Henry turned to him and said 'I am very much rejoiced that some, who are present, should hear these words; they are not at their ease.' He also later rebuked Kemp for not having spoken 'words of greater friendship'. Henry's apparently outlandish response to the French ambassadors was thus a result of his own perception that the careful diplomatic language of his councillors had not adequately captured the strength of his personal desire for peace. Finally, in some ways Henry's demeanour in these meetings was a conscious echo of his father's style of government. When the ambassadors met the king for a second time in his privy chamber they found him leaning against a cupboard, the manner in which Henry V had regularly received petitioners and a symbol of the informality and ease of their forthcoming audience.[21] Rather than revealing Henry's inanity, the French ambassadors' report of their 1445 meeting reveals a king meeting many contemporary expectations, albeit in an idiosyncratic fashion. He ostentatiously took counsel and then pronounced his will, he appeared both magnificent and informal, depending on circumstances, while his demeanour towards the ambassadors underlined his genuine affection for his uncle and commitment to peace to men who were, in both a real and symbolic sense, representatives of the French king.

If the intricate formality and symbolism of the king's behaviour were apparent to visitors from other princely courts, Henry's behaviour was at times inexplicable to his subjects and troubled them greatly. It could be argued that the majority of Englishmen and women had a relatively unsophisticated view of kingship. Successful kings were those under whom justice was seen to be done, the economy prospered, and England's foreign enemies received their just deserts. These three key indicators of 'good kingship' were clearly lacking during the 1440s and Henry's reputation suffered accordingly. The accounts of seditious speech during that decade reveal a degree of consistency in the criticisms levelled at him and suggest that Henry's peculiar approach to rule critically undermined his subjects' confidence in the Lancastrian regime. Most telling perhaps are the comments on Henry's physical appearance and behaviour. As early as 1442 a Kentish yeoman was accused of stating that the 'king is a lunatic, as his father was' and that the duke of Gloucester should have the governance of the realm.[22] Presumably the accused had confused his genealogy and was referring to Henry's grandfather, Charles VI of France, rather than Henry V, while the slander had been spoken in the context of the arrest on charges of witchcraft of Eleanor Cobham, duchess of Gloucester, the previous year; but the accusation that Henry VI was mentally deficient resurfaced throughout the decade. In 1446 a London draper claimed that Henry was 'not in his person as his noble progenitors have been, for his visage was not favoured, for he had got unto a child's face and is not steadfast of wit as other kings have been before'.[23] This was a charge repeated three years later by a Dutchman in Ely who stated that the king 'looked more like a child than a man'.[24] Some reports of seditious speech contained compellingly vivid descriptions of the king's alleged idiocy: a Sussex man claimed in 1450 that 'the king was a natural fool and would often times hold a staff in his hand with a bird on the end playing therewith as a fool'. He went on to state 'that another king must be ordained to rule the land saying that the king was no person able to rule'.[25] These statements are difficult to interpret. First, many of those accused of uttering treasonable words against the king were either acquitted by a jury or pardoned. Moreover, their descriptions of the king match contemporary astrological predictions of his character arising from his birth in December, under the influence of the moon. As Jonathan Hughes has observed, to contemporary observers 'Henry was destined to have a feminine, watery, changeable character, the opposite of the fiery Martian temperament of his father . . . As he entered adulthood with his pallid, childlike face, Henry grew more phlegmatic, lacking passion, hating violence, withdrawn and forgetful. Most disturbing, his extreme phlegmatic withdrawal threatened to tip him into a state of idiocy, the simplicity of the moon child.'[26] Faced with a prince who did not fulfil their simplistic ideals of kingship, his subjects turned to culturally ingrained explanations of appearance and behaviour to find meaning in his actions.

Yet these descriptions of the king, apparently influenced by widely held astrological beliefs, could easily develop into more dangerous ideas of sedition and treason. After 1445 the king's virility and his failure to produce an heir were repeatedly called into question. Interestingly, however, the blame for this was more commonly apportioned to his servants or to Queen Margaret herself. In 1446 a Suffolk man accused the marquis of Suffolk and Bishop Aiscough of Salisbury of ruling the king and preventing him from enjoying conjugal relations with his wife: when 'the king would have his sport with our sovereign lady the queen, then the said bishop of Salisbury and others that were about our said sovereign lord the king counselled him that he should not come near her, the which is cause that she is not confined and so the land is defaced of a prince'.[27] Two years later a Kentish man stated that if 'he were a peer or a lord of this realm he would be one of them that should help to put her down for because she bears no child and because that we have no prince in this land'.[28] Another recurrent motif in reports of treasonable speech was the irony of the image of a ship, symbolic of England's military and commercial strength, in the English noble (a gold coin worth 6s. 8d.) In 1449 a Dutchman in Cambridgeshire allegedly said that the king would shortly 'lose the imprint of the ship in the noble and set instead the sheep'.[29] The previous year a Kentish farmer had said 'the king is nought to bear the form of the ship or the *fleur-de-lis* in the noble nor in his arms'.[30] Significantly, this motif had appeared more than a decade earlier in *The Libelle of Englysche Polycye*, a poem written in the aftermath of the Burgundian siege of Calais and associated with the aggressive foreign policy championed by Humphrey, duke of Gloucester. The author lamented the decline of English arms and the English navy during Henry VI's minority:

> For iij. thynges our noble sheweth to me,
> King, shype and swerde and power of see.
> Where bene oure shippes, where bene oure swerdes become?
> Owre enemyes bid for the shippe sette a shepe.
>
> (ll. 34–37)

The analogy of Henry with a sheep would become more direct as the English position in France worsened and the Lancastrian regime faced unrest at home. In 1453 a Southwark man claimed 'the king is but a sheep and has lost all that his father won, and would to God he had died soon after he was born'.[31] Most importantly, though, it demonstrated how Lancastrian political discourse shaped popular perceptions of the king and his rule.

One of the most notorious incidents of seditious speech came in April 1444 and involved Thomas Kerver, a Berkshire gentleman. He was alleged to have said that Henry's incompetence had cost the realm more than £100,000 and if the king had been more like Charles VII, who had recently been engaged on campaign in Gascony, the English would not be involved in an expensive war defending Lancastrian France. Kerver's case is significant on a number of levels. First, his outburst was prompted by a sermon preached to the Lancastrian court by Friar John Curtays at Abingdon earlier that year. Kerver repeated in English Curtays's Latin theme of 'Woe to the realm that has a child king'. It was a good example of the public nature of political discourse within Lancastrian England. Second, it shows how well-known discursive themes (in this case Henry's childlike nature) could be discussed and given focus by immediate events (Charles VII's recent campaign in Gascony). Finally, the regime's response demonstrates their anxiety around these public perceptions of Henry's fitness to rule and perhaps reveals their own misgivings over his effectiveness. Kerver was accused of imagining the king's death and of inciting his subjects to rebellion. The charges were drawn up by William Tresham, a lawyer and Lancastrian servant closely linked to Henry's household, and investigated by a special commission led by Sir Thomas Stanley, controller of the king's household. At the beginning of July Kerver was arrested, imprisoned in the Tower of London, tried for treason in the court of King's Bench, and found guilty. At this stage, however, there was an unusual turn of events. On 30 July the original trial and verdict were scrapped in favour of a special commission of *oyer et terminer* (empowered to hear and determine criminal matters independent of the jurisdiction of King's Bench) led by the earl of Suffolk and Chief Justice Fortescue. Kerver was again found guilty and sentenced to be drawn through Maidenhead and Reading before being hanged on a Berkshire gallows. He was then to be cut down while still alive and taken to Tyburn, where he was to be beheaded and his body quartered. On 4 August the king intervened: under his Eagle signet he issued letters stating that Kerver was to be drawn and hanged but spared the final stages of a traitor's death, remitting him to prison instead. The letters captured the confusion and anxiety around Kerver's case. They promised that in future offenders, 'even of the royal blood, could expect neither favour nor grace' from the king, while the messenger was warned that 'this our pardon be in no wise openly noised but kept as secret as you may'. Indeed, that the king had taken a personal interest in Kerver's fate and intervened to save his life is clear from another signet letter, dated 25 August 1447, ordering his release from Wallingford castle. The preamble to the writ explained that Henry had originally given oral instructions to Sir John Fortescue to release Kerver, only to be told that such an action could be expedited only by writ.[32]

It was not only the king's ordinary subjects who struggled to come to terms with the idiosyncratic nature of Henry's kingship. Established Lancastrian authors also came up with strangely ambiguous accounts of the king. Perhaps the best example is the account of Henry VI's life by John Capgrave, presented to the king on the occasion of his visit to the Austin Friary at Lynn in 1446. Capgrave was an Augustinian friar and Cambridge-educated theologian who wrote a number of prose and verse religious texts. In the late 1430s and early 1440s he had dedicated a number of theological works to Humphrey, duke of Gloucester, but by the time Henry visited Lynn, Capgrave, like his former patron, was no longer close to the Lancastrian regime. His account of Henry's life was contained within a collection of lives of exemplary kings named Henry, the *Liber de Illustribus Henricis* ('Book of Illustrious Henries'). Henry VI's inclusion in this company may appear odd and it has been suggested that it was done at the king's insistence. Alternatively, Capgrave's account of Henry VI's reign to date allowed him the opportunity to critique the regime, voicing many of the common complaints about Henry's kingship while simultaneously offering praise and advice. As Karen Winstead observes, the *Liber* is 'a diabolically subversive text whose praise of the sovereign masks a critique of his government'.[33] Capgrave's Henry was notable for doing very little. In the twenty-five years since he had come to the throne only six incidents were considered of note: his birth, his two coronations, his foundation of King's and Eton colleges, his marriage to Margaret of Anjou, and his visit to Lynn. Henry had demonstrated great devotion to the Holy Cross but little else. His 1431 coronation expedition was typical of a reign that was marked by the king's passivity: 'On the journey he harmed none, neither did anyone trouble him.' Capgrave even included a long passage on the importance of proper marital relations, amidst rumours of the king's celibacy. He repeated the words of those of a 'malignant disposition' who 'continue to sow among the people such murmuring words as these, – "Alas for thee, O land, whose king is a boy and whose princes eat in the morning."' While offering arguments to refute this notion, by articulating such sentiments Capgrave voiced his own concerns over Henry's kingship. Similarly, he reminded his readers of the jibes of England's enemies: 'Our enemies laugh at us and say, – "Take the 'ship' off your precious money, and stamp a 'sheep' upon it, showing thereby your own cowardice," – we, since who used to be the conquerors of all nations, are now being conquered.' Capgrave asked 'What does it avail us to read of the examples of these illustrious men, and not to imitate them?' in an unmistakable and direct criticism of Henry's kingship. By repeating apparently widely held criticisms of the king, Capgrave added to the growing sense of unease around the nature and effectiveness of Henry's kingship. Predictably enough Capgrave offered the king's father, Henry V, as the true exemplar, a prince who successfully combined martial prowess, a pious devotion to the Church, and a love of good government and justice. Yet he also offered more ambiguous exemplars, such as the Anglo-Saxon boy kings Edward the Martyr and Kenelm, both of whom were murdered amidst questions over their fitness to rule.[34]

Defeat in France and the end of a regime

When the Londoner John Vale sat down to compose his short chronicle of events from 1431 until 1471 one event stood out as a watershed. After noting Henry's coronation in Paris, he observed that the king was 'governed and ruled by divers of his council such as were not come from royal blood, but they that were brought up of nought'. Their 'sinister counsel, envy and premeditated malice' were the root cause of the civil wars that had blighted Vale's own career and led the realm to the 'extreme point of utmost destruction and depopulation of subjects and people'. They had been responsible for the event that had begun this sorry collapse into anarchy: the murder of the king's uncle, Humphrey, duke of Gloucester, on 22 February 1447 at the Bury St Edmunds Parliament. 'After whose death', Vale related, 'many divers sorrows and lamentable heavinesses were practised and put in use.'[35] Vale was not alone in reaching this conclusion. Many of the chronicles written in the third quarter of the fifteenth century traced the origins of the civil war to Gloucester's death, drawing on the myth of 'Good Duke Humphrey' that was to loom large in Yorkist propaganda during the 1450s and 1460s. The period from 1447 until 1450 did indeed witness a series of crises and catastrophes from which Henry VI's reign never really recovered. Three factors combined, leading to the collapse of Suffolk's regime and the duke's murder in the spring of 1450. First, and most importantly, the loss of Normandy was an unequivocal demonstration of the regime's failure and its betrayal of the Lancastrian legacy. Second, the worsening fiscal and economic situation provided the Commons in parliament with an opportunity to deploy established Lancastrian notions of good government against the regime, building upon growing popular discontent to develop a programme of reform that proved irresistible in the crisis of 1449/50. Finally, the latter half of the 1440s saw a change of personnel at both a national and local level that further destabilised an already precarious political balance.

Henry VI's uncle, the duke of Gloucester, had been one of the most divisive figures of the reign. From his claim to act as protector in 1422, through his continuing personal antipathy to Cardinal Beaufort and Archbishop Kemp and his aggressive foreign policy (towards both Lancastrian France and his own dynastic interests in the Low Countries), he had repeatedly clashed with other leading figures around the king. In 1439/40 he had mounted a final, concerted attack on Cardinal Beaufort, combining opposition to the release of the duke of Orléans with personal attacks on Beaufort's loyalty to the king, but this had been largely ignored by his fellow councillors. Gloucester's efforts in 1439/40 may have contributed to Beaufort's retirement from public life, but they also highlighted the irrelevance of Duke Humphrey to the developing thrust of Lancastrian policy both in England and in France. Gloucester's own marginalisation was assured in 1441 when his wife, Eleanor Cobham, was accused of witchcraft and treason, employing astrologers to predict the king's death. This resulted in Eleanor's public penance, her divorce and imprisonment. Gloucester was disgraced and appears to have lost whatever trust the king still had in him. Although the duke remained a regular attendee at court, he took no active role in any of the negotiations that led to the truce of Tours and the king's marriage in 1445. By the middle of 1446, however, Gloucester again threatened to provide a focus for those unhappy with the course of Lancastrian policy in France. As we shall see, the difficult and unpopular decision to surrender the county of Maine to the French had been made and plans were afoot to arrange a personal meeting between Henry and Charles VII with a view to concluding a final peace. There were also concerns over Gloucester's continuing role as heir presumptive and possible plans to rescue Duchess Eleanor: in July the council ordered that she be moved to the Isle of Man.

On 14 December 1446 writs were issued for a parliament to assemble at Cambridge on the following 10 February; on 20 January further summons were issued changing the location to Bury

St Edmunds. The ostensible reason for the change of venue was an outbreak of plague, and the abbey at Bury (which the king knew well from his visit there in the winter of 1433/34) offered a suitable place to hold a parliament. Yet more sinister motives may have been at play. On 30 January, in an unprecedented move, the king ordered the royal justices to suspend hearings in London, as their presence was required at parliament. It may be that a decision had been made to move against Gloucester and that a location outside London, where Duke Humphrey enjoyed popular support, was politically expedient. In late 1446 Gloucester had visited his Welsh estates, before spending the Christmas season in his castle at Devizes in Wiltshire. The previous year had seen some notable instances of anti-Welsh sentiment in England and there were parliamentary petitions against the Welsh in the parliaments of 1445 and 1447. The duke travelled to Bury with a large contingent of Welsh retainers and this may have fuelled fears that he planned to move against the king and his council. Gloucester arrived in Bury in the morning of 18 February, ten days after the assembly had opened, and on his arrival he was persuaded to go to his lodgings rather than seeking an immediate audience with the king. Later that day a group of peers, led by John, Viscount Beaumount, steward of England and a prominent courtier, visited the duke in his lodgings and placed him under arrest. Gloucester's arrest was closely followed by that of several members of his retinue, but on 23 February the duke died suddenly. The following day his body was displayed to the Lords and members of the House of Commons. The precise circumstances of Gloucester's death are unclear. There is no formal record of either his arrest or any charges of treason, but chroniclers writing in the 1450s were in unanimous agreement that the Bury Parliament had been summoned with the principal aim of destroying the duke and that he was unaware of the plots against him. Indeed the nature of the parliament (at three weeks, the shortest of the reign) and the few records that relate to it suggest that it was, as Anne Curry has observed, 'an exceptional meeting engineered for an unusual purpose'.[36] Similarly, the king's role in the events that led to his uncle's death is obscure; had he become convinced, or persuaded, of Gloucester's malign designs towards him? What is clear, however, is that plans were already well advanced to appropriate the duke's wealth and political power at the time of his death. Parts of his estate were quickly granted to the queen, the king's foundations at Cambridge and Eton, and leading members of the household. On the day after Gloucester's death Sir James Fiennes, one of those directly implicated in his murder by later chroniclers, was made warden of the Cinque Ports and charged with the administration of the duke's goods. He was also elevated to the peerage as Lord Saye and Sele. On 3 March Duchess Eleanor was formally disbarred from receiving any dower from her late husband, making the king the sole heir to his uncle's considerable estates.

Gloucester's death marked an important watershed in the reign of Henry VI, if not in terms of its immediate practical impact then at least in the popular imagination. The duke's death coincided with other deaths and retirements from public life that gave the late 1440s a tangible air of disquieting change. In April 1447 Cardinal Beaufort died. Although he had effectively retired from public life following the debacle of Somerset's expedition to France in 1443, his death marked the end of a career that had spanned the reign of all three Lancastrian kings. In August the same year Henry's kinsman John Holand, duke of Exeter, died. Exeter too had served both Henry V and Henry VI loyally at both home and abroad for four decades. In August 1449 yet another Lancastrian stalwart, Walter, Lord Hungerford died, and in the following month Marmaduke Lumley, bishop of Carlisle and the treasurer who had done so much to try to rescue the crown's dire financial position in the mid-1440s, resigned his position due to ill-health. His successor was none other than James Fiennes, Lord Saye and Sele. At a local level the change of generation may also have had an unsettling effect. More research is needed on the dynamics of local politics throughout England in the 1440s, but in Kent the middle years of that decade saw the deaths of several leading figures who had held local office since the first or second decade of the century. These men had headed families whose estates had been in the east of the county, and the resulting shift in the locus of political power towards the west of the county (based around Sevenoaks and James Fiennes's seat at Knole) contributed greatly to the uncertainty and unrest that gripped Kent in 1450.

The crisis of 1450 had its origins in part in the events of the Bury Parliament of 1447, but it stemmed principally from the collapse of the Lancastrian position in France. The years after Henry's marriage to Margaret of Anjou in April 1445 were marked by a curious mixture of conviction and confusion. On the one hand was the king's determination to conclude a peace with France; on the other was confusion over how that was to be implemented and how this reversal of a central pillar of Lancastrian policy was to be made palatable to the king's subjects both in England and in France. Implicit in the marriage between Henry and Margaret was the idea that the Lancastrians would surrender the county of Maine to Margaret's father, René of Anjou. This was initially René's idea and Henry appears to have made verbal promises to that end in the summer of 1445, but by November the plan had been taken up by Charles VII as a tangible signal of Henry's commitment to peace. On 22 December in a secret letter to Charles, sealed with his own signet, Henry promised to surrender the county of Maine by 30 April 1446 in return for a twenty-year truce.[37] Henry also undertook to travel to France and meet his uncle in person to conclude a final peace. There is no doubt that the English ambassadors, led by the earl of Suffolk and Bishop Moleyns, who were charged with delivering this vital document to the French, knew of its contents and Henry's wishes, but the plan to surrender Maine was the king's own. It was a personal agreement concluded between princes and such an initiative could only have come from Henry himself. Queen Margaret may have played an important role in counselling the king at this juncture (indeed, her letters to Charles VII insisted she had done all she could to further the cause of peace), but the desire for peace which the agreement to surrender Maine expressed had been a consistent part of Henry's kingship since the late 1430s.[38]

In practice the surrender of Maine proved impossible to achieve satisfactorily, while the proposed meeting between Henry and his uncle the king of France never took place. The trouble-free cessation of the county relied on the cooperation of the Lancastrian officials and captains serving in the county itself, while the cost of mounting a royal visit to France was clearly prohibitive. The initial dates set for both the surrender and the meeting passed and on 22 February 1447 the English ambassadors, Bishop Moleyns, Lord Dudley, and the experienced war captain Matthew Gough, secured an extension of the truce to 1 January 1448.

Meanwhile, the Lancastrian policy towards their French possessions appeared increasingly confused. Edmund Beaufort, marquis of Dorset, was appointed the king's lieutenant in Normandy in December 1446 in succession to the duke of York. He was also the titular count of Maine and any surrender of it to René of Anjou would have to involve his willing participation. In the event Dorset did not cross the Channel until March 1448. In July 1447 French ambassadors travelled to London, securing a promise that Maine would be surrendered by 1 November 1447 in return for a further extension of the truce to 1 May 1448. Henry ordered Gough and another Lancastrian war captain, Fulk Eyton, to take delivery of the county from Dorset, but they dragged their heels, inventing various technicalities to delay a surrender which they and many of their fellow Lancastrian captains felt demeaning. In October Henry wrote under his signet to Dorset stating that the failure to deliver the county of Maine by the agreed date was 'to us an occasion of bitter displeasure' and ordering him to compel those under his command to assist in the surrender.[39] Nevertheless, in the face of the refusal of the men on the ground to cooperate, the agreed date for the surrender was extended once more to 8 February 1448. By now, however, Charles VII's patience was wearing thin. By 10 February his army was encamped outside Le Mans, the capital of Maine, preparing for war. Faced with such a show of force, the English capitulated and on 11 March the treaty of Lavardin finalised the terms of the surrender of Maine. Henry's determination to surrender the territory in the cause of peace was deeply unpopular in Normandy and the *pays de conquête*. On 15 March, at the gates of Le Mans, Gough and Eyton made a solemn declaration that their actions were driven solely by the king's desire for peace; the surrender of Maine in no way compromised Henry's sovereignty as king of France. On the following 12 June, in order to acquit his servants of any taint of treason, Henry himself issued letters patent declaring that Gough and Eyton had performed their duties as loyal subjects in delivering various towns and fortresses to the French.[40]

The surrender of Maine was a confused and squalid business. It had revealed the political weakness of the English to the French and the lack of commitment to defend Lancastrian France among many of the king's leading English subjects, but it had at least been motivated by a genuine desire for peace on behalf of the king. Attention now turned to Brittany, where Henry's policy was driven by less rational considerations. In 1427 John V, duke of Brittany, one of Henry V's key supporters at the Treaty of Troyes, had returned to the English allegiance, giving a personal commitment to the young Henry VI. As a sign of his allegiance to the Lancastrian Dual Monarchy, Duke John had sent his younger and favourite son, the eight-year-old Gilles, to England to grow up in Henry's household. The two boys apparently became great friends before Gilles returned to Brittany in 1434. Nine years later he arrived back at the English court to promise his service to Henry VI. By this time the duchy of Brittany had passed to Gilles's elder brother Francis. Duke Francis had been persuaded by Charles VII to appear at the negotiations at Tours as his ally and the commitment of the duke to Lancastrian Dual Monarchy was questionable, to say the least. By 1446, moreover, a rift had developed between the two brothers which meant that Henry, in effect, supported Gilles's claim to the duchy against his brother, who was supported by the French king. In June that year Gilles was arrested by servants of Charles VII (whom he had met at his castle of Le Guildo, believing them to be a peaceful embassy from the French king) and delivered to his brother, who promptly imprisoned him. Henry became convinced, helped by Gilles's servants who had fled to England, that the French actions constituted a breach of truce. The Lancastrians began a course of fevered diplomacy to secure Gilles's release, but when this failed the regime embarked on a course of action that would have disastrous consequences. On 24 March 1449 an Aragonese captain in English service, François de Surienne, captured the key Breton fortress of Fougères. Surienne later claimed that he had been encouraged by Matthew Gough and other key figures in the Lancastrian establishment in Normandy to secure the fortress as a prelude to an audacious attempt to rescue Gilles.

The effect of the attack on Fougères was almost immediate. Duke Francis called upon Charles VII for assistance in recovering the castle and to resist English aggression. On 27 June the two concluded a treaty to drive the Lancastrians from Normandy and on 31 July 1449 King Charles declared himself absolved from the truce of Tours. The campaign that followed was even more devastating than had been Henry V's capture of the duchy some thirty years previously. The French had used the years of truce well, assembling a powerful artillery train under the guidance of Jean and Gaspard Bureau and reorganising their fighting forces. The English, on the other hand, had done nothing to renew their defences, despite Suffolk's advice as early as 1445 that the Norman garrisons be 'fortified and repaired sufficiently that they may be strong and able to resist the king's enemies'.[41] In October the French began the siege of Rouen and within six days Edmund Beaufort (since March 1448 duke of Somerset) had made ignominious terms for its surrender. Thereafter the collapse of Lancastrian Normandy was rapid, while the English response was typically confused and dilatory. By the beginning of 1450 only the fortresses of Bayeux, Caen, Cherbourg, Falaise, and a handful of others remained in English hands. It was not until 9 March 1450 that a small expeditionary army, commanded by the veteran Sir Thomas Kiriell, left Portsmouth for Cherbourg. On 15 April Kiriell's small army was destroyed at the battle of Formingy, marking the effective end of Lancastrian Normandy. On 19 August James Gresham wrote to John Paston that 'it was told that Cherbourg is gone, and we have now not a foot of land in Normandy.'[42]

The loss of Normandy and the collapse of the Dual Monarchy, that defining achievement of the Lancastrian dynasty, could not have had anything other than catastrophic consequences for Henry VI's regime at home. The parliament of February 1449 had done little to meet the financial crisis in either Normandy or England, despite a personal request for funds from Somerset, delivered by Abbot Boulers of Gloucester, and a reported crown debt of £372,000. In response to the government's demands for money the Commons appear to have resurrected their call for the resumption of royal grants so that the king could 'live upon his right and inheritance and so as a king of royal power to reign upon his people'.[43] They certainly hedged with provisos their grants of two half fifteenths-and-tenths, along with poll taxes on aliens and priests and a renewal of the wool subsidy. According to one well-informed contemporary, during the parliament's second session (held at Winchester from 16 June until 16 July) popular anger began to concentrate on the duke of Suffolk, blaming him personally for the worsening situation in France.[44] Faced with the intransigence of the Commons' demands for resumption, King Henry dissolved parliament. During the summer the military situation worsened and popular discontent grew and writs for the new assembly were issued only nine weeks after the dissolution of the February parliament. The parliament that assembled at Westminster on 6 November 1449 thus did so amidst growing popular anger. This was fuelled by the course of the war in France, a deepening fiscal crisis caused by the economic situation, and also by the collapse of the regime's political credit and a growing disquiet over the role of the king's household in the government of the realm.

By the end of 1449 Suffolk had emerged as the scapegoat for the regime's various failings of the previous decade. The principal charges against him related to the impending defeat in France and his part in the diplomatic and military bungling that had given Charles VII his *casus belli*. It was not the first time, however, that Suffolk had been forced to defend himself against such popular accusations. In February 1444 he had requested a public declaration, made under the king's letters patent, that no blame should accrue to him or his fellow ambassadors if the Anjou marriage failed to bring peace.[45] In June the following year he made a statement in parliament that he had acted by the king's command.[46] Finally, on 25 May 1447, Henry affirmed before Queen Margaret and other lords in the king's chamber that the duke had acted in accordance with his wishes to secure peace through the surrender of the county of Maine.[47] There can be little doubt that in relation to Lancastrian France Suffolk had pursued a policy that was instigated by the king himself and in which he had enjoyed broad support from his fellow lords. In April 1446, they had formally declared to the king in parliament that the desire for peace and the planned meeting between Henry and Charles VII had originated with Henry himself: 'which said motions and stirrings only our Lord has liked to stir and move you too, he knows, without that any of the lords or other of your subjects of this your realm, in any way have stirred you so to do'.[48] By the time the second session of parliament convened at London's Dominican Friary by Ludgate on 22 January the noble consensus was in tatters. It had been torn apart not only by events in France and the clear failure of the policy that Suffolk was associated with, but also by the strength of popular feeling against the regime. Discontent expressed through verse and slanderous bills, 'the odious and horrible words that runs through your land in the mouth of almost every commoner', as Suffolk described it, was also fuelled by specific events that had nothing to do with the course of the war, but which gave credence to the notion that greed, self-interest, and 'covetise' had replaced the common profit as the organising principle at the centre of royal government.[49] Early in 1449 the Dartmouth shipowner Robert Wennyngton and two members of the royal affinity from Kent had been commissioned to guard the seas. Ships had been provided by other household men, such as Thomas Daniel, but instead of protecting the coast from French raids they had embarked on a campaign of privateering, notoriously robbing the Hanseatic, Flemish, and Dutch ships of the Bay Fleet and exacerbating the economic crisis that gripped the southeast of England.

On 9 January 1450 Adam Moleyns, the unpopular bishop of Chichester and a man thoroughly complicit in the king's peace policy, was murdered by a mob of decommissioned soldiers and sailors at Portsmouth. Rumours abounded that he had implicated Suffolk in treasonable dealings with the French. When parliament reconvened later that month the Commons were determined to move against the duke. On 28 January they presented detailed, yet scarcely believable, charges that Suffolk had conspired with the French ambassadors and encouraged Charles VII to invade England. The duke, they claimed, had already fortified his castle at Wallingford in preparation. He also had designs on the throne himself, evidenced by the plan to marry his son to Margaret Beaufort, then his ward. The following day Suffolk was committed to the Tower. A little over a week later, on 7 February, the speaker of the Commons, William Tresham, presented a detailed bill of impeachment, but the king intervened, preventing the lords from sending it to the judges. Finally, on 9 March the Commons submitted another bill against Suffolk, in the main repeating the charge that the whole French policy of the 1440s had been of the duke's making, but also listing offences that related to the domestic government of the kingdom. He had, they alleged, helped himself to funds from the exchequer, distributing them 'to himself, his friends, and his well-wishers', and contributed to the general law-lessness of the realm by appointing his own servants as sheriffs in various counties throughout the realm. On that day Suffolk came to the parliament chamber, refuted the allegations with the same confidence he had shown in rebutting earlier claims, and submitted himself to the king. At this point Henry made another of his characteristically disastrous interventions. On 17 March, in the king's 'innermost chamber' within the palace of Westminster and in the presence of the lords, Henry listened to and dismissed the charges of treason against Suffolk out of hand. The duke instead was to be banished from England to reside in France for five years from 1 May. There is evidence that Henry's decision was made against the advice of his lords. Viscount Beaumont 'on the behalf of the said lords both spiritual and temporal, and by their advice, assent and desire, recited, said and declared to the king's highness that what was thus decreed and effected by his excellence concerning the person of the said duke did not proceed by their advice and counsel, but was done by the king's own direction and rule'.[50] He then asked for this statement to be enrolled on the Parliament Roll as a formal record of the king's wilfulness and the Lords' misgivings. If Henry's decision was reluctantly accepted by the Lords, the Commons were even less inclined to be generous. On 30 March parliament was prorogued and the king moved to Leicester. When the new session opened on 29 April the Commons at last received an Act of resumption of royal grants, albeit one compromised by no less than fifteen modifying clauses and 186 individual exemptions, in return for a modest tax on incomes.

Suffolk's impeachment and his punishment did not, however, assuage popular opinion. In fact, if anything, it made it worse. The duke was granted a safe conduct to the Low Countries and set sail on 30 March, but his ship was intercepted by the *Nicholas of the Tower* in the Channel. Suffolk was subjected to an impromptu trial and beheaded by the crew with half a dozen strokes of a rusty sword. His body was then thrown ashore on Dover beach. The duke's murder was an extraordinary demonstration of popular political engagement and how deeply ingrained Lancastrian political traditions were within England by the mid fifteenth century. According to their indictment, Suffolk's murderers had a clear

understanding of the constitutional position and the king's obligation to listen to the community of the realm. When presented
with the king's letters of safe conduct, they supposedly replied
that 'they did not know the said king, but they knew well the
crown of England, saying that the aforesaid crown was the community of the realm and that the community of the realm was
the crown of the realm'.[51]

Conclusion

The crisis of 1449/50 represented the failure of the policies that
Henry VI had followed since he had come into his majority in
1437. On the crucial question of the war in France and the future
of the Dual Monarchy the king had followed a consistent policy:
peace, even at the expense of the territorial and personal legacy
left to him by his father, Henry V. In his willingness to sacrifice
his title and some of his lands, Henry was turning his back on a
central component of the Lancastrian legacy, one that had been
won and defended with the blood and wealth of his servants and
subjects. It was a policy born of the king's naïve idealism, but
given extra impetus by the very real practical difficulties of maintaining the conquests of Henry V. By the 1440s some compromise
over the question and extent of the Dual Monarchy was the only
realistic option left to the Lancastrian regime in England. In practice the policy was a shambles. The inability to strengthen the
Lancastrian diplomatic position through successful and coordi-
nated military action was due to three factors: first, a failure of
leadership on the part of the king; second, an unwillingness of
the king's servants and subjects, both in England and in France,
to agree on a united response to Charles VII; and third, the acute
fiscal and political crisis in England that worsened as the decade
went on.

There can be little doubt that it was Henry himself who was
responsible for the direction of Lancastrian policy in the 1440s.
Suffolk, Moleyns, and others gave substance to a broad aspiration
on the part of the king. The king's household servants were, above
all else, committed servants of Henry and the House of Lancaster,
but they were also practical politicians who recognised that some
part of the Lancastrian legacy would have to be sacrificed to

maintain the dynasty. The regular protestations of Suffolk and others that they were following the king's wishes were not an elaborate charade designed to mask the truth of Henry's inability to rule. Rather, they represented a realisation that the policy followed in the 1440s was one that was unpopular and ran contrary to other, entirely legitimate interpretations of the Lancastrian legacy. In making such statements Henry's ministers spoke not only to their aristocratic peers, but to the wider political nation and the commons of England, among whom the regime's legitimacy ultimately rested.

That the king's preference for peace and compromise was controversial among his greater subjects should not be a surprise. The English aristocracy were a military caste whose reputation and claim to political power rested in part on their conduct in war. Moreover, many of them had gained materially from the Lancastrian conquests in France. What is perhaps more surprising, and distinctly Lancastrian, about the crisis of 1449/50 is that it was driven principally by popular opposition to the king's policies. Rumours and whispered complaints about the nature of Henry's kingship gave way in 1449/50 to a groundswell of popular anger directed at the men most closely associated with the peace policy and the household regime of the 1440s led by the duke of Suffolk. Unable to legitimately attack the king, their anointed sovereign lord, the commons made scapegoats of Henry's ministers, voicing their anger in a sustained campaign of seditious ballads and handbills. As one contemporary remembered, 'the name of the lord of Suffolk was destroyed by bills made against him and set up'.[52] In this crucial respect the crisis of 1449/50 was distinctly Lancastrian in character: Henry VI and his ministers had been judged and found guilty by the commons of England.

Notes

1 *PROME*, ix, 178.
2 *POPC*, v, 112–13.
3 *Foedera, Conventiones, Literae . . .* , ed. Thomas Rymer (12 vols, The Hague, 1745), x, 724, 732.
4 *POPC*, v, 394–5.
5 *Paston Letters and Papers of the Fifteenth Century*, ed. N. Davies (2 vols, Early English Text Society, 1971–6), i, 40.

6 *Letters and Papers Illustrative of the Wars of the English in France*, ed. Stevenson ii(2), 453.
7 G.L. Harriss, *Cardinal Beaufort: A Study of Lancastrian Ascendancy and Decline* (Oxford, 1988), 317.
8 M.K. Jones, 'John Beaufort, Duke of Somerset and the French Expedition of 1443', in *Patronage, the Crown and the Provinces in Later Medieval England*, ed. R.A. Griffiths (Gloucester, 1981), 89.
9 TNA, E101/71/4/916.
10 Harriss, *Cardinal Beaufort*, 337; John Watts, *Henry VI and the Politics of Kingship* (Cambridge, 1996), 193.
11 *POPC*, v, 409–14.
12 *POPC*, vi, 32–35.
13 *A Journal by One of the Suite of Thomas Beckington*, ed. N.H. Nicolas (1828), 6.
14 *POPC*, vi, 323–4.
15 B.P. Wolffe, *Henry VI* (1981), 171.
16 Watts, *Politics of Kingship*, 103; J.W. McKenna, 'Piety and Propaganda: The Cult of Henry VI', in *Chaucer and Middle English Studies in Honour of Rossell Hope Robbins*, ed. Beryl Rowland (1974), 78–79.
17 Jack Lander, *Conflict and Stability in Fifteenth-Century England* 1969, 68.
18 Karen A. Winstead, *John Capgrave's Fifteenth Century* (Philadelphia, PA, 2007), 135–6.
19 *Official Correspondence of Thomas Bekyngton*, ed. George Williams (2 vols, Rolls Series, 1872), i, 155–9.
20 Watts, *Politics of Kingship*, 104.
21 *Letters and Papers Illustrative of the Wars of the English in France*, ed. Stevenson, i, 103–24.
22 TNA, KB27/742, rex rot. 7.
23 Ibid., KB9/260/40.
24 Ibid., KB9/262/1–2.
25 Ibid., KB9/122/78.
26 Jonathan Hughes, *Arthurian Myths and Alchemy* (Stroud, 2002), 47–48.
27 TNA, KB9/260/85.
28 Canterbury Cathedral Archives, DCc-ChAnt/C/239.
29 TNA, KB9/262, m. 1.
30 Canterbury Cathedral Archives, DCc-ChAnt/C/239.
31 TNA, KB9/273, m. 103.
32 C.A.F. Meekings, 'Thomas Kerver's Case, 1444', *English Historical Review* 90 (1975), 331–46.
33 Winstead, *John Capgrave's Fifteenth Century*, 159.
34 John Capgrave, *Liber de Illustribus Henricis* ed. F.C. Hingeston (1858), 125–37.
35 *The Politics of Fifteenth Century England: John Vale's Book*, ed. Margaret Kekewich Coilin Richmond, Anne E. Sutton, Livia Visser-Fuchs and John L. Watts (Stroud, 1995), 178–80.
36 *PROME*, xii, 7.
37 *Letters and Papers Illustrative of the Wars of the English in France*, ed. Stevenson, ii(2), 639–42.

38 Ibid., i, 183–6.
39 Ibid., ii(2), 694.
40 *Foedera*, ed. Rymer, xi, 215.
41 *Letters and Papers Illustrative of the Wars of the English in France*, ed. Stevenson, ii. (2), 592–3.
42 *Paston Letters*, ed. Davies, ii. 455.
43 *Six Town Chronicles*, ed. R. Flenley (Oxford, 1908), 125.
44 'John Benet's Chronicle', ed. G.L. and M.A. Harriss, *Camden Miscellany XXIV* (Camden Society, 1972), 195, 212.
45 *Foedera*, ed. Rymer, xi, 53.
46 *PROME*, xi, 395.
47 *Foedera*, ed. Rymer, xi, 176–7.
48 *PROME*, xi, 471.
49 Ibid., xii, 92.
50 Ibid., 92–106.
51 Roger Virgoe, 'The Death of William de la Pole, Duke of Suffolk', in *East Anglian Political Society and the Political Community of Late Medieval England*, ed. Caroline Barron, Carole Rawcliffe and Joel Rosenthal (Norwich, 1997), 253.
52 TNA, C47/7/8.

8   A regime in crisis

Jack Cade and the Duke of York, 1450–55

The death of William de la Pole, duke of Suffolk, in March 1450 initiated a new and prolonged political crisis from which the House of Lancaster and the kingship of Henry VI never recovered. 'The fall of Suffolk', as John Watts has remarked, 'was the fall of the king himself.'[1] It marked the beginning of the end of Henry's kingship not because Suffolk was the only individual capable of maintaining a façade of princely authority in the face of the king's obvious inadequacies, but because the policies associated with the duke and the royal household were the king's policies and the rejection of those policies by the political nation was the rejection of the particular strands of Lancastrianism within which Henry had chosen to position himself. Yet the years that followed revealed both the strength of Lancastrian kingship and the nation's broad commitment to the conveniently ambiguous Lancastrian project. The situation was transformed not by any concerted or coherent opposition to Lancastrian ideals or policies, but by the sudden, if temporary, collapse of the king into insanity in the autumn of 1453. It was Henry's absence, rather than his inadequacy, that allowed the regime's most outspoken critic, Richard, duke of York, to emerge as the leader of a credible and powerful opposition and that made possible the outbreak of civil war at St Albans in May 1455.

Jack Cade's rebellion and the Duke of York

News of Suffolk's death had an immediate and electrifying effect on the commons, particularly in Kent, where news of the duke's murder apparently prompted the sheriff, William Cromer, to

threaten to turn the county into a 'wild forest' in retribution.[2] By
the spring of 1450 the county was already in a disordered state,
doubtless prompted by the rumours and slanders that were circulating in the wake of the House of Commons' accusations against
Suffolk. In January Thomas Cheyne had led a rising in the east
of the county, calling for the death not only of Suffolk but also
of James Fiennes, Lord Saye and Sele, and other local figures
associated with the court. His rebellion was stopped only by the
determination of the citizens of Canterbury to keep the city's
gates closed to the rebels. Suffolk's death and the threats made in
its aftermath only amplified the calls for justice to be meted out
to the traitors around the king. As the duke's body was carried
from Dover up the Pilgrims' Way to London, the atmosphere of
fear and retribution forced people to take events into their own
hands. By the end of May Kent was in uproar. Under cover of
the religious festival of Whitsunday (24 May), in the area around
Ashford, local communities, using existing institutions of com-
munal organisation such as the commission of array (designed to
organise local defence against invasion or to raise men for service
in France), gathered themselves to march upon London under the
leadership of Jack Cade. Cade's identity remains a mystery, but it
was later claimed that he was an Irishman who had served in
France and had fallen foul of the authorities. The exact size of
the rebel host is unknown, but judging from the pardons issued
in July and the evidence of various contemporary chronicles it
may have numbered in excess of 10,000 men. News had reached
the king at Leicester by 6 June, when the duke of Buckingham
and the earls of Oxford, Devon, and Arundel were commissioned
to ride against the traitors and rebels in Kent. In the circumstances
'parliament was not so much dissolved as faded away', and Henry
and his lords returned to London to meet the crisis.[3]

By 11 June the rebels were encamped on Blackheath, their camp
'diked and staked well about, as it was in the land of war'.[4] By Sat-
urday, 13 June, the king and his lords had established themselves at
St John's Hospital, Clerkenwell. On Monday royal heralds rode out
to Blackheath and confronted the rebels. The Kentishmen came not
as rebels, they said, but as 'public petitioners for public justice to be
done, and demonstrators of their own grievances and those of the
realm'.[5] At first, Henry's reaction seemed forthright. On the return

of the royal messengers, the king apparently ordered his own host, a considerable force comprising not only the men of his own household but also those of the dukes of Exeter and Buckingham and at least eleven other lords, to move in sight of the rebels on the heath. The earl of Northumberland led a mounted force to scout the camp and returned to report that Cade's force easily outnumbered the king's men. On 15 June a delegation led by Archbishops Stafford and Kemp, and including Bishop Waynflete of Winchester, the duke of Buckingham and the constable of England, Viscount Beaumont, met the rebels, received their petitions, and promised to return with the king's answer. Henry, however, refused to entertain the rebels' demands and Cade, fearing that the king proposed to lead the royal host against them in person, retreated from Blackheath. Perhaps encouraged by rumours that the king was to ride against the rebels himself, certain members of the royal party decided to pursue Cade and his men into Kent. On the afternoon of 18 June the king's camp received the news that Sir Humphrey Stafford of Grafton and William Stafford, kinsmen of the duke of Buckingham, had been ambushed and killed by the rebels near Sevenoaks. The following morning Henry assembled his army on Blackheath, reinforced by fresh contingents from Cheshire and Lancashire, but rather than riding into Kent to confront the rebels, the royal host wavered and 'made then a sudden shout and noise upon the heath, saying destroy we these traitors about the king which that the said captain has intended to do or ever we will do it'.[6]

At this crucial juncture Henry's nerve failed him. Rather than facing the rebels himself, he ordered the arrest of several of his household servants, including his chamberlain, the treasurer of England Lord Saye and Sele. On 25 June the king decided to abandon the capital altogether and four days later Cade's rebels were back on Blackheath. On 3 July they crossed London Bridge into the city and wreaked their vengeance on the supposed traitors around the king: Saye and Cromer, his son-in-law as well as sheriff of Kent, were summarily tried and executed, while proceedings were begun at the Guildhall against Thomas Daniel and other courtiers. The unrest spread beyond the South-East and on the same day that Cade entered the capital a mob lynched Bishop Aiscough of Salisbury while he celebrated mass in Wiltshire. Cade's rebels, amidst much looting, had, however, outstayed their welcome in London, and on 5–6 July they were expelled from the city. On 7 July a royal pardon was offered to them, with the exception of their leader, and most seem to have dispersed peacefully. Cade was eventually captured on the Kent/Sussex border on 12 July and died of his wounds.

Henry's response to the events of the early summer of 1450 was crucial and ultimately disastrous for the remainder of his reign. Cade's rebels claimed to be the 'true commons' representing the commonweal. They lamented the loss of Normandy, the impoverishment of the king and the commons, and the exclusion of the 'true blood of the realm' from the king's counsels.[7] As such, they were articulating a widely held and entirely legitimate component of the Lancastrian legacy that gave political agency to the commons and saw government properly constituted in a representative council of noblemen. This was recognised by some of the lords and royal servants about the king on Blackheath and it was this that led them to echo Cade's call for justice on the traitors (just as they had backed the Commons' demands against Suffolk earlier in the year). Yet, in responding to these calls Henry also revealed his own inconstancy. By abandoning Lord Saye, his closest surviving household servant and a man whose personal commitment to the Lancastrian cause had spanned over three decades, Henry undermined those other Lancastrian principles of loyalty and service. Contemporaries were aware of the personal failings of the king at this moment of crisis. Instead of facing the rebels in battle or demanding their submission to royal authority (as the young Richard II had done at Blackheath against Wat Tyler and the peasants in 1381), Henry decided to abandon the capital for the duchy of Lancaster heartland of Kenilworth castle. As one contemporary chronicler observed, Henry 'left his people and fled', rather than face the rebels in battle.[8]

Henry's failure of leadership during Cade's rebellion provided the circumstances for others to emerge as true defenders of the Lancastrian legacy. Principal among these, of course, was Richard, duke of York, the greatest magnate of his age. York was descended from Edward III through both the paternal and maternal lines, enjoyed the largest baronial income of the mid fifteenth century (some £5,000 *per annum*), and was a man acutely aware of his own status and lineage. Yet, more importantly perhaps for the politics of the 1450s, others too were aware of his pedigree. To Cade's rebels he was the 'high and mighty prince' who along with the other 'true lords' would restore good government, that fundamental pillar of Lancastrian legitimacy. York's status as the guarantor of good government had been suggested in April 1450 when Henry VI had been confronted on his way to the Leicester parliament by John Harries, a Yorkshire shipman. Threshing the air with a flail, Harries had announced that 'the duke of York then in Ireland should in like manner fight with traitors at the Leicester Parliament and so thrash them down as he had thrashed the clods of earth in that town'.[9] Harries was hanged, drawn, and quartered for his ill-considered outburst, but the incident revealed an apparently widely held opinion among the commons that York was the champion of reform. In 1450 Duke Richard found himself, at first reluctantly, thrust forward as the saviour of the commonweal and defender of a Lancastrian legacy that was fast becoming disconnected from the person of the king himself.

In many ways York was an unlikely candidate to lead the opposition to Henry. Born around 1411, he had known the king since the mid 1420s, when he had taken up residence at court, and in 1433 he had been elected to the Order of the Garter in expectation of great things to come. His first real taste of responsibility was three years later when he was appointed the king's lieutenant in France. He appears to have relied on his elder brother-in-law, Richard Neville, earl of Salisbury, and the experienced commander, John, Lord Talbot (from 1442 earl of Shrewsbury), for both advice and practical assistance, but his first period of office was reasonably successful. A second period in command (from 1441 until 1445) was less auspicious militarily, but the duke proved himself a capable administrator and diplomat. He was fully complicit in the negotiations for the truce of Tours in 1444, and he received the backing of his fellow lords two years later when Bishop Moleyns accused him of embezzlement. From that point he was among the leading figures in domestic government and benefitted personally, in terms of land and office, from the demise of Humphrey, duke of Gloucester. Thus up to the point of his departure as lieutenant-general of Ireland in June 1449 he was a loyal and integral part of the Lancastrian regime. Yet there were problems.

Despite his large income, he was living beyond his means and by 1450 the arrears of wages and debts owed to him by the crown had reached £26,000. Although York had not fared worse than many of the crown's other creditors – indeed, he had fared much better than some – his own financial problems may have confirmed for him the more widely held sense of crisis in 1449–50. There is also evidence that the duke may have left England for Ireland under something of a cloud. It was certainly not the exile that Cade's followers were later to claim, but on his return to England the following year York claimed that certain members of the king's household in north Wales had planned to ambush him both on his departure and when he returned to England. In Ireland York appears to have been worried about the lack of money to fund his campaign against the rebellious Gaelic chieftains and that the same accusations of incompetence and treason levelled against those in charge of the war in Normandy would be made against him. In June 1450 he wrote to the earl of Salisbury (and possibly to other lords) complaining that without more money he would be forced to abandon his command. His letter hints at the fear that dogged York's actions at this time: 'it shall never be chronicled, nor remain in scripture, by the grace of God', he declared, 'that Ireland was lost by my negligence'.[10]

Thus, in the summer of 1450 York found himself in the middle of an acute political crisis and thrust centre stage by the actions and expectations of others. Cade's rebels had identified him as an antidote to the traitors around the king, while the king's household and the other targets of the commons' anger similarly identified the duke as their chief enemy. York himself feared that he would be indicted for treason for giving support to Cade (who apparently claimed kinship with him and took the alias John Mortimer) and that his position as heir presumptive would be undermined or worse. It was into this atmosphere of suspicion and rumours that York returned to England, probably in the last week of August. One contemporary reported that the king's household were 'afraid right sore' of the duke's return.[11] It was this fear of Duke Richard's motives that explains the failed attempt by some members of the king's household to way-lay him on his route from north Wales and the duke's protestation of loyalty to the king in September. York's 'first bill', as it has become known, addressed those who had spoken out against him, challenging them to confront him publicly before the king. He protested his loyalty and declared himself 'a true knight'. Henry appears to have accepted York's protestations of good faith at face value, the two were reconciled, and the king admitted him 'as our true faithful subject and as our well beloved cousin'.

Shortly afterwards, however, in early October, York moved from being a private petitioner, seeking a confirmation of his own loyalty, into a public spokesman calling for reform of the commonweal. The precise reasons for this shift are unclear, but it marked a significant change and forced the king and his council to reconsider their approach to the duke's complaints. A second bill, addressed to the king but circulated widely and intended to be a public document, took up the call of Cade's rebels and York offered his services to ensure 'justice be had against all such that have been so indicted or openly so noised' of treason. It was an extraordinary and inflammatory statement that called into question Henry's fitness to rule and marked an acceptance by the duke that the commons' calls for justice on the traitors were indeed justified. The king's response was forthright. He did not accept the duke's offer; instead the problems were to be addressed by a 'sad and substantial council' which York was invited to join but on which he was to have no special importance. York was disappointed but not defeated.[12] A third bill, addressed to the king and the lords, outlined the need for reform but, crucially, introduced a new angle of attack. For the first time the duke introduced the defeat in France as a result of the greed and evil counsel of those 'brought up of nought' and called, in language taken directly from Cade's manifestos, for counsel to be given by 'the true lords and especially the lords of the mighty royal blood'.[13] This was doubly significant: it aligned York with the commons' diagnosis of the regime's failure and also identified good government not as a narrowly Lancastrian attribute but as something which pertained to lords of the royal blood more generally. This bill seems to have been met with the same response as his previous complaint. York's campaign was reactive and sought its legitimacy in two contradictory ways: first, by an appeal to his position as a prince of the royal blood of Edward III and (implicitly) as heir presumptive, and second, by an appeal to the commons and fundamental principles of Lancastrian government. It failed because the duke badly misjudged the mood of his fellow peers and the king's apparently new-found resolve to show loyalty to those around him. On 6 November 1450 a new parliament assembled at Westminster and the dynamics of politics shifted again.

Henry's commitment to uphold the integrity of his household and defend it against accusations of treason was especially important to York as the accusations revolved around the king's defence of Edmund Beaufort, duke of Somerset. He was the younger son of John Beaufort, earl of Somerset, John of Gaunt's eldest son by Katherine Swynford, and he soon emerged as York's arch-rival, a rivalry that was undoubtedly personal but that soon merged with issues of principle. Like York, Somerset had been a key figure in the Lancastrian regime in the 1430s and 1440s, but his Beaufort blood – he was the king's half-uncle – may in part have driven the king's unswerving loyalty towards him. York had not objected to Somerset's appointment as lieutenant of France in December 1447, but the latter's conduct, especially his surrender of the castle of Rouen (of which York was still nominally captain) without a fight in October 1449, was considered dishonourable and treasonable by Duke Richard. For York this was a personal affront and his rival personified the self-interested and dishonourable men who had undermined government at home and caused defeat in France. His dispute with Somerset was not the main reason for his intervention in domestic politics in the summer of 1450, but by the autumn it was giving York's public campaign a much-needed focus. Duke Richard arrived in parliament around 23 November in great pomp, with a sword carried before him and at the head of a large retinue. One of his leading servants, Sir William Oldhall, was elected Speaker. A parliamentary petition in late November called for the banishment of thirty-one individuals, headed by Somerset, from court. It must be assumed that York was behind, or at least supported, this petition. The king's reply was hesitant. He stated that he had not yet been informed of the precise reasons why these individuals should be removed, yet he agreed that certain (unnamed) persons should indeed be sent away for a year, reserving only his right to call upon them to face his enemies or rebels in the field. Somerset was sent to the Tower (albeit briefly and probably for his own safety), yet the extent to which Henry's reply represented a victory for York is unclear. The names of those the Commons sought to banish were, with the important exception of Somerset, largely those identified by Cade's rebels earlier in the year, and around the same time Speaker Oldhall found himself accused of treason and conspiring with the men of Kent to murder the king. Indeed during the following months whatever support Duke Richard could command among his fellow peers drifted away; the excluded courtiers returned to their posts and the inquiries in Kent failed to satisfy the Commons or punish the so-called traitors. In May 1451 Thomas Young, one of the MPs for Bristol, called for York to be formally recognised as heir to the throne. His call appears to have been backed by the House of Commons but was rejected out of hand by Henry, who responded by immediately dissolving parliament. Whether this was a desperate attempt by York to recover his position or an unsolicited intervention by one of his supporters, its effect was to eclipse the duke's political power and return the control of the government to Henry, his household, and those peers in attendance upon him.

York's interventions in politics had now lost all semblance of legitimacy. His armed involvement on behalf of Thomas Courtenay, earl of Devon, in his dispute with Lord Bonville in Somerset in September 1451 confirmed the duke's growing reputation among his peers as a disruptive and self-interested individual. York and his new ally, Devon, refused the king's summons to attend a council meeting in the Midlands. In London and elsewhere attacks on his servants and proceedings for treason against Sir William Oldhall gathered pace. The king's household doubled the guard around Henry's person in the winter of 1451/52 amidst fears of a rising and an attempt on the king's life by York's supporters. Duke Richard now attempted to repeat the events of 1450. He dispatched open letters to the king protesting his loyalty and called for the removal of Somerset as a danger to the commonweal. In February 1452 he sent calls for his servants and tenants to attend upon him as he marched under arms to demonstrate his loyalty to the king and to remove Somerset. The king reacted promptly, ordering towns to close their gates to the duke, and assembling the lords around him. By 27 February York was encamped at Dartford, supported only by Devon and Lord Cobham. The royal host was three times larger than the duke's, and the earls of Salisbury and

Warwick and many other peers accompanied the king. On 3 March Duke Richard submitted himself to the king and presented a set of now familiar articles against Somerset. Henry dismissed them and York was taken, under escort, back to the capital. A few days later, at the high altar of St Paul's cathedral York solemnly swore that he would attend upon the king whenever summoned and never attempt anything by force of arms against Henry or his subjects in the future. His humiliation was complete. He had posed as the champion of reform, driven by fear and his own exalted sense of himself; he had hijacked the commons' call for justice on the traitors, using their language to pursue his own personal dispute with Somerset; and he had appealed to his fellow peers to support him and they, almost to a man, had failed to do so.

The year 1450 had been a crucial one in the kingship of Henry VI. In the face of military defeat abroad and political crisis at home, the king's commitment to his version of the Lancastrian legacy wavered. His banishment of Suffolk, while saving the duke from judicial execution at the hands of the Commons, unwittingly set in train events that would eventually destroy the Lancastrian monarchy. Perhaps aware of what his commitment to Suffolk had led to, the king decided not to face down the rebels on Blackheath in June and instead surrendered his closest servants to their less-than-tender mercies. Henry appears to have recovered from this moment of panic to defend himself and those around him from York's attacks in the autumn and winter of 1450 and into the spring of 1451. Yet his kingship was undermined by a public recognition that the Lancastrian legacy was contested and that Henry had failed to enforce his own version of it. The lords' response to the crisis was also crucial in determining the outcome of events between 1450 and 1452: it reaffirmed their commitment as a body to the Lancastrian regime and to Henry personally. Equally, York's emergence as the principal opponent of Henry's government in 1450 was vital in defining the character of the remaining years of the reign. In making the claim to embody good government, the duke was disassociating one of the fundamental principles of the Lancastrian legacy from the person of the king and the Lancastrian royal family. In March 1452 York tried and failed to assert his claims to be the king's chief counsellor and guardian of the Lancastrian legacy; little could he have imagined that within eighteen months the fates would have intervened again, that Henry would be reduced to total madness, and that he would preside over the government as protector and defender of the realm of England.

The king's madness and York's first protectorate

In the summer of 1452 Henry VI's kingship looked to have recovered from the most serious crisis of the reign thus far. The king had seen off the challenges to his authority by rebellious subjects and troublesome magnates alike and he had agreed to an Act of Resumption in an effort to rescue the royal finances. Indeed, since the summer of 1451 Henry and his council had tried hard to reverse the damage done to his kingship by the events of 1450. From June to August the king took part in a series of judicial perambulations through Surrey, Sussex, Hampshire, and Kent to punish those involved in the recent rebellions. At Lewes, Salisbury, and Canterbury Henry personally sat in judgement alongside his justices. While not on progress the king appears to have shifted the location of his main residence from Windsor and Eltham to Westminster. Between 1450 and 1452 he spent 263 days at Westminster and 145 at Windsor and Eltham, compared with 28 and 323 respectively between 1446 and 1448.[14] Henry thus played a more prominent and public role in the government of the realm in the two years following Cade's rebellion, and it was this display of personal kingship, as much as anything else, that probably accounted for York's failure to gain the political ascendancy.

The situation in France, however, still caused concern. Charles VII threatened to attack English-held Calais and in January 1452 the council discussed the idea that Henry should lead an army there in person. This appears to have been a serious consideration and a series of letters to Thomas, Lord Clifford, the man tasked with the relief of Calais should it come under French attack, made clear the king's intended role in the expected campaign. With the help of his subjects, Henry hoped to 'do our part in such wise as it shall be to the pleasure of God, to the worship and wealth of us and this our realm and to the rebuke and shame of our said adversaries' and evil willers' purpose'.[15] While this may be dismissed as empty rhetoric on the part of the council, it also spoke to the realm's expectations of an apparently reinvigorated king. In June commissions were even issued in anticipation of the king's imminent departure for Calais. In the event, Henry did not embark for France, but loans were collected and in January the following year writs were issued for a new parliament. In the meantime Henry further exerted his influence by promoting his half-brothers, Edmund and Jasper Tudor, to the rank of earls. They took the titles of Richmond and Pembroke, respectively, honours previously held by the dukes of Bedford and Gloucester. The king now appeared to have regained control of the polity after the events of 1449–50: he was surrounded by a loyal household and a nobility led by members of the extended Lancastrian royal family.

The parliament that assembled at Reading on 6 March 1453 represented the high-water mark of Henry VI's kingship. Expectations were still high that Henry would lead an expedition to France in person, following the earl of Shrewsbury's remarkable success in recapturing much of Gascony during the previous autumn. A grateful Commons made a life grant of the customs of tunnage and poundage (recalling the grant made to Henry V after Agincourt) and devised a generous subsidy to equip 20,000 archers for six months' service overseas, as well as attainting Sir William Oldhall and denouncing Jack Cade as a traitor. The duke of Somerset was back in the ascendancy, while his rival, York, was conspicuous by his absence from the first two sessions of parliament (6–28 March and 25 April–2 July 1453). As the parliament's second session moved towards a close, plans were afoot for the king to travel to the South-West and to Yorkshire to deal in person with his squabbling subjects. Henry had maintained a very visible presence during the assembly. He thanked the Commons in person for their grant of a subsidy, promising to be 'a gracious and benevolent lord to you' and handing over 'certain schedules of parchment signed by his own hand' exempting certain named individuals from the provisions of various Acts passed by the parliament.[16] The king continued to play an important role in government after the parliament's prorogation, and on 21 July he was present at a council meeting that discussed certain disputed manors in south Wales between the duke of Somerset and earl of Warwick. Events, however, would soon take a startling turn. Four days earlier the earl of Shrewsbury had been killed leading an ill-advised attack on French gun emplacements laying siege to the Gascon town of Castillon. Whether or not news of this abrupt reversal provided the catalyst is unclear, but in early August Henry, returning to the royal hunting lodge at Clarendon near Salisbury from a judicial progress through Dorset and Wiltshire and attended only by his riding household, collapsed into a stupor, totally unable to speak, act, or even at first to eat.

The circumstances and diagnosis of the affliction that removed Henry from the political scene for over a year are mysterious. Indeed even the precise date on which the king fell ill is uncertain. He was at Clarendon by 5 August and it is likely that the news of Talbot's defeat reached him around this time. On the 7th of that month he was able to receive the kiss of homage from a local landowner, Sir William Stourton, but it seems that by the second week of August he had been taken ill and that the onset of his condition was alarmingly sudden. From 11 August the steady flow of royal writs and missives from Clarendon stopped and routine administrative matters (and more extraordinary concerns such as the mounting tension between the Neville and Percy families in Yorkshire) were handled by the council at Westminster. The king was moved from Clarendon to Windsor, where he remained in seclusion throughout the winter of 1453/54.

If little evidence survives of the timing and circumstances of Henry's collapse, then the precise nature of the king's illness is even more obscure. Much has been made of the recurrent bouts of mental illness suffered by his maternal grandfather, Charles VI of France, and it has been suggested that Henry suffered from a psychotic episode, perhaps schizophrenic, that was in part at least hereditary. While the fact of Henry's illness is mentioned in several mid fifteenth-century chronicles, none offers any real insights into the king's condition. In fact, there are only three strictly contemporary accounts that shed light on his symptoms. On 19 January 1454 John Stodeley, a London merchant, wrote a long and detailed newsletter outlining political events in the capital to his unidentified correspondent in the provinces. He described how, around New Year's Day, the queen and the duke of Buckingham had presented the new-born Prince Edward to the king at Windsor. First the duke introduced Henry to his son with no response, then the queen tried before they left, 'saying only that once he looked on the Prince and cast down his eyes again, without any more'.[17] In March parliament sent a delegation of twelve lords and churchmen to visit the king at Windsor and bring news of the death of Archbishop Kemp, among other things. They saw Henry on three occasions; on each he was utterly unresponsive and had to be supported from room to room by two men. The delegation reported that 'they could obtain no answer, word or sign; and therefore with sorrowful hearts they came away'.[18] The final contemporary account is that of Abbot Whethamstede of St Albans. It is unclear whether he saw the king in person, but his description accords with the other two sources. Whethamstede described how the king had lost his sense of time, his memory, and even control over his limbs, unable to keep his head upright and remaining in a slumped position.[19] From these accounts it is difficult to suggest any firm diagnosis, but the response of those who saw him suggests that the king's collapse was both sudden and unexpected, and that its manifestation was as much physical as it was mental.

The medical response to Henry's affliction similarly suggests that the onset of the illness was unforeseen. On 15 March 1454 the lords appointed a commission of three physicians and two surgeons to attend upon the king. They were empowered to administer a range of treatments, including potions, waters, unguents, laxatives, head-purges (administering heat to the scalp, which sometimes involved shaving the scalp completely), gargles, baths, poultices, and embrocations, as well as blood-letting by incision or other methods.[20] The men appointed to this commission were led by John Arundell, an Oxford medical graduate and canon of St George's chapel, Windsor, who had served as one of the king's physicians since the early 1440s, and William Hattecliffe, a fellow of King's College, Cambridge, who had taken a medical doctorate at the fashionable university of Padua and had been a member of the king's household since November 1452. Their appointment to a special commission (which also included John Faceby, a Southwark physician who would later be licensed by the king to practise alchemy) suggests that the symptoms the king exhibited in 1453/54 were unprecedented and lay outside the normal routine of their attendance upon the king as royal physicians. The treatments prescribed were, however, entirely conventional in a fifteenth-century context. Diet, blood-letting, head-purges, and laxatives were designed to restore the balance of the four humours (black bile, yellow bile, phlegm, and blood), a system of medical understanding that had its origins in ancient Greece and that still dominated medieval theories of the body and mind. According to this theory Henry's condition was most likely due to an excess of cold and wet humours (phlegm, black bile, and blood) and the treatment (such as a diet of warm chicken broth or blood-letting) was designed to restore balance.

Fifteenth-century medicine, however, also concerned itself with the welfare of the patient's soul and took note of astrology and other indicators of a patient's well-being. Henry, born in December and vulnerable to the influence of the moon, was, in theory at least, predisposed towards a phlegmatic constitution, one that was 'watery, changeable, cold and unstable' and also essentially feminine.[21] These astrologically based concerns over Henry's health and character may have had a much longer pedigree than the physical and mental affliction that gripped him in 1453. In 1441 the duke of Gloucester's wife, Eleanor Cobham, had been arrested partly because she had cast horoscopes predicting the king's illness and death, prompting the king's chief physician, John Somerset, to commission his own, more optimistic reading of Henry's stars. This interest in the astrological dimensions of Henry's condition and long-term concerns for the king's health may have led to the employment of Gilbert Kymer, sometime chancellor of the University of Oxford and one of the leading physicians in the country, to attend upon the king in June 1455. Kymer had a long-standing connection to the House of Lancaster, having penned a regimen of health for the duke of Gloucester in 1424, and in 1456 he was among a group of physicians, including Hattecliffe and Faceby, licensed to practise alchemy, not only to produce gold from base metal but also to distil pure alcohol (*aqua vitae*) and other liquids for medicinal purposes. Thus, while Henry's collapse in 1453 was sudden and his symptoms unprecedented, his illness may have confirmed long-standing concerns over his constitution and a humoral imbalance that threatened his ability to rule effectively.

If the causes, and even the course, of the king's affliction remain obscure, its consequences for the government of the realm and for the Lancastrian monarchy are clear. By the autumn of 1453 a small group of councillors, dominated by the bishop of Winchester and the treasurer of England, the earl of Worcester, were effectively in control, but it was not until 23 October that the duke of York was summoned to London to attend their meetings. The councillors had initially, it seems, omitted to invite Duke Richard, but the birth of the king's son on 13 October (named Edward after Edward the Confessor, whose feast day he shared) removed the tension around York's position as the heir presumptive. The letter requesting the duke's presence simply apologised for the councillors' oversight, and York arrived in London on 12 November. Almost immediately his ally, the duke of Norfolk, launched a fierce attack on Somerset, who was again accused of responsibility for the loss of Normandy and Gascony. Somerset was committed to the Tower on 23 November and York set about building a new regime. This new regime was, ostensibly at least, built on consensus and compromise. Duke Richard promised to do all 'that should or might be to the welfare of the king and his subjects', and there was to be no repeat of the attempted household purges of 1450.[22] The birth of a son to the king and queen in October had raised the spectre of Margaret of Anjou ruling as regent, something which the majority of lords had been keen to dismiss. Thus York's passage to pre-eminence among his fellow councillors was eased by his acceptance on 15 March 1454 of the young Prince Edward as heir to the throne, and on 27 March it was agreed in parliament that the duke should assume the title and duties of 'protector and governor of the realm' during the king's incapacity. York protested that this had arisen not from his own ambitions but from his acceptance of the necessity of the situation and in response to pleas from his fellow peers.[23] As Ralph Griffiths has observed: 'To make him protector in the constitutional uncertainty of 1454 might be deemed by some a dynastic challenge on York's part and the duke may have regarded it in precisely the same light.'[24] In any case it seems certain that the protectorate was something arrived at only reluctantly by the lords, evidenced by the protestations of infirmity, old age, or youthfulness which several peers offered as excuses not to serve on the council.

Indeed, the expressions of unity made in parliament and council masked deepening and dangerous divisions among the nobility, some of which had already escalated into violent feuds by the winter of 1453/54. The Bonville/Courtenay dispute in the West Country, in which York had intervened in September 1451, rumbled on, complicated by the involvement of the earl of Wiltshire, a nobleman close to the court, on the side of Lord Bonville. In 1452 the feckless Henry Holand, duke of Exeter (who was also York's son-in-law), had seized Ralph, Lord Cromwell's manor of Ampthill in Bedfordshire. Cromwell's attempt to recover the property at law had met a violent response from Exeter, who had attacked his rival in Westminster Hall in July 1453. Cromwell now looked for help and allied himself, through marriage, to the powerful Neville family. Maud Stanhope, Cromwell's niece and joint-heiress, was betrothed to the earl of Salisbury's second son, Sir Thomas Neville. In August, having celebrated their nuptials at Tattershall castle in Lincolnshire, the couple and their wedding party were attacked on their way north by Thomas Percy, Lord Egremont, the somewhat unstable younger son of the earl of Northumberland, and his brother, Sir Richard Percy. The Percy/Neville feud, between the two greatest magnate families in the North, had its origins in the 1440s over the families' respective influence on the Anglo-Scottish marches, but it had reached a crisis because Lord Cromwell held some former Percy lands that the current earl now hoped to recover. This hope was now seriously threatened by the alliance between Cromwell and the ambitious Nevilles. The Nevilles' ambitions caused problems elsewhere too. In the Midlands Salisbury's eldest son, Richard Neville, had married Anne, the sister and principal heiress of Henry Beauchamp, late duke of Warwick. This worsened his existing dispute with the duke of Somerset, who was married to one of Anne's half-sisters, Eleanor. Richard, now earl of Warwick through the right of his wife, clashed with Somerset over custody of the Despenser lands in Glamorgan, south Wales. Warwick had held these during the minority of his cousin, George Neville, Lord Bergavenny, but in June 1453 the king had granted the custody to Somerset. By the autumn, Warwick was holding them by force against Somerset and Lord Dudley, to whom the earl had been ordered to surrender them. While tensions simmered in the Midlands, south Wales and the West Country, it was in the North that matters came to a head. Early in 1454 the duke of Exeter allied himself with the Percy Lord Egremont, and in the spring, having opposed York's appointment and claimed the office of protector for himself, he went north to join his Percy allies. The renegade lords attempted to seize the city of York in May, but fled as the duke of York travelled north with a large retinue to enforce justice. Exeter claimed sanctuary in Westminster Abbey, but the judicial proceedings failed to punish the Percies and their servants. Instead, they were defeated by Sir Thomas and Sir John Neville at Stamford Bridge at the end of October; Egremont and his brother, Sir Richard Percy, were captured and imprisoned in Newgate in London, while Exeter was taken from sanctuary and incarcerated, under Salisbury's guard, in Pontefract castle.

The king's illness, and York's protectorate, had thus been marked by an alarming breakdown in order. While later Yorkist chroniclers would conclude that 'for a whole year [Duke Richard] governed most nobly and in the best way' and modern historians can congratulate him on his commitment to 'rule consultatively and representatively with the lords', the fact remains that a significant proportion of the political nation probably regarded the protectorate as partisan government at its worst, driven by self-interest rather than the good of the commonweal.[25] In part this was the inevitable conclusion of any government that was not led by the impartial authority of an active king, but it was also an impression reinforced by York's activities and the decisions made during his protectorate. On 2 April 1454 he secured the appointment of the earl of Salisbury as chancellor of England to replace the recently deceased archbishop of Canterbury, Cardinal John Kemp. Kemp had been a stalwart of the Lancastrian regime, a churchman who had served Henry V and had been a voice of moderation throughout Henry VI's reign; the contrast with Salisbury could not have been lost on the regime's opponents. York's record at dealing with local disorder was mixed. Although he moved quickly and forcefully to quell disorder in Yorkshire, elsewhere the duke was less successful. The quarrelsome Derbyshire gentry who had sacked Sir William Blount's manor of Elvaston simply refused to answer the protector's summons, making the unfortunate messenger eat the writ, seal and all, while in Wales York failed to control Gruffyd ap Nicholas, whose violent behaviour made a mockery of the protector's authority. Even where he did intervene forcefully, such as in the West Country, where he bound over his erstwhile ally the earl of Devon to keep the peace, York's policies backfired and lost him much-needed support. More damning perhaps was the long imprisonment of Somerset without a trial. In the autumn of 1454 the protector attempted to instigate proceedings against his rival, but found little support among the other lords.

The end of York's first protectorate was signalled by the recovery of the king around Christmas 1454. Henry had in fact been returning to some semblance of normality since the autumn. In September he had been conscious enough to participate when Thomas Bourchier, the new archbishop of Canterbury, took up his crozier and paid homage at Windsor. On 27 December he was well enough to command his almoner to ride to Canterbury to give thanks at the shrine of St Thomas Becket. Four days later Queen Margaret presented their son to the king. Edmund Clere, writing to John Paston a few days later, described the scene: 'And then [Henry] asked what the prince's name was, and the Queen told him Edward; and then he held up his hands and thanked God thereof. And he said that he never knew until that time, nor what was said to him, nor knew what where he had been while he had been sick until now.' The king also asked who the prince's godfathers were and learnt of the death of Archbishop Kemp. Soon afterwards the bishop of Winchester and prior of St John of Jerusalem were able to have a long conversation with the king, reporting that 'he spoke to them as well as ever he did', weeping with joy at the conclusion of the audience.[26] With the king's apparently complete recovery the basis for York's government dissolved and calls for the release of his rival, Somerset, grew. On 26 January Duke Edmund was released from the Tower on condition that he remained at least twenty miles distant from the king. This was probably small consolation to York, who surrendered his office, possibly at the same council meeting that settled terms for Somerset's release. Power now passed back to Henry and his household. On 4 March the council, in the presence of the king, lifted the restrictions on Somerset's movement and repudiated the charges against him. York was forced to submit the matters between him and his rival, now reduced to a private squabble rather than a fundamental question of public government, to the arbitration of his fellow peers. Moreover, the office of captain of Calais, granted to York in July 1454, was taken back into the king's hands, only to be bestowed on Somerset two days later. This was a deliberate affront to York, who had accused Somerset of military incompetence and worse, only to see the most important command in the realm given to his rival, but it also demonstrated a reassertion of the royal authority.

Henry's recovery from illness and the reassertion of direct royal authority ended York's period of ascendancy. It is unclear, however, whether Duke Richard and his allies retired from government or whether they were ousted by their rivals. On 7 March Salisbury resigned the Great Seal; a week later Exeter was released from Pontefract castle; and on 15 March the earl of Wiltshire, Somerset's ally, replaced the earl of Worcester as treasurer of England. Grants of office and patronage that had been made to York and his allies during the protectorate were now cancelled and redistributed among men close to the king. In mid-April Henry and his council resolved to summon a Great Council to meet at Leicester, in the heart of the duchy of Lancaster lands. York and his Neville allies, perhaps justifiably, feared a repeat of the events of February 1447 when Humphrey, duke of Gloucester, had been summoned to the Bury Parliament only to be arrested on charges of treason. They decided to withdraw from Westminster, leaving without apparently asking permission of the king. The battle lines for the opening engagement of the Wars of the Roses were now drawn.

The first battle of St Albans

If there had been an expectation that the king's recovery at Christmas 1454 would mark a return to the stable, consensual government that had characterised much of Henry's adult reign, then these hopes were soon dashed. The nature of Henry's affliction was such that it appears his involvement in the major decisions of government was even more restricted than it had been before the onset of his illness in August 1453. The letter summoning Gilbert Kymer on 5 June stated 'we be occupied and laboured as ye know well with sickness and infirmities', suggesting a less than complete recovery from his affliction, and between 3 February and 21 April 1455 the king had not signed any official documents.[27] In these circumstances York and his allies, perhaps rightly, feared the influence of their enemies at court and on the council and for their own safety. The king's council had met at Westminster in April and determined to summon a Great Council to meet at Leicester the following month. Its ostensible purpose was to provide for the king's safety, but it was most probably designed to settle once and for all the dispute between York and Somerset, almost certainly in the latter's favour. According to their letter to the chancellor, Archbishop Bourchier, on 20 May, the Yorkist lords feared they had been deliberately excluded from the meeting and complained that 'we conceive a jealousy had against us'.[28] Duke Richard's whereabouts in early May are far from clear but he probably went north, to his castle at Sandal in Yorkshire, and set about raising an army with the help of his Neville allies. The court's response was dilatory and confused. The king remained in Westminster and only on 18 May despatched letters asking for armed men to be sent to him in all possible haste. The following day York, Salisbury, and Warwick received letters under the Great Seal ordering them to disband their forces under pain of forfeiture.

On 21 May the king and his household, accompanied by the duke of Buckingham and a handful of other lords, left Westminster for Leicester. By this time the Yorkists were encamped at Ware. The sequence of events that followed is uncertain: the Yorkist lords answered the chancellor's orders for them to disband and wrote directly to the king (enclosing a copy of their earlier letter to Archbishop Bourchier for good measure and probably circulating copies of both letters to other lords). They protested their loyalty, their concern for Henry's safety, and their determination to have justice against their enemies and traitors to the commonweal who sheltered 'under the wing of your majesty royal'.[29] The letters were allegedly handed to the king's confessor, who delivered them to the earl of Devon in the king's quarters in the early hours of 22 May. It was later alleged that this communication was concealed from the king by two household servants, Thomas Thorpe and William Joseph, acting on the instructions of the duke of Somerset. It also appears that York was in direct contact with the duke of Buckingham, to whom he renewed his accusations against Somerset. Buckingham probably did communicate these demands to the king, but Henry did not reply, probably wishing to take counsel more widely before responding.

At this point Henry appears to have made one of his characteristically idiosyncratic interventions. As Somerset rode north to join the royal party, the king, aware that York was determined to settle his score with the duke, replaced him with the duke of Buckingham as constable of England and commander of the royal forces. This may have been a clumsy attempt to appease the rebel lords, or it might simply indicate Henry's commitment to hear the Yorkists' legitimate concerns. In any case, it made no difference; York, it seems, was determined on revenge. Buckingham argued against meeting the Yorkists in open battle and instead the royal party prepared to travel the seven miles from Watford to St Albans, with plans to be there around midday. Buckingham perhaps hoped that in this way York would put off his attack and instead negotiate when more lords and bishops arrived from London. Duke Richard, however, had already moved to St Albans and his forces, superior to the king's in both number and prowess, awaited the royal party's arrival in the town. A brief attempt at further negotiation followed but it seems that York, and perhaps more importantly the Nevilles, had decided that their ends were only to be met by violence. The fighting, in which the earl of Warwick and the northerners, led by the Neville retainer Sir Robert Ogle, played a leading role, was short lived. The king's banner was unfurled in the market-place but it seems that his household showed little taste for the fight (indeed, it is possible that some of those close to the king were sympathetic to York). The battle soon developed into a rout, with some of the king's men shedding their armour and fleeing. Henry was himself wounded in the neck and took refuge in a tanner's house, while Somerset was cut down attempting to flee the house in which he found himself besieged. Buckingham was also seized, but another of the rebel lords' targets, the treasurer of England, the earl of Wiltshire, escaped disguised as a monk. There were probably few other casualties, but the earl of Northumberland and Thomas, Lord Clifford, were cut down, perhaps targeted in a deliberate act of vendetta by the Nevilles. Indeed, after the battle, while York was ordered to provide prayers for the deceased and pay compensation to Somerset's widow, Warwick was ordered to compensate the children of the dead Lord Clifford. This aspect of personal feud is further highlighted by one later Yorkist chronicler who observed that 'when the said

Duke Edmund [of Somerset] and the lords were slain the battle was ceased'.[30]

Once the fighting was done, Henry was escorted to St Albans Abbey by York. There Duke Richard and the earls of Warwick and Salisbury submitted themselves to the king as his loyal subjects, 'saying that they never intended hurt to his own person. And therefore the king our sovereign lord took them to grace, and desired them to stop their followers, and see that no more harm should be done.' The king, in a characteristic act of mercy, pardoned the rebel lords and the following day he left, accompanied by York and other lords, for London, where they remained, 'with joy and solemnity', before summoning another parliament to assemble at Westminster on 9 July.[31]

Conclusion

The years between 1450 and 1455 had been the most turbulent of Henry's reign to date. They had begun with popular rebellion, which had led to the emergence of a powerful noble opposition to the king's closest advisors and the royal household (if not yet the king himself). Yet the crisis of 1450–52 had been averted, it seems, by a reassertion of royal authority and a reaffirmation of the king's own role at the centre of government. This answered a widely held desire for royal leadership and spoke of the nation's broad commitment to Lancastrian principles of government. The situation had collapsed, however, in the summer of 1453 with the king's sudden and total physical and mental breakdown. There is no indication that the events of 1453 were expected or that the king's illness was of a nature that could be accommodated within the structures already in place to meet the demands of a king whose involvement in government had previously been fitful and idiosyncratic. It was the extraordinary nature of Henry's total absence for over a year, from the summer of 1453 until Christmas 1454, that allowed the duke of York and his allies to wreck the consensual, conciliar government that had characterised Lancastrian rule since 1422. The Henry that emerged from his stupor in December 1454 appears to have been a man even less capable than before of uniting and leading the disparate strands of the Lancastrian legacy. Yet he was still the king, and his interventions, however sporadic and ill-considered, still seemed to command the respect and obedience of the majority of his subjects. Certainly, and crucially, even his opponents still operated within a political framework which was recognisably and distinctly Lancastrian in character. Thus control of the king, both physical and political, emerged as the defining element in English politics in the months after the first battle of St Albans. Equally important, however, was the fact that Henry himself, despite evidence of a recurrent and occasionally debilitating illness, remained capable of exercising his royal will and indicating whose counsel (and ultimately control) he wished to receive. It was this paradox, of a king both incapable of day-to-day rule yet able sporadically to make his will felt, that gradually led an increasing number of his subjects to imagine and eventually accept his deposition.

Notes

1 John Watts, *Henry VI and the Politics of Kingship* (Cambridge, 1996) 254.
2 Isabel Harvey, *Jack Cade's Rebellion of 1450* (Oxford, 1991), 186.
3 B.P. Wolffe, *Henry VI* (1981), 231.
4 *The Historical Collections of a Citizen of London in the Fifteenth Century*, ed. James Gairdner (Camden Society, 1876), 190.
5 Thomas Gascoigne, *Loci e Libro Veritatum*, ed. J.E.T. Rogers (Oxford, 1881), 189.
6 *Six Town Chronicles*, ed. R. Flenley (Oxford, 1908) 132.
7 Harvey, *Cade's Rebellion*, 186–91.
8 *Six Town Chronicles*, ed. Flenley, 132.
9 C.L. Kingsford, *English Historical Literature in the Fifteenth Century* (Oxford, 1913), 371.
10 Historical Manuscripts Commission, *Calendar of Carew Manuscripts*, v, 258–9.
11 *Paston Letters and Papers of the Fifteenth Century*, ed. N. Davies (2 vols, Early English Text Society, ii, 460.
12 R.A. Griffiths, 'Duke Richard of York's Intentions in 1450 and the Origins of the Wars of the Roses', in *King and Country: England and Wales in the Fifteenth Century* (1991), 299–304.
13 *The Politics of Fifteenth Century England: John Vale's Book*, ed. Margaret Kekewich Coilin Richmond, Anne E. Sutton, Livia Visser-Fuchs and John L. Watts (Stroud, 1995), 187–9.
14 G.L. Harriss, 'The Court of the Lancastrian Kings', in *The Lancastrian Court*, ed. Jenny Stratford (Donington, 2003), 15.
15 *POPC*, vi, 119.
16 *PROME*, xii, 248–9.
17 *The Paston Letters,* ed. James Gairdner (6 vols, 1904), ii, 295–6.
18 *PROME*, xii, 258–9.

19 *Registrum Abbatiae Johannis Whethamstede*, ed. H.T. Riley (2 vols, Rolls Series, 1872–3), i, 163.
20 *POPC*, vi, 166–7.
21 Carole Rawcliffe, 'The Insanity of Henry VI', *The Historian* 50 (1996), 11.
22 *Calendar of Patent Rolls, 1452–1461*, 143.
23 *PROME*, xii, 259–63.
24 R. Griffiths, *Reign of Henry VI* (1981), 725.
25 'John Benet's Chronicle', ed. G.L. and M.A. Harriss *Camden Miscellany xxiv* (Camden Society, 1972) 212; John Watts, 'Richard, Duke of York (1411–1460)', in *Oxford Dictionary of National Biography*, xlvi, 754.
26 *Paston Letters*, ed. Gairdner, iii, 13.
27 J.R. Lander, 'Henry VI and the Duke of York's Second Protectorate, 1455–6', in *Crown and Nobility 1450–1509* (1976), 78–80.
28 *PROME*, xii, 340.
29 Ibid., 341.
30 *An English Chronicle 1377–1461*, ed. W. Marx (Woodbridge, 2003), 79, 73.
31 *English Historical Documents, Volume IV 1327–1485*, ed. A.R. Myers (1969), 276.

9 Civil war and the end of the House of Lancaster, 1455–61

While the first battle of St Albans in 1455 should be regarded as the opening engagement of the Wars of the Roses, the journey to Lancastrian defeat and Henry VI's deposition in March 1461 was a slow and hesitant one. The natural reluctance to remove an anointed king and the political nation's commitment to a broadly Lancastrian vision of good government combined with the simple fact of the king's involvement, however sporadic, in the affairs of the kingdom to delay the eventual day of reckoning. It was not until the Lancastrian lords, rallying around the figureheads of Prince Edward and Queen Margaret, forced their Yorkist opponents' hands in the autumn of 1459 that open conflict was renewed. Even then, it was not until the Accord of 1460, which disinherited Prince Edward in favour of the duke of York, that all hopes of a peaceful settlement were finally extinguished. That the death throes of Lancastrian monarchy were so prolonged and so painful was due in part to the determination of the king himself and his commitment to widely shared principles of consensual government that were recognisably Lancastrian in nature.

Queen Margaret and the Lancastrian court

Henry's role at the battle of St Albans had been crucial: he had refused to parley with the Yorkist lords and had replaced Somerset as commander of the royal forces with the duke of Buckingham. He had not, however, participated in the fighting (although clearly he was close enough to it to be wounded by a stray arrow), and his return to London highlighted the new political order imposed upon him by the victors. He entered the capital flanked by York and Salisbury, with Warwick ahead of them bearing the royal sword. On 25 May York placed the crown on Henry's head in a solemn crown-wearing ceremony at St Paul's. The following day the king despatched writs summoning a parliament for 9 July. The mood was ostensibly one of conciliation, yet York and his allies were keen to apportion blame for the events of the previous spring, identifying Somerset, Thomas Thorpe, and William Joseph as architects of the bloodshed. This was not a universally held perception: as one well-informed contemporary noted, after the bill attributing blame to Somerset had passed, 'many a man grudged full sore'.[1] A major redistribution of offices demonstrated that political power had been transferred to York, at least temporarily, and a bill seeking to rehabilitate the reputation of Humphrey, duke of Gloucester, testified to the partisan agenda of the assembly. By associating himself with Gloucester, fast emerging as the erstwhile champion of reform and leader of the opposition to Henry VI's corrupt counsellors, York laid claim to one important part of the Lancastrian political legacy.

Nevertheless, Henry VI was still king, even if his royal presence was becoming an increasingly negligible component of the political scene. York's government appears to have enjoyed little support among his fellow peers, at least if the parlous nature of their attendance at parliament is any measure of their commitment to the new regime. It may have been to consolidate his position and transfer real power to an aristocratic council led by himself that York engineered the events of the second session of the parliament of 1455. This assembled at Westminster on 12 November amidst news of further, violent disorder in the localities. In Henry's absence, York was named as the king's lieutenant in parliament, but the Commons demanded that the duke once more be appointed protector to deal with the disorder; the hearing of petitions for justice, they argued, 'should be too burdensome and wearisome to his highness'.[2] It seems likely that Henry had suffered some form of relapse of the illness that affected him in 1453; not a total collapse, but one sufficient to remove him once again from the day-to-day business of government. Thus on 17 November the lords reluctantly agreed to York's appointment as protector until such time as the king, with the advice of the Lords in parliament, ended it.

Five days later the government of the realm passed formally to the council with York as protector and chief counsellor. This was not so much a personal triumph for Duke Richard as a reassertion by the lords of those principles of conciliar government that were central to Lancastrian monarchy. Yet even under these circumstances the duke's ability to govern was circumscribed by the presence of the king. In all matters touching 'the honour, worship and security' of the king's person, a deliberately broad and undefined term, the council was to notify Henry of its decisions, presumably so he might, if he chose to, alter them.[3]

These arrangements, however, did not end the discord between York and his supporters and the other lords. The Commons were once again pressing for an act of resumption of royal grants. Ostensibly this was a familiar attempt to restore sound royal finances, but it also sought to limit expenditure on the royal household and the king's freedom to control the revenue of the duchy of Lancaster lands. This once again highlighted the tension between the private lordship exercised by the king as duke of Lancaster and wider principles of good government. York threw his weight behind the Commons' call for resumption when parliament reassembled in January. Attendance among the Lords seems to have been no better than before and both York and the earl of Warwick turned up with large armed retinues. All sides appear to have recognised that the continuation of York's position as protector depended on his ability to push through the Act of Resumption.[4] Although this measure eventually passed, it found little support among the Lords, and those aspects of the original petition designed to curtail royal freedom were omitted. The duchy of Lancaster lands held in trust for the royal foundations were untouched, the plan to limit the queen's dower to 10,000 marks (£6,666 13s. 4d.) was dropped, and the king was not required to submit exemptions from the Act for scrutiny by the Commons. Indeed, Henry's reply that he understood the aims of the bill but reserved the right to make exemptions from its terms undermined its real effectiveness.[5] This was a clear failure for York. On 25 February 1456, in accordance with the terms of his appointment, he was removed by the king in person, acting upon the advice of his lords spiritual and temporal. Although the duke was compensated financially, he had failed to establish the type of political ascendancy his victory at St Albans had promised. York was certainly aware that his ambitions had been thwarted and he left Westminster before the parliament ended on 9 March.

At this point the king and his supporters made a decision that would have far-reaching consequences for the House of Lancaster. In the summer of 1456 Queen Margaret accompanied the young Prince Edward on a tour of his patrimony, including the earldom of Chester, before settling herself and her son in the duchy of Lancaster heartland at Kenilworth castle. In August Henry joined his wife at Coventry. Bertram Wolffe characterised this retreat to the Midlands as 'the actions of the rash and despotic queen',[6] but it may also have arisen from a real fear for the royal family's safety. In any case, this relocation to the Midlands marked a major shift in the political situation. By so doing Henry was distancing himself from the public, national duties of kingship, and repositioning himself physically and symbolically at the centre of an essentially private, ducal household. The king's role in this decision-making process can have been only minimal and the driving force, almost certainly, must have been Queen Margaret and her desire to protect her husband (and perhaps more importantly her son) from York and his allies. Until 1453 Margaret appears to have played a conventional role as queen consort, acting as mediator and patron, as well as developing close connections to the duke of Suffolk and other leading members of the Lancastrian affinity. The king's illness in the summer of 1453 and the birth of their son transformed her situation. Her attempts to establish a regency in January 1454 were thwarted by a lack of support among the lords, and there can be little doubt that from this time Margaret considered York's ambitions to be a threat to the Lancastrian dynasty in general and to her son in particular. These fears can only have been exacerbated by the events that followed Henry's recovery at Christmas 1454. Contemporaries recognised her importance in the opposition to York's second protectorate: one observer characterised her as 'a great and strong laboured woman, for she spares no pain to sue her things to an intent and conclusion to her benefit'.[7] The summer and autumn of 1456 were characterised by fear and rumour. Tales spread of an armed clash in which Viscount Beaumont had been killed and the earl of Warwick injured, while the violent actions of York's servants and supporters in Wales only served to justify the defensive measures taken by the Lancastrian court.

Thus, by the autumn of 1456 Henry's role in government and in the formulation of a Lancastrian response to the Yorkist challenge had been seriously diminished. Yet, as was the case in the parliament of 1455, his interventions were still important. The king's own role in events in these last years of the reign is even more difficult to discern than it had been previously. His signature still appeared on bills and petitions for grace, but the tendency for these to relate to matters concerning the clergy, religious houses, and his own household became more marked than ever. Endorsements by the king's chamberlain, Sir Thomas Stanley, noting 'the king has granted this' suggest Henry's personal involvement, but such notes also reveal that he was willing to pass increasing amounts of business to the discretion of the council, which was still in formal control of royal government, following the decision made in parliament in November 1455. In August 1458 a petition from Thomas Stratton, clerk of the king's work, was endorsed with the words 'the king wills that his chancellor and the lords of his council see this bill and if they seem it behoveful that then his letters patent be made'.[8] The following year a petition from John Hillesdon, one of the yeomen of the king's chamber, was annotated by Stanley to the effect that 'the king wills this bill be sent to his chancellor to have his advice therein'.[9] Kings, of course, were required to seek counsel and then to make their decisions accordingly. Yet these annotations were testimony to the fact that by the late 1450s both the king and his councillors had openly accepted his basic inability to exercise his royal will in all but the most mundane matters. However, there are suggestions that, at times, Henry may still have enjoyed periods of greater energy. In April 1457 he and the queen moved to Hereford and presided over a commission of oyer and terminer appointed to hear charges against York's allies, Sir William Herbert and Sir Walter Devereux. Similarly, in September that year he felt able to return to Westminster (although much of the next six months was actually spent at Abingdon, Chertsey, and Reading Abbey, probably out of financial necessity). Although the king ideally should have functioned as an impartial authority to whom the lords could submit their disputes, his continued yet only occasionally active presence at the centre of government in fact worked against the settlement of the deep divisions within the polity.

Although government was naturally carried out in Henry's name, real power was widely assumed to lie with Margaret. Indeed, the queen emerged as the rallying point for those whose primary loyalty was to the House of Lancaster itself, not some abstract notion of the crown or commonwealth. Lancastrian identity re-emerged as one based upon the royal/ducal household, just as it had been in the reigns of Henry's father and grandfather. This was evident in a transfer of positions of responsibility to those men already intimately connected to the households of the king and queen. On 26 September the queen's chancellor, Lawrence Booth, became keeper of the privy seal, while on 5 October the earl of Shrewsbury replaced Viscount Bourchier as treasurer. Six days later Archbishop Bourchier surrendered the Great Seal to William Waynflete, bishop of Winchester, the king's confessor and a man devoted to the personal service of Henry VI. Further institutional changes sought to protect the interests of the Lancastrian royal family. In February 1457 the newly established council of the Prince of Wales was given formal control of his patrimony. It included Booth, his brother Archbishop William of York, Waynflete, Humphrey Stafford, son and heir of the duke of Buckingham, the earls of Shrewsbury and Wiltshire, Viscount Beaumont, and Lords Dudley and Stanley. Elsewhere Lancastrians ousted the duke of York and his allies from important offices. In April the disputed castles of Aberystwyth and Carmarthen were taken from York and granted to the king's half-brother, Jasper Tudor. Money remained an overriding concern for the Lancastrians. The parliament of 1455 had not granted supply and the royal households were forced to rely on their prerogative of purveyance. This, of course, risked engendering popular opposition and it may be these fears that explain why the king spent at least a third of his time between August 1456 and July 1460 enjoying the hospitality of various religious houses. In many ways the normal mechanisms of royal finance broke down in these years. The Lancastrian court refashioned itself from a public, royal household into a private, ducal one. As the volume of government business diminished, its costs were increasingly met by the private resources of the duchy of Lancaster. A good example of this is the increased importance of William Grimsby, the treasurer of the king's chamber and keeper of his jewels, who, from the autumn of 1456 until September 1457, when Henry returned to the Home Counties and London, regularly travelled between the Midlands and the exchequer at Westminster, taking cash for the use of the king. In October 1458 he became deputy-treasurer of England, an indication of how ostensibly public offices were being subjugated to the private needs of the Lancastrian royal family.

It is, however, simplistic to assume that power had passed completely to the queen and the group of committed Lancastrians who now emerged to support her and her son, the Prince of Wales. Many, if not most, of the lords remained uncommitted either to the duke of York or to the Lancastrian party solidifying around the queen. The council at Westminster continued to meet regularly and transact business, even if this had contracted in volume. Judicial business, in particular, seems to have continued under the guidance of the council, with special commissions of inquiry attempting to dispense impartial justice on a range of local disputes. The earl of Salisbury, absent from the council since the middle of 1456, had returned in November, while York also played a prominent part in its deliberations. At the end of February 1457 a large and representative Great Council met at Coventry. It was the occasion for a concerted attack on the Yorkist lords, led by Chancellor Waynflete. Nevertheless, the French raid on the Kentish port of Sandwich at the end of August that year put the brake on any immediate slide into faction. This coincided with the return of the king and many lords to London. John Watts has suggested that it was most likely the broadly based, inclusive council of nobles and leading churchmen then gathered at Westminster who initiated the attempt at reconciliation between the Yorkist lords, on the one hand, and the queen and the relatives of those lords killed at St Albans, on the other.[10] Yet it is equally likely that it was the return of Henry himself to the political process in the autumn of 1457 that made this possible. For more than two years the moderate lords and bishops had tried in vain to reconcile the two parties; the most compelling explanation for the duke of York's agreement to submit to the lords' arbitration (and Warwick's decision to ignore death threats to participate in the process) is the presence of Henry himself at the negotiations. On 27 January 1458 Henry addressed the assembled lords in person on the dangers of dissension among their ranks, a familiar theme of Lancastrian political discourse.[11] This process culminated in the so-called 'Loveday' of March 1458.

If there were high hopes for the projected reconciliation they were soon to be disappointed. One reason for this was the continued fear and suspicion of each other that dominated the thoughts and actions of the principals, particularly York and his allies. A more immediate reason was that both the settlement brokered and its formal recognition at the 'Loveday' ceremony at St Paul's on 25 March 1458 highlighted the essentially private and personal nature of the dispute between the rival camps. The arbitration award, made in the king's name, in effect attributed blame to York and his adherents, going some way to reversing the account presented in the parliament of 1455. The Yorkists had been the first to draw blood and the award required them to make amends by endowing a chantry chapel at St Albans for the souls of the deceased. Both Somerset's heir and widow and Clifford's heir were compensated, while the damages due to the Nevilles from the Percies for their actions in 1453/54 were forgotten in an effort to end that dispute. While the earl of Salisbury seems to have acquiesced in the council's decision, for York it represented his failure to convince his fellow lords of the justice of his cause. It also confirmed the obstinacy of the king and the partisan nature of Lancastrian government. The duke's platform for reform, his stand against Somerset as a traitor, and his defence of the commonweal were reduced to a petty, personal squabble. The symbolism of the 'Loveday' itself was telling. Salisbury processed to St Paul's hand-in-hand with the new duke of Somerset, and York likewise with Queen Margaret. This charade both explicitly recognised the existence of two, rival armed camps and ignored the public nature of York's grievances, presenting the political crisis purely and simply as one of private feud. Ostensibly the 'Loveday' was a triumph for the Lancastrians in as much as it upheld the legitimacy of Henry VI's government and its ability to resolve conflicts between the king's greatest subjects. Ironically, however, it also marked the beginning of the end for any real prospect of a peaceful resolution of the crisis.

The failure of compromise and the road to war

When York, Salisbury, and Warwick had arrived in London early in 1458 they had done so at the head of large armed retinues. They had thus threatened to impose their will by force, as well as to defend themselves from the rival retinues of the dukes of Somerset and Exeter and the Percies. Strenuous efforts were made by the city authorities to keep the rival camps apart, employing 5,000 soldiers to patrol London's streets. This was indicative of the deep atmosphere of distrust that had grown up between the rival parties since the events of 1455. Nevertheless, events did not descend into violent chaos and the sham reconciliation of the 'Loveday' took place on 25 March. Henry's brief bursts of energy, such as his apparently long address to the lords in January, may have facilitated this moment of false optimism. The Yorkist lords remained in and around the capital in the wake of the 'Loveday' while the queen retired again to the Midlands (leaving Henry to travel pointlessly between St Albans, Windsor, and various royal lodges in the Thames Valley), but soon the Lancastrians were making active preparations to oppose York and his allies. Margaret returned to London in the autumn. Purchases of weaponry continued to strengthen the royal household, while appointments to local office attempted to secure the provinces against the Yorkist lords. In November an attempt on Warwick's life by members of the royal household almost succeeded. Around the same time the earl of Salisbury committed himself formally to York. He met the duke's counsellors and retainers at his seat of Middleham in Yorkshire and agreed that they 'should take full part with the full noble prince the duke of York'.[12] Salisbury's decision at this time is evidence of the justifiable need for self-preservation among York and his allies. Indeed, the prominence of the new Percy earl of Northumberland in the queen's counsels and the violence planned against both Warwick and York were enough to convince Salisbury that only Duke Richard's eventual victory could safeguard his own position and power.

In May 1459 Henry joined Margaret in the Midlands. Royal letters were sent to several counties ordering the gentry to attend upon the king at Leicester on 10 May with as many men defensibly arrayed as they could muster. The king ordered the purchase of

3,000 bow staves 'considering the enemies on every side approaching upon us, as well upon the sea as on land'.[13] Some of these
letters were initialled by the king himself, but his active involvement
in the formulation of Lancastrian policy in these months must be
doubted and, as was widely believed by contemporaries, it is almost
certain that Queen Margaret had taken day-to-day control of the
Lancastrian cause. These preparations were the prelude to another
Great Council meeting summoned to meet at Coventry in June.
The assembly, to which the Yorkist lords and their allies (such as
Archbishop and Viscount Bourchier, and Bishop Neville of Exeter)
had not been summoned, proceeded to accuse them of treason.
The parallels with 1455 are obvious, but this time the initiative lay
with the Lancastrians. It was not until 20 September, however,
that Warwick arrived in London from Calais. The queen and her
party were now anxious to prevent a rendezvous between the
Yorkist lords. Somerset was sent to track Warwick's progress north,
which he did from a safe distance, while another royal army
attempted to prevent Salisbury from reaching the duke of York
at Ludlow. Warwick escaped their clutches, but on 23 September
another royal force, perhaps 10,000 men strong and led by the
elderly James, Lord Audley and John, Lord Dudley, halted Salisbury's progress at Blore Heath, just south of Newcastle-under-
Lyme. The battle lasted some four hours, but the Yorkists eventually
prevailed, killing Lord Audley in the melee. The fighting was fierce,
however, and Salisbury only narrowly escaped capture; his two
younger sons were less fortunate and were imprisoned in Chester
castle.

Salisbury now pressed on to Worcester, where he was joined by
the duke of York. There York and Salisbury entered into a solemn
agreement, an indenture signed and sealed in the cathedral, the
contents of which are now unfortunately lost but which presumably bound them to assist one other, saving only their allegiance
to the king. They thus maintained the fiction that they were acting
in the interests of the commonwealth, saving Henry from his evil
counsellors. This agreement, along with their demands, was now
taken to the king by the prior of Worcester cathedral priory and
other churchmen. The Yorkist articles repeated the charges that
had formed the core of criticism levelled at the Lancastrian regime
for the past decade. They accused the traitors about the king of

subverting justice, impoverishing the crown, and ignoring the king's wishes. Their remedy was an equally familiar and unconvincing one: York and the Nevilles offered to set aside their personal grievances and insisted that the king once again take advice from 'the great lords of his blood'.[14] Once Warwick had joined his father, Salisbury, and York at Worcester, the three lords retreated to the duke's stronghold of Ludlow. Now there could be no hope of compromise. York and Warwick declined the offer of a royal pardon if they surrendered within six days. Although the pardon had omitted Salisbury for his part in Audley's death and would thus have been unthinkable, given the lords' recent commitments to each other, its acceptance would also have admitted some guilt on their part. The Yorkists had now played their hand, yet despite their military successes their cause had attracted little support from their fellow peers. As they marched across country to Ludlow they were accompanied only by York's two sons, the earls of Rutland and March, and Lords Clinton and Grey of Powis.

On 9 October writs went out summoning a parliament to gather at Coventry on 20 November. York, Salisbury, and Warwick were not summoned and it seems certain that the intention was to attaint the Yorkist lords of treason. Accordingly, the rebels sought to come to the king's presence to present their grievances directly to him, much as they had done in 1455. On 12 October the royal host found itself confronted by the Yorkists in defensive positions at Ludford Bridge, on the River Teme just south of Ludlow. The Yorkists faced the king's army, which was accompanied by at least twenty members of the parliamentary peerage. Henry was present on the field, seated on a horse with his banners displayed. According-ing to the later Lancastrian narrative of events, he addressed his host in person, exhorting them 'in so witty, so knightly, so manly and so cheering a style, with such a princely bearing and assured manner, in which the lords and people took such joy and comfort that their only desire was to hasten the fulfilment of your coura-geous knightly wish'.[15] While this display of dynamic leadership on the king's part may seem unlikely, the mere fact of his presence proved too much for many among the Yorkist ranks, including a contingent of professional soldiers from the Calais garrison led by the veteran soldier Andrew Trollope, and they promptly went over to the king in return for a pardon. This, as one chronicler observed, 'made the duke [of York] full sore afraid when he saw that some old soldiers went from him unto the king'.[16] Duke Richard and his allies decided that discretion was the better part of valour. They returned to Ludlow, leaving their army in the field leaderless, and from there went their separate ways. York and his second son, the earl of Rutland, fled to Ireland, while Salisbury, Warwick, and York's eldest son, the earl of March, travelled via Devon and the Channel Islands to the safe haven of Calais.

Defeat and the deposition of Henry VI

The parliament that met at Coventry on 20 November 1459 had been summoned before the defeat of the Yorkist lords at Ludford Bridge. It had been called to condemn them and their allies, but it was not an overtly partisan gathering. Although York, Salisbury, and Warwick were not summoned, attendance by the remaining peers was strong and, while many of the known 186 members of the Commons were later to emerge as supporters of the House of Lancaster, a significant minority are known to have remained neutral or even to have supported the Yorkists. It was decided to proceed against the rebellious lords by way of attainder: they were to be stripped of their estates and their heirs disinherited. In all, twenty-seven rebels were attainted, but this was certainly fewer than had originally been mooted and some notable Yorkist supporters, such as Sir Walter Devereux, William Herbert, and William Hastings, were pardoned. The conclusion must be that most of the lords wished to maintain the broad consensus that had kept the peace during most of the 1450s. In this, they had the crucial support of the king, whose professed willingness to pardon all those willing to submit must have tempered the mood. There may also have been disquiet about the process of attainder itself. Although not unknown previously, its use on this scale was unprecedented and its consequences may have unnerved several among the Lords and Commons.

It was probably to counter growing disquiet over the process of attainder that the tract known as the *Somnium Vigilantis* was written. It set out the case against York and his allies in no uncertain terms. No matter how grave the problems facing the realm, it insisted, rebellion against the king could never be justified.

Moreover, the Yorkist lords had broken their oaths of allegiance to Henry on more than one occasion and failure to punish them severely would now dangerously undermine royal authority. The author of this tract is unknown, but its intended audience may well have been moderate lords, like the duke of Buckingham, and perhaps even the king himself. It took the form of an imagined conversation between representatives of the Yorkist lords who had come to court seeking clemency and a royal spokesman. The beginning of the text is now lost, but it clear that the debate (which probably both reflected and shaped the real debate that took place in parliament) was couched in terms that had been familiar components of Lancastrian political discourse for more than half a century. The Yorkist lords claimed legitimacy by representing the commonwealth and stressed the royal virtue of mercy. The Lancastrian rebuttal of these claims was unambiguous. The Yorkist lords had forfeited their right to mercy as they had acted out of 'pure malice', bent on the 'final destruction of this gracious king'. It rejected their claims to act for commonwealth, arguing instead that the Yorkist lords' actions were driven by their own ambitions. Significantly, the tract also dismissed the 'foolish commons' who still sympathised with the Yorkist lords' call for reform, despite their broken oaths and rebellion. In so doing, the author was consciously rejecting the legitimacy of the commons' role in shaping the Lancastrian polity and abandoning a central component of the Lancastrian political legacy.[17] Abbot Whethamstede of St Albans also recorded the arguments for and against mercy being shown to the Yorkist lords as they were rehearsed before the king in parliament. Crucially, while the majority of lords were swayed by the arguments made for justice, Henry favoured mercy. Once again the king's character was crucial in determining the outcome of events. While the Yorkist lords were duly attainted, Henry reserved the right to pardon freely those who would submit to his grace in the future.[18] Indeed, some who had fought for the Yorkists at Ludford Bridge had already submitted themselves 'in their shirts and halters in their hands, falling before the king', thus escaping the rigours of parliamentary justice.[19] As a final act of the parliament, on 11 December, sixty-six lords, bishops and heads of religious houses swore solemn oaths of allegiance to the king, and significantly to Queen Margaret and Prince Edward as well.[20]

The effect of the somewhat ambiguous message of the Coventry Parliament was reinforced by the regime's utter failure to turn the military victory at Ludford Bridge into a decisive strategic advantage. In Calais, where the duke of Somerset had been appointed captain on 5 October, Warwick successfully defeated all attempts to dislodge him. In January 1460 Lancastrian attempts to reinforce Somerset were thwarted by a raid on Sandwich, led by John Dynham, the West Country esquire who had helped Warwick and March escape from England the previous October but whom the king had subsequently pardoned. Warwick's ships, impounded at Sandwich in November 1459, were retaken, giving an important strategic boost to the Yorkist earls. Warwick then defeated Somerset at Newembridge, just outside Calais, and the duke was forced to retire to the Lancastrian-held castle of Guînes, where he remained, impotent to intervene in English affairs, until the autumn of 1460. Similarly, Jasper Tudor, earl of Pembroke, who was responsible for re-asserting royal authority in Wales, enjoyed little success in attempting to reduce the Yorkist-held castle of Denbigh. York remained safe in Ireland, supported both militarily and financially by the Anglo-Irish establishment, and in March 1460 the earl of Warwick travelled to Waterford to meet with Duke Richard to discuss their next move.

Warwick returned to Calais in June 1460. Shortly afterwards, his kinsmen and deputy, William Neville, Lord Fauconberg, led another raid on Sandwich, destroying a Lancastrian fleet poised to sail to Calais and securing the port in preparation for a Yorkist invasion. On 26 June the earls of Salisbury, Warwick, and March landed in Kent and began their march on London. The Yorkist agenda was a familiar one: their lives endangered by traitors about the king, they were marching for justice, both for themselves and for the commonwealth. This message was reinforced by their re-issue of one of Jack Cade's manifestos of 1450. The so-called 'Articles of the Commons of Kent' may have been an attempt to garner popular support as they marched to London, but it also revealed the ideological poverty of the Yorkist position. Nothing had changed since 1450: Henry VI still failed to offer any effective royal leadership and the realm remained impoverished and ungoverned, yet Yorkist rhetoric and their proposed remedy for the realm's ills was still couched in a recognisably Lancastrian political vocabulary. The Yorkists' explanation for this parlous state of affairs was the corrupt government of the 'traitors' who remained at court and the fact that lords loyal to the commonwealth were excluded from counselling the king. The earls of Shrewsbury and Wiltshire, and Viscount Beaumont had replaced the dukes of Suffolk and Somerset as the villains in the Yorkist imagination, but the language of complaint had a depressingly familiar tone. The rebel lords' protestations of loyalty to the king must have been wearing thin but, as yet, there was still no real alternative to Henry on the political horizon, nor any new Yorkist policies to address the issues of counsel, royal finance, and law and order.

On 10 July the Yorkists engaged the royal army, led by the duke of Buckingham and earl of Shrewsbury and with Henry present, at Northampton. Once again, treachery influenced the outcome and Lord Grey of Ruthin's timely defection led to a crushing Yorkist victory. Henry appears to have played no part in proceedings: after the battle, the Yorkists found him alone in his tent, apparently deserted by his advisors. Buckingham, Shrewsbury, and Lord Egremont had been killed in an echo of events at St Albans five years previously and Henry once again fell under the control of the Yorkist lords. Queen Margaret and her son, who had wisely remained in Coventry, fled to Denbigh castle, held by Jasper Tudor, before sailing for Scotland, where they threw themselves on the mercy of the new Scottish King James III and his mother, the Queen Dowager Mary of Guelders. By 16 July the victorious Yorkists were back in London and in the same position they had found themselves five years earlier; in control of the king and government by force of arms. Their response was similar: George Neville, bishop of Exeter, replaced Archbishop Bourchier as chancellor, while Viscount Bourchier was appointed treasurer in place of the dead Shrewsbury. On this occasion, however, the king's household was also purged and Salisbury's younger son, John Neville, was appointed chamberlain. On 30 July the chancellor despatched writs summoning a new parliament to assemble at Westminster on 7 October. In the meantime Henry continued as king. Writs continued to be sent out in his name and there is evidence of the same sporadic personal involvement in the affairs of government as before. For example, on 28 September 1460 he signed a writ ordering Viscount

Bourchier to deliver £100 each in cash to the earls of March and Salisbury.[21] While Henry travelled between Eltham, Greenwich, and the bishop of London's palace near St Paul's cathedral, the realm waited for the duke of York's return from Ireland and his response to the latest turn in events.

For reasons unknown, York delayed his return from Ireland until early September. This may have been because he was aware of the difficulty and unpopularity of the course of action he had now decided upon. As he made his way to Westminster he carried a sword borne upright before him, usual practice for the king's lieutenant in Ireland but unknown in England. As he neared his destination he adopted the undifferentiated royal arms, dropped Henry VI's regnal year from the dating clause of his letters, and retained individuals in his service without the usual clause reserving their allegiance to the king. The message was clear: Duke Richard had come to claim the throne, rightfully his by inheritance based upon his maternal descent from Lionel, duke of Clarence, the second son of Edward III. Quite when York had decided to claim the throne remains one of the great unanswered questions of the fifteenth century. Rumours, of course, had circulated since 1450 and the duke's own recognition of his position had been implicit in his claim to exercise the office of Protector of the Realm and in the production of several elaborate genealogies stressing his royal blood. The Act of Attainder passed against him in 1459 had claimed that one of the duke's servants, Robert Radcliff, had, with his dying breath, revealed York's designs on the crown. Once back in Ireland after the debacle of Ludford Bridge, York had exercised his quasi-regal powers without reference to Henry VI's regime, summoning a parliament that had passed a law making rebellion against the governor treason and initiating a separate coinage for Ireland. If, however, Duke Richard had revealed his intentions to his allies at their conference in March 1460 he may have met with little immediate support. Warwick, in particular, appears to have emerged as a conciliatory force in the wake of the victory at Northampton. In July the Milanese ambassador praised his efforts to 'keep the country in peace and unity', while four months later one of John Paston's correspondents warned that the realm would be 'utterly undone' without Warwick's guiding hand.[22]

When York arrived in Westminster on 10 October 1460 he immediately made his way to parliament. There, in the presence of the lords, he laid his hand on the throne and announced 'that he determined not to lie down his sword but to challenge his right . . . and determined that no man should have denied the crown from his head'.[23] But instead of popular acclamation, Duke Richard met with general consternation. Archbishop Bourchier asked if he wished to see the king, to which York replied that he could think of no one who ought not rather come to see him. The duke's bold, even brash, move had backfired; it did not meet with the public support of even his closest friends, never mind the many lords hostile to him then present in parliament. His desire to be crowned king was probably in the first instance undone by the refusal of Archbishop Bourchier to participate in any coronation, but Duke Richard almost certainly also faced opposition from the earl of Warwick. Accordingly, he was forced to submit a formal, written case. This was based entirely on his descent from Lionel of Clarence, but the Lords hesitated and passed the matter to the king. Henry, needless to say, prevaricated further: the Lords begged him to remember if there were any objections to York's title 'because his said highness had seen and understood many different writings and chronicles'.[24] Two days later the Lords passed the matter to the judges, who claimed that matters touching the king's estate were for the Lords, not them. The Lords turned next to the sergeants of law, who, unsurprisingly, said that matters outside the competence of the judges were also too high for them. York's own defence of his position was feeble: he was absolved from breaking the oaths of allegiance and promised to eschew 'the way of fate' he had made throughout the 1450s because they were against God's law. He had, in fact, been rightfully king all along and would be guided by 'truth, right and justice' rather than oaths made to a usurper.[25]

It was a sentiment that few appear to have shared. Finally, on 25 October the Lords came up with a compromise, reminiscent of the Treaty of Troyes in 1420. Henry was to remain king, but on his death the throne was to be settled on York and his heirs. In effect, just as Charles VI of France had done forty years previously, Henry had resigned any last vestiges of royal authority: he admitted that York's title was 'just, lawful, true and adequate'.

Moreover, while the 'Accord' recognised that Henry should enjoy the crown during his natural life, it also admitted the possibility that it might, in future, 'please his highness to lay down or yield the said crowns' to York. The Parliament Roll also recorded that the new heir to the throne should receive the same obedience from royal officers as the king himself, and that offenders against the duke and his family should be subject to the same penalties of treason as if they had offended against the king.[26]

While York and his allies savoured their victory in parliament, the Lancastrians had not been idle. Queen Margaret had been negotiating with the Scots for assistance against the rebels; the price of their support was the town of Berwick-upon-Tweed. In October the duke of Somerset had returned from the Continent and, with the earl of Devon, he mustered his forces alongside the earls of Northumberland, Westmorland, and other Lancastrian lords at Hull. The Yorkist lords had little choice but to move north to face the Lancastrian threat and restore order and stability in the king's name. York and Salisbury left London on 2 December, while Warwick remained in the capital. It seems likely that York misjudged the size of the Lancastrian army, and he soon took refuge in his castle at Sandal. On 30 December 1460 Duke Richard's army was caught in the field by a much larger Lancastrian force. The battle of Wakefield was a disaster for the Yorkists. York had been outwitted by his Lancastrian opponents, and left the safety of his stronghold unaware of the true size of the enemy host. Duke Richard, his son the earl of Rutland, and Salisbury's son, Sir Thomas Neville, all fell in the mêlée. Salisbury was taken alive and beheaded at Pontefract the next day. Their remains were then taken to York and their severed heads were displayed on the city's walls. York's, in mockery of his royal pretensions, was adorned with a paper crown. The events at Wakefield underlined the inherent risks of pursuing political goals through violence. The king once again played no part in these events. While the Accord was being violently discarded by his queen and her supporters, Henry remained at the Bishop of London's palace, under the control of the earl of Warwick.

Leadership of the Yorkist cause now passed to the eighteen-year-old Edward of Rouen, earl of March, the eldest surviving son of Richard, duke of York. Edward was born in the Norman capital on 28 April 1442, and his early years are obscure. In 1452 rumours abounded that he was marching on London to free his father in the wake of Dartford, and he certainly accompanied York to parliament in 1454. After the rout at Ludford Bridge he accompanied his uncle, the earl of Salisbury, and cousin, the earl of Warwick, to Calais, but appears to have played only a minor role in affairs during the crucial months that followed. He was present at the battle of Northampton in July, but remained in London throughout the autumn, neither travelling to the Midlands with Warwick in September nor accompanying his mother to meet the duke of York when the latter returned from Ireland. He nevertheless featured in popular pro-Yorkist poetry of the time as the 'Rose of Rouen'. March's reaction to his father's claim to the throne is unknown: he may have initially opposed York's claim and he certainly kept a low profile during the negotiations that resulted in the Accord of October 1460. On 1 November, at the solemn crown-wearing to mark the settlement, March carried Henry VI's train, while York walked in procession alongside the king. Edward was spending Christmas at Shrewsbury when he received news of his father's death. He had been sent west in December to raise men from the family estates in Wales and the Marches, while Warwick had remained in London to guard the capital. On receiving of the news of the disaster at Wakefield, Edward, now duke of York himself, prepared to intercept the Lancastrian army marching south. News, however, reached him of a second Lancastrian force, commanded by the earls of Pembroke and Wiltshire, coming from Wales. Now Edward demonstrated the vigour that would characterise his actions over the coming months. He turned his army around and on 2 or 3 February he intercepted the Lancastrian earls at Mortimer's Cross, on the old Roman road to Wales between Leominster and Wigmore. Ably assisted by Sir William Herbert and Sir Walter Devereux, he routed the Lancastrian army. Pembroke and Wiltshire escaped, but Henry VI's step-father, Owen Tudor, was taken and later executed.

Elsewhere, however, the Yorkists were dealt a further blow when, on 17 February, Warwick suffered a heavy defeat at the hands of Queen Margaret's army at St Albans. This battle of St Albans was a much larger affair than its predecessor some five years earlier. Warwick was accompanied by the duke of Norfolk, the earls of

Arundel and Suffolk, and six other lords. The earl also, of course, had in his custody Henry VI himself. The Lancastrian army, on the other hand, had a distinctly northern character but, alongside the earl of Northumberland and Westmorland, it numbered among its ranks the dukes of Exeter and Somerset, the earls of Devon, Oxford, and Shrewsbury, and five other lords. Its legitimacy as truly representative of the house of Lancaster was reinforced by the presence of the recently disinherited Prince Edward. The Yorkists, it seems, were defeated by sheer weight of numbers as much as anything, although poor communication may have meant that many, perhaps including Warwick himself, were never engaged. By the end of the day, Warwick was in flight and the king had been reunited with his supporters. One contemporary chronicle, apparently written within weeks of the battle, stated that Henry re-joined his wife and son 'by his own assent and will', in effect demonstrating his personal rejection of the recently negotiated Accord.[27] The way now seemed clear for the Lancastrians to enter London and regain the reins of royal government, but at this crucial juncture the city authorities stood firm and barred the gates. The principal reason for this was probably fear of the northerners, who had quickly gained a reputation for pillage from their passage along the Great North Road into Hertfordshire. Another possibility is that the mayor and aldermen of London had already committed themselves firmly to the Yorkist cause. Bertram Wolffe suggested that the presence of Henry himself in the Lancastrian army actually hurt the Lancastrian cause. The dynamic leadership offered by Andrew Trollope, acting as Queen Margaret's commander in the field, was replaced by an 'immediate military and political paralysis' as the king joined the army. Henry's inability to direct events, while the Lancastrian host looked to him for direction, ensured that 'havering and uncertainty now followed decisive military success'.[28] Instead it was Edward and Warwick, who had met at Chipping Norton in Oxfordshire, who entered the capital on 27 February.

Only one course of action now lay open to the remaining Yorkist lords: by killing the duke of York, the Lancastrians had broken the Accord negotiated the previous October. Edward had to make amends by claiming the throne for himself. Thus, on 1 March Bishop Neville of Exeter declared Edward's just title to the throne to a presumably sympathetic gathering of some three to four thousand in St John's Field. The assembly was asked if Henry, an anointed king and representative of a dynasty universally accepted as rightful kings until only a few months earlier, had forfeited his right to be king and Bishop Neville demanded to know if they would accept Edward in his stead as their king. The answer, of course, was affirmative. For the first time since his accession as a baby in 1422, Henry's fitness and right to rule was formally called into question. The assembly at St John's Field was in some ways similar to the parliament of 1399, which had seen the accession of Henry's grandfather. On that occasion the earl of Northumberland had catalogued Richard II's tyranny and asked if the assembled Lords and Commons would accept Henry Bolingbroke as their king. Now the assembled crowd merely assented to Edward's *de jure* right to be king of England.

Edward's election as king, if it can be called such, was the decision by the small Yorkist council, which met at Baynard's Castle two days later, that they would support and defend his right. This council summoned people to gather outside St Paul's on the morning of 4 March. Edward processed to the cathedral and at St Paul's Cross the people were again asked if they accepted him as their king. Having been universally acclaimed, he made his way to Westminster Hall, where he took his place upon the king's seat and assumed the royal regalia. Edward then made a declaration of his own title to the throne and the crowd acclaimed his accession, much as they would have done at a more regular coronation. Nevertheless, by stressing the notion of popular support for the new king, the Yorkists were appropriating one of the pillars of Lancastrian kingship. York himself, and later Warwick, had staked their claim for political power on the basis that they were representing the commons and the commonweal; it played into the new regime's hands to foster the idea that Edward had 'took upon himself the crown of England by the advice of the lords spiritual and temporal, and by the election of the commons'.[29]

Edward now needed to establish his authority and this meant defeating the Lancastrians in battle. On 11 March Lord Fauconberg went north with an army funded by generous loans from the Londoners and two days later Edward himself left the capital, accompanied by the duke of Norfolk, to join forces with the earl of Warwick in the Midlands. By 28 March Edward had reached

Pontefract and the following day, Palm Sunday, the Yorkist host clashed with the Lancastrians between the villages of Saxton and Towton. Towton was the largest and bloodiest battle of the Wars of the Roses and may well have been the largest fought on English soil, with over 20,000 combatants on the field. The Lancastrian army was larger than Edward's and contained the majority of the nobles and gentlemen present on the field. Edward was accompanied by Norfolk, Warwick, and Lords Montagu, Scrope of Bolton, Fauconberg, and Fitzwalter. The battle took place in a blizzard and was notable for the aggressive tactics employed by the Yorkist army, with Edward himself in the thick of the fighting. The contrast with Henry, who remained impotently awaiting the outcome of the battle with his family at York, could not have been more marked. The result was a catastrophic defeat for the Lancastrians: the earl of Northumberland and Lords Clifford, Dacre, Neville, Richemont-Gray, and Welles were killed in action, alongside many of their retainers, while the earls of Devon and Wiltshire were taken and subsequently executed. The slaughter was immense and contemporaries were shocked at the scale and significance of the Lancastrian defeat. Upon hearing of the defeat, Henry, Margaret, Prince Edward, and a small band of followers fled York and managed to slip quietly across the border into Scotland. As the final, shameful act of Lancastrian kingship, the town of Berwick-upon-Tweed was handed over to the Scots in fulfilment of the arrangement Margaret had made with the young James III the previous December. Edward IV entered York the next day and the following weeks were spent touring those northern counties still loyal to the house of Lancaster. On 26 June the new king returned to London in state, amidst great celebrations, and two days later he was crowned at Westminster Abbey.

Conclusion

It took a period of eighteen months of civil war, seven pitched battles (at three of which the king himself was present), and the death of more than a quarter of the parliamentary peerage, not to mention hundreds if not thousands of ordinary Englishmen and women, to finally end the reign of Henry VI. The slaughter underlines the fact that the Yorkist victory was a close-run thing and, numerically at least, one achieved against the odds. Yet this victory removed a king whose adult reign, it has been argued, was defined by his own 'inanity' and failure to offer any effective direction or leadership.[30] The question, then, of why the deposition of Henry VI was so protracted and painful a process is a compelling one.

First, and foremost, is the question of the nature of Henry's kingship. Unlike the previously deposed kings, Edward II and Richard II, no one could claim (at least before December 1460 and York's death at Wakefield) that he had ruled as a tyrant or acted against the law. The duke of York's claim to the throne did not make any explicit comment on Henry's kingship, merely stating that his own line, descended from the third son of Edward III, Lionel of Clarence, was superior to that of Henry's, descended from John of Gaunt, Edward's fourth son. Only in Edward IV's first parliament was it necessary to construct a narrative that questioned Henry's fitness to rule and the consequences of his decades of misgovernance: the Commons recalled that 'extortion, murder, rape, the shedding of innocent blood, riot and unrighteousness were commonly practised in your said realm without punishment' during his predecessor's reign but their petition did not catalogue his misdeeds in any detail. This same tone was adopted by contemporary Yorkist chroniclers. Edward's right to the throne came from his descent through Lionel of Clarence, a right taken from him by the 'unrightful usurpation and intrusion' of Henry VI's grandfather in 1399. Although Henry VI too was thus a usurper, it was Henry IV's crime of deposing Richard II that had directly led to the calamities that had befallen the realm during the years of Lancastrian rule, not the nature of Henry VI's kingship per se.

Indeed Henry's own actions in the final years of his reign did little to help his opponents construe him as the active agent of the troubles that had beset the realm. Only retrospectively, in Edward IV's first parliament, could the blame for the events of 1459–61 be laid at Henry's door. According to the Act declaring Edward's royal title, realising that the crown rightly pertained to the duke of York, Henry had 'planned and laboured continually by devious schemes, frauds, deceits and outrageous means, to bring about the complete and final destruction of the same noble Prince

Richard and his issue', instigating their attainder at the Coventry Parliament of 1459. The following year he had been compelled to accept York as heir to the throne, but 'continuing in his old rancour and malice, using fraud and malicious deceit and dissimulation contrary to truth and conscience', he had 'covertly urged, incited and instigated the final destruction, murder and death of the said Duke Richard and his sons', leading to the murder of York at Wakefield by the duke of Somerset. He had then, 'greatly and amazingly rejoicing in the said sorrowful and piteous murder of the same noble prince and worthy lords', ordered his followers to dispossess Edward, earl of March of his father's duchy of York and break the terms of the Accord.[31] It was thus Henry's breaking of the agreement made in the parliament of 1460 that finally forfeited any legitimate claim to reign as king and absolved Edward and his subjects of obedience to him.

The Yorkist charges against Henry VI identified him as the principal agent of events in 1459–61 out of necessity. The new regime could justify his deposition only by presenting him as the architect of the recent divisions, not merely as a passive figure but as one who actively incited others to carry out his designs. Had the king played no role at all in the public affairs of the realm since his recovery from illness at Christmas 1454, this would have presented a far bigger challenge to the Yorkists. In fact, Henry's occasional but public and significant interventions in politics between 1455 and 1460 may have made the narrative presented in the 1461 parliament more credible. In the autumn of 1457 an apparently re-energised king returned to London to break the deadlock between the opposing parties, convincing York and Warwick to appear before the council, and resulting in the 'Loveday' of March 1458. The nature of that award, which reduced York's public and political grievances to the level of a private vendetta, may represent the victory of the queen's party, but it may equally reflect Henry's own view of the sacred nature of his own authority. He rejected York's claims to represent the interests of the commonweal as forcefully in 1458 as he had done in 1450, 1452, and 1455. Yet Henry's steadfast views on royal authority were tempered by a propensity towards mercy. It was his reluctance to condemn the Yorkist rebels at the Coventry Parliament that explains the heated nature of the debate at that assembly and the ambiguity of its outcome which allowed the Yorkists to fight another day. Henry remained a real presence in the government of the realm until, in effect, he surrendered his authority totally at the parliament of 1460. This presence allowed both Lancastrians and Yorkists to alternately employ the same rhetoric, to claim that Henry was effectively held prisoner by the opposite side and forced to make decisions against his will, during the final decade of his reign.[32]

It was thus the Accord of 1460, an agreement in which Henry appears to have played a prominent role, that finally sounded the death knell of Lancastrian kingship. The lords, the majority of whom had previously refused to commit themselves to either Lancaster or York, were now forced to choose: recognise York as the true heir and rightful king or refuse to accept the authority of the decision made in parliament. In either case, as the principal architect of the Accord and as a king who had presided over the emasculation of his royal authority, Henry's reign was effectively over. With the Accord signed, any real authority that he still enjoyed vanished as those closest to him refused to accept the judgement made in his name. In reality he was powerless to prevent York's death at Wakefield and was marginalised at the second battle of St Albans and at Towton. The future of the Lancastrian monarchy was decided at Towton by the English nobility, some three-quarters of whom were present on the field. It was a battle fought between those who held on to a personal Lancastrian view of the polity, represented by Queen Margaret and her son, and those who subscribed to a more abstract vision of good government, represented by Edward IV. Both sides, however, defined their motives and actions in terms that were recognisably Lancastrian in origin.

Notes

1 *Paston Letter and Papers of the Fifteenth Century Part III,* ed. Richard Beadle and Colin Richmond (Early English Text Society, 2005), 158.
2 *PROME,* xii, 349.
3 Ibid., 359.
4 *Paston Letters,* ed. Beadle and Richmond, 161.
5 *PROME,* xii, 386–7.
6 B.P. Wolffe, *Henry VI* (1981), 302.
7 *Paston Letters,* ed. Beadle and Richmond, 161.

8   TNA, C81/1468/16.

9   Ibid., C81/1467/5.

10 John Watts, *Henry VI and the Politics of Kingship* (Cambridge, 1996), 342–5.

11 *Registrum Abbatiae Johannis Whethamstede*, ed. H.T. Riley (2 vols, Rolls Series, 1872–3), i, 296–7.

12 A.J. Pollard, 'The Northern Retainers of Richard Nevill, Earl of Salisbury', *Northern History* 11 (1975–6), 52.

13 *Letters and Papers Illustrative of the Wars of the English in France during the Reign of Henry VI*, ed. J. Stevenson (2 vols in 3, Rolls Series, 1861–4), ii.(2), 511.

14 R. Griffiths, *Reign of King Henry VI* (1981), 818.

15 *PROME*, xii, 459.

16 *The Historical Collections of a Citizen of London in the Fifteenth Century*, ed. James Gairdner (Camden Society, 1876), 205.

17 J.P. Gilson, 'A Defence of the Proscription of the Yorkists in 1459', *English Historical Review*, 26 (1911), 512–25.

18 *Registrum Abbatiae Johannis Whethamstede*, ed. Riley, i, 345–56.

19 *Historical Collections*, ed. Gairdner, 207.

20 *PROME*, xii, 464–7.

21 TNA, E404/71/5/2.

22 Michael Hicks, *Warwick the Kingmaker* (Oxford, 1998), 184.

23 P.A. Johnson, *Duke Richard of York 1411–1460* (Oxford, 1988), 214.

24 *PROME*, xii, 517–18.

25 Ibid., 520.

26 Ibid., 524–5.

27 Hannes Kleineke, 'Robert Bale's Chronicle and the Second Battle of St Albans', *Historical Research* 87 (2014), 744–50.

28 Wolffe, *Henry VI*, 329.

29 *Historical Collections*, ed. Gairdner, 215.

30 K.B. McFarlane, 'The Wars of the Roses', in *England in the Fifteenth Century*, ed. G.L. Harriss (1981), 240.

31 *PROME*, xiii, 11–21.

32 John Watts, 'Polemic and Politics in the 1450', in *The Politics of Fifteenth Century England*, ed. Margaret Kekewich, Colin Richmond, Anne E. Sutton, Livia Visser-Fuchs and John L. Watts, 26–38.

10 Exile, imprisonment, and the Readeption, 1461–71

It is a measure of the peculiar nature of Henry VI's reign that he survived his deposition in 1461 by more than a decade. Moreover, for half that period he was kept as a prisoner in the Tower of London. Henry's last years are almost totally bereft of any evidence of his own agency. Indeed, his impotence (in contrast to the active scheming of Queen Margaret on behalf of their son, Prince Edward) probably saved his life. Edward IV simply had nothing to gain by killing the former king and focusing Lancastrian loyalty on the far more promising Edward of Lancaster. Henry remained in the eyes of his many Lancastrian supporters the rightful king and, due to disputes within the Yorkist ranks and an unholy alliance between Margaret of Anjou and the earl of Warwick, he found himself reinstated on the throne in October 1470. During his brief 'Readeption' Henry cut a forlorn and tragic figure and he appears to have played little or no active role in the events of these months. He remained in London while Edward IV first defeated the earl of Warwick and then moved to counter Queen Margaret and Prince Edward when they returned from France. With the total defeat of the Lancastrian cause, and the death of Prince Edward, at the battle of Tewkesbury, Henry's utility to his Yorkist rivals was finally at an end. On the night of 21/22 May 1471 he was put to death in the Tower of London.

Exile and imprisonment

After the debacle at Towton, Henry, Margaret, and their son, accompanied by a small group of perhaps two dozen followers, made the journey north to Scotland. At the invitation of Mary of Gueldres, the Lancastrian party took up residence at the Guest House of the Dominican Friars in Edinburgh, the customary place to lodge distinguished guests of the Scottish king. From here Henry and Margaret held a court in exile. The former chief justice, Sir John Fortescue, was appointed chancellor and emerged as their principal 'man of business'. Henry was apparently pleased with their reception and in January 1464 he made a grant to the provost and citizens of Edinburgh, entitling them to trade freely with England as if they were the king's own subjects, in recognition of their generosity towards him during his exile. Money was clearly an issue and his supporters appear to have financed the Lancastrian royal family out of their own pockets. While plotting began almost immediately to enlist foreign support against the Yorkists, and Lancastrian agents were dispatched to the Continent, the former king and queen initially remained in Edinburgh. By August Margaret was still holding court at the Blackfriars' and in correspondence with Lancastrian servants in France and Burgundy. According to those Lancastrian agents, Henry, accompanied by only four men and a boy, had moved to Kirkcudbright on the south-west coast of Scotland during the summer, probably staying at the Franciscan friary.[1] Henry's presence there is curious. The town was in the part of Scotland under the lordship of the earls of Douglas. James, the 8th earl, had been an exile in England since 1455 and had supported the Lancastrian cause in 1459–60, yet he still had important friends in south-west Scotland. The region was also close to the English border and the many Lancastrian sympathisers in Westmorland and Cumberland. It is possible, however, that Henry had taken up residence in the town after visiting the nearby abbeys of Sweetheart and Lincluden near Dumfries, the latter having already played host to Queen Margaret during her stay in Scotland the previous year. Significantly, in the late fourteenth and early fifteenth centuries the 'Black Douglases' had championed a form of lay piety which had very much in common with that practised by the Lancastrians, and the earls had been important patrons of both religious houses. Henry's visit to Kirkcudbright may reveal therefore something of his concerns at this time, which may have been more to do with his own personal piety than the wider political and dynastic concerns of the House of Lancaster.[2]

In England, meanwhile, the Lancastrian loyalists maintained an armed and effective resistance to the new regime. In Wales, Carreg Cennen and Harlech castles held out against Edward's forces and in the north, where servants and supporters of the Percies contested the new regional hegemony of the Neville family, the Lancastrians still commanded substantial support. In July 1461 Queen Margaret sent the duke of Somerset and Lord Moleyns to France to negotiate support from the ailing Charles VII. Charles, however, died on the 22nd of that month and his successor, Louis XI, was more cautious in his support for the House of Lancaster. On Good Friday 1462 Margaret herself landed in Brittany in order to secure French support for her husband. Meeting with the new king at Tours, site of the ill-fated truce between Henry and Charles VII some eighteen years previously, she received limited assistance in the form of forty-three ships and 800 men led by Pierre de Brézé (already infamous in England for his raid on Sandwich in 1457). She then returned to Scotland with her French army, collected Henry, and landed near Bamburgh in Northumberland on 25 October. Bamburgh castle surrendered to the invaders and before long the neighbouring castles of Alnwick and Dunstanburgh had also fallen. However, on their return journey to Scotland Margaret's fleet was wrecked by storms. The French soldiers accompanying them, some half of the original force, were marooned on Lindisfarne, while Henry, Margaret, and de Brézé managed to make safe haven in Berwick-upon-Tweed. The Lancastrian campaign met with a swift response from Edward IV's lieutenant in the north, the earl of Warwick, and his brother Lord Montagu. They immediately invested the Lancastrian-held castles and by December Alnwick, Bamburgh, and Dunstanburgh were all back in Yorkist hands. The Yorkist regime's tenuous hold on these northern strongholds, however, probably convinced Edward of the efficacy of a policy of reconciliation towards the leading Lancastrian rebels, most notably Henry Beaufort, duke of Somerset and Sir Ralph Percy, head of that family during the minority of the fourth earl of Northumberland. Indeed, it seems that the recent Lancastrian reversal had persuaded Somerset that his interests were best served by accommodating himself to the Yorkist regime.

Margaret, however, was not to be so easily dissuaded from her cause. In March 1463 she crossed the border again at the head of a joint Lancastrian and Scottish army. Sir Ralph Percy immediately returned to the Lancastrian fold and surrendered Bamburgh and Dunstanburgh, while Sir Ralph Gray, another recently pardoned Lancastrian, also changed sides and betrayed Alnwick. By June, Margaret and Henry were both resident at Bamburgh. In the same month, however, a large Yorkist army, well equipped with ordnance from Calais and the Tower of London, marched north under Warwick to join Lord Montagu, the recently appointed warden of the East and Middle Marches. Faced with an overwhelming response from Edward IV's government and without the prospect of Scottish support, Queen Margaret fled for the Continent. In early August she landed at Sluys in the Low Countries, accompanied by her son, the duke of Exeter, Sir John Fortescue, and as many as 200 other Lancastrian loyalists. She threw herself upon the mercy of Philip the Good, duke of Burgundy, who arranged her travel to the duchy of Bar, where her father provided the means to establish a Lancastrian court in exile at the castle of Koeur, near the town of Saint-Mihiell. Henry now appears to have been abandoned by his wife and the remainder of the Lancastrian 'inner-circle'. By this stage they seem to have considered Prince Edward their best chance of restoring the fortunes of the House of Lancaster. The ex-king made his way back to Edinburgh and celebrated the New Year there under the protection of James Kennedy, bishop of St Andrews (who had apparently some years earlier been instructed by Charles VII of France to look after his nephew).

On 9 December 1463 James III had promised Edward IV that Scotland would not give any further assistance to the Lancastrian cause. Henry now faced the prospect of extradition from Scotland to England. In early January 1464 Bishop Kennedy helped Henry escape from Edinburgh, first to St Andrews, and by the third week in February he was ensconced in the Lancastrian stronghold of Bamburgh castle. Henry had received a boost to his cause, however, in January when the duke of Somerset reneged on his oath to Edward IV and travelled north, eventually (after a narrow escape at Durham) joining the defenders of Bamburgh. Between the beginning of February and the end of March, and accompanied by Sir Ralph Gray, Sir Ralph Percy, and Lords Hungerford and Roos, Somerset conducted a campaign which resulted in the capture of Norham castle as well as several Northumbrian towns. However, fortune would soon intervene once more: on 25 April Lord Montagu was en route to meet representatives of James III when he was intercepted by a Lancastrian force, commanded by Somerset, at Hedgley Moor. The battle was a short-lived affair: Lords Hungerford and Roos quickly fled, while the Lancastrian vanguard, commanded by Percy, was overwhelmed and Percy himself was killed. Somerset and Gray escaped and regrouped at Alnwick, but on 15 May they were surprised at Hexham by a Yorkist force commanded by Lords Montagu, Greystoke, and Willoughby. The duke was taken and executed the following day. Only Gray evaded capture and made for Bamburgh, which he held with another rebel, Sir Humphrey Neville. Following an artillery bombardment, the garrison surrendered, delivering the treacherous Gray to his fate. During all this time Henry remained at the small castle of Bywell, on the north bank of the River Tyne.

Quite how Henry escaped his Yorkist pursuers is unclear. Lord Montagu took Bywell and found only the former king's hat, which he dutifully presented to Edward IV at Pontefract later in the month. Rumours abounded that Henry had returned to Scotland, but it seems more likely that he travelled around Westmorland, Lancashire, and West Yorkshire, perhaps exploiting connections strengthened when he had stayed in south-west Scotland during the summer of 1461. He certainly stayed several times at the home of John Maychell of Crackenthorpe near Appleby in Westmorland. In 1466 Maychell received a pardon for sheltering the ex-king. Finally, in July 1465, Henry was discovered hiding in Waddington Hall near Clitheroe in Lancashire, seat of Sir Richard Tempest. Unbeknown to his host, Henry's whereabouts were betrayed by Sir Richard's brother, John, who burst into dinner, along with a group of local Yorkists led by Sir James Harrington. There was a struggle, yet somehow Henry managed to make his escape. He fled into nearby Clitherwood, but it seems he was again betrayed, this time by one William Cantelowe, a monk of the Benedictine abbey of St Mary's in Abingdon. Henry, accompanied by two chaplains and a squire, was eventually captured on 13 July at Bungerly Hippingstones, a ford on the River Ribble. He was brought to the capital and rode 'through Cheapside and so through all London to the Tower' with his feet bound under his horse. There he was met by the earl of Warwick, recently returned from Calais, who formally arrested him in the name of Edward IV.

Henry now began a period of imprisonment that would last more than five years. 'Henry of Windsor, late in deed but not of right king of England' was apparently well looked after during his confinement. A chaplain, William Kimberley, received a generous salary of 7½d. a day to say mass daily for the royal prisoner. He was looked after by two squires and two yeomen of the crown, with a small band of servants, 'and every man was suffered to come and speak with him by licence of the keepers'.[3] According to his hagiographer John Blacman, if any of his visitors asked Henry why he had unjustly occupied the throne he would reply: 'My father was king of England, and peacefully possessed of the crown of England for the whole time of his reign. And his father and my grandfather was king of the same realm. And I, as a child in the cradle, was peaceably and without any protest crowned and approved as king by the whole realm, and wore the crown of England some forty years, and each and all of my lords did me royal homage and plighted me their faith, as was also done to other my predecessors.' Henry appears to have resigned himself to the inevitability of his fate: 'Wherefore I too can say with the Psalmist: The lot is fallen unto me in a fair ground: yea, I have a goodly heritage. For my right help is of the Lord, who preserveth them that are true of heart.'[4]

The Lancastrian court in exile

While her husband skulked around the Anglo-Scottish borders and then languished in the Tower of London, Queen Margaret and her son struggled to keep alive the vision of the House of Lancaster as a European princely dynasty of the first rank. Based at her father's castle of Koeur in Lorraine, she and her small band of Lancastrian loyalists maintained close contact with many of the ruling houses of Europe and worked tirelessly to remove the usurper Edward IV from the English throne. Their efforts were successful, in as much as Edward was forced into exile and Henry VI restored to the English throne in September 1471. The short-lived, but ultimately disastrous, Readeption regime should not obscure the fact that the Lancastrian court in exile between 1463 and 1471 succeeded in maintaining a central component of the Lancastrian legacy, namely the image of the House of Lancaster as one of the foremost European princely dynasties. Moreover, the ideas that emanated from it, mostly through the writings of Sir John Fortescue, reveal its members' commitment to Lancastrian principles of good government.

Margaret's Lancastrian court in exile was in reality a paltry affair. King René of Anjou allowed his daughter a pension of 6,000 crowns a year, barely enough to feed her and her servants, but in 1465 this was supplemented by an annuity of 5,000 francs from the French king, Louis XI. The size of her establishment is uncertain, but it numbered no more than 200 and may have been as few as 50. Its most important members were often away on embassy. Occasionally members of the court were invited to dine at the nearby abbey of Saint-Mihiell, but as John Fortescue warned John Butler, the titular earl of Ormond, in December 1464 'we are all in great poverty, but yet the queen sustains us in meat and drink, so that we are not in extreme necessity. Her Highness may do no more for us than she does'. Ormond was advised to come to Koeur with a full purse. The court's principal members were all committed Lancastrians who had previously served in the households of the royal family. Sir Robert Whittingham, keeper of the queen's wardrobe and treasurer of the household, for instance, had been an usher of the king's chamber and receiver of the prince's rents before being appointed keeper of Margaret's Great Wardrobe in 1458. William Grimsby and William Joseph, as we have seen, had both been intimate servants of the king and queen during the 1450s, while Sir John Fortescue, the former chief justice, was a long-standing servant of the House of Lancaster. The Lancastrian cause was also represented by the presence of exiles at various other European princely courts. From 1465 Edmund Beaufort, the titular duke of Somerset, and his brother John, as well as Henry Holand, duke of Exeter, stayed at the Burgundian court, while the Beaufort brothers also visited the Breton court. Similarly, John Butler, earl of Ormond, travelled to the court of John II of Portugal, while Jasper Tudor, earl of Pembroke, visited the French court. While the degree to which these men were solely agents of Queen Margaret and not merely representatives of their own personal interests may be questioned, the presence of such nobles of royal blood at foreign courts reminded Continental observers of the contested nature of the Yorkist regime and that Henry VI, an anointed king, remained a prisoner in the Tower.

It is probably with Fortescue and the queen that the credit lies for maintaining the Lancastrian vision of a European princely dynasty in the face of such difficulties. Fortescue himself travelled to Paris to meet with representatives of the French king at least three times, in 1462, 1464, and 1470, but more importantly, as chancellor, he was responsible for drafting the stream of letters sent from Koeur to Lancastrian supporters in England and on the Continent and to foreign princes. He also wrote a series of four memoranda to the French chancellor, Guillaume Juvenal des Ursins, that presented practical arguments why Louis XI should support the Lancastrians in removing Edward IV from the English throne. The vision of Lancastrianism which developed at Kouer was one that attempted to reconcile the various constituent parts of the Lancastrian legacy. To this end Fortescue also penned several tracts where he defended the Lancastrian right to the throne by prescription alone and envisioned a future polity shaped by distinctly Lancastrian concerns. Significantly, Fortescue's imagined future for the Lancastrian polity, still ruled over by Henry VI, was one of conciliar government. In his 'Articles sent fro the prince to therle of Warrewic', a set of instructions ostensibly from Prince Edward to the turncoat earl of Warwick in 1470 to be relayed to his recently released father, Fortescue stated that the king should be counselled by a formal council of twelve laymen and twelve clerics, and that he should 'do no great thing touching the rule of this realm . . . but first his intent therein be communed and disputed in that council'. This would ensure that 'the king not be counselled by men of his chamber, of his household, nor other which cannot counsel'.[5] This was not merely a response to some of the Yorkist grievances of the 1450s, but a viewpoint wholly consistent with the concerns of Lancastrian government in the 1420s, 1430s, and 1440s. Fortescue's other writings reinforced a vision of good government firmly grounded in Lancastrian precedents. His concern for justice and the primacy of the common law, as well as his plans for fiscal stability based on the proper management of the crown's resources, echoed the debates that had characterised Lancastrian parliament and council meetings since 1399.

For the exiles in Saint-Mihiell en Bar, the focus of their imagined Lancastrian future was, of course, the young Edward of Lancaster. There is evidence of a concerted attempt to educate the prince in the three dominant strands of Lancastrianism: martial prowess, justice and good government, and piety. While these were the standard elements of princely education in the late Middle Ages, to the exiles these virtues had taken on a decidedly Lancastrian identity. In the first of these it seems their efforts were made easier by Edward's own rather bloodthirsty bellicosity. In his *De Laudibus Legum Anglie* ('In Praise of the Laws of England') Fortescue described how the prince, by the late 1460s, 'gave himself over entirely to martial exercises', taming steeds with his spurs and delighting in attacking his companions 'sometimes with a lance, sometimes with a sword, sometimes with other weapons'.[6] In 1467 the Milanese ambassador reported that Edward spoke of 'nothing but cutting heads off and making war'.[7] It was to temper this side of his character and to prepare him to be a Lancastrian prince that Fortescue penned *De Laudibus* and other authors prepared similarly didactic material for the prince. These texts reveal their authors' attempts to reconcile the various strands of Lancastrianism. Fortescue, for instance, stressed that the study of law was as important a princely virtue as martial prowess, and that law and justice itself was 'the object of all royal administration'.[8] Moreover, he argued that justice arising from a secure knowledge of the law had been practised by the biblical kings of Israel, thus emphasising the sacral nature of Lancastrian kingship. It is likely that the finely illustrated copy of the *New Statutes of England*, now in the library of the Yale Law School, was commissioned around this time for Prince Edward, designed to enable the prince to put Fortescue's teachings into practice. Its illustrations showed English kings in prayer, reinforcing the link between prayer and justice offered in Fortescue's work. This concept had been intrinsic to the idea of kingship during the reigns of Edward's father, grandfather, and great-grandfather.[9] These themes also occur in *The Active Policy of a Prince*, an advice poem written in the mid 1460s by George Ashby, a Lancastrian servant recently released from Yorkist captivity. Ashby's poem draws upon a tradition of Lancastrian poetic counsel that stretched back to Gower, Hoccleve, and Lydgate, who were explicitly and implicitly referenced by the author. Like Fortescue, Ashby stressed the importance of law and justice as the foundations of Lancastrian kingship, but he also highlighted the true royal blood and legitimacy of the Lancastrian dynasty in contrast to the usurping Yorkists.

Yet, before the Lancastrian polity could be rebuilt, the usurper Edward IV had to be deposed and Henry VI restored to the throne. To this end Fortescue and Queen Margaret followed twin paths: first, to exploit and foster opposition to the Yorkist regime at home, and second, to elicit support among European princes. The latter was assisted by the marriage in 1464 of Edward IV to an English widow, Elizabeth Wydeville. This ended the negotiations for a marriage between Edward and a French princess which had been pursued by the earl of Warwick. The gulf between England and France was confirmed in 1468 by the marriage of Edward's sister, Margaret, to Charles the Bold, the new duke of Burgundy, and the English king's announcement of his intention to reopen the Hundred Years' War. Queen Margaret's policy since the start of her exile on the Continent had been to prevent an alliance between Yorkist England and the other European powers. In August 1463 a visit to Duke Philip (where she had turned up poorly dressed and with only a small entourage) had resulted only in fair words and gifts. Similarly, she received little comfort from the Holy Roman Emperor or King Henry IV of Castile. From 1467, however, with the assistance of her brother Duke John of Calabria, the Lancastrians began to receive more encouraging signs from Louis XI. In his memoranda, written around this time for a French audience, Fortescue was keen to point out the very real benefits France would enjoy if Henry VI was restored to the throne. He pointed out the natural affinity between the Houses of Valois and Lancaster (something Fortescue was equally keen to play down to his English audience) and promised a treaty of perpetual peace. To Louis XI, one of the most consummate politicians of the fifteenth century, the Lancastrians offered another opportunity to divide his enemies. His growing support for Margaret's cause was part of a wider policy that saw him invade the duchy of Brittany, forcing the feeble Duke Francis II to abandon his treaty obligations to Edward IV and make his own treaty with Charles the Bold. Moreover, Louis XI fostered his friendship with the earl of Warwick, Edward IV's erstwhile chief counsellor, whose relationship with the king was becoming increasingly strained as a result of the Burgundian alliance and the growing influence of the Wydevilles at court.

The earl of Warwick's growing unease at Edward's policy was also a principal target of Lancastrian plans to foment discord in England. As early as February 1467, according to the pro-Yorkist Milanese ambassador, Duke John of Calabria was already suggesting that Warwick's unhappiness could drive him into an alliance with the Lancastrians. In the following year a major conspiracy was unearthed in London, involving the former mayor Sir Thomas Cook, which linked the earl to the exiled Lancastrians. In the spring of 1469 Queen Margaret's chancellor, Dr Ralph Makerell, was arrested in Norfolk. It has been argued that he was instrumental in arranging an accommodation between Warwick and Margaret and it is perhaps significant that he was pardoned in the autumn of that year, when English government was effectively in the hands of the earl. Historians have traditionally given the credit to Louis XI for reconciling Warwick with his former queen, highlighting the way in which the French king had courted the earl, aware of his disaffection with Edward's pro-Burgundian policy. Yet it seems this underestimates the powerful arguments made by Fortescue and other Lancastrians to the French court and their efforts in encouraging Lancastrian sympathies and Warwick's discontent at home. Whatever the machinations of the various parties involved, during the summer of 1470 a settlement was reached between Margaret, Warwick, and Louis XI to the effect that the earl would support Margaret in restoring Henry VI to the English throne.

The treaty of Angers on 22 July 1470 represented the most extraordinary turnaround in Lancastrian fortunes. Formally brokered by Louis XI, the meeting saw Margaret reconciled with Warwick and Edward IV's brother, George, duke of Clarence, who had allied himself with the rebel earl a year earlier by marrying Warwick's daughter, Isabel. The pact was sealed with another marriage alliance, this time between Prince Edward and Warwick's younger daughter, Anne. It was stage-managed to highlight the regal status of the House of Lancaster, but also to underline that Warwick, in helping to depose Henry VI in 1461, had acted in accordance with Lancastrian principles of good government and in the interest of the commonwealth. A newsletter, *The maner and guyding bitwene the quene Margarete and of here soone and therle of Warrewic*, designed for circulation in England, was composed to demonstrate the good grace of both parties. As the two parties were introduced, Margaret explained how she would struggle to pardon the earl 'which has been the greatest cause of the fall of King Henry, her and of her son'. Hearing this, Warwick confessed on bended knee to his part in the downfall of the House of Lancaster, but claimed that Henry and Margaret 'by their false counsel' had attempted to destroy him and his fellow rebel lords. He defended his actions, saying he had a 'rightwise cause to labour their undoing' and that he had done nothing 'but that a noble man outraged and despaired ought to have done'. Nevertheless, given his shameful treatment at the hands of Edward IV, he was now determined to assist Henry in regaining his throne and offered the bond of the French king as surety. Margaret, taking the advice of Louis, as well as that of her father's servants, then pardoned Warwick. It was agreed that Anne Neville should remain with Margaret and that her marriage to Prince Edward would not be concluded until Warwick had returned to England with an army and defeated Edward IV.[10]

Angers was the culmination of almost a decade of effort on the part of Margaret and her fellow Lancastrian loyalists to see Henry VI restored to the English throne. She had achieved this partly through her own dogged determination and sense of duty to her husband and son, but also because she had been able to employ aspects of the Lancastrian legacy to appeal to potential supporters both in the British Isles and on the Continent. She had exploited the status of the House of Lancaster as a European princely dynasty to build contacts at other princely courts and used her own family relations to enlist French support. The extended Lancastrian royal family, the Beauforts and the duke of Exeter, even if they at times pursued an agenda driven by personal concerns rather than wider dynastic ones and even if their status was problematic in the eyes of Fortescue and other Lancastrian supporters, reminded the princely courts of Europe of the regality of the Lancastrian line. The political writings of Sir John Fortescue during the 1460s also highlighted the long-standing connections (and differences) between England and France, setting Lancastrian kingship firmly in a European context. Yet Fortescue also brought to the fore other aspects of the Lancastrian legacy: the importance of common law, themes of justice, good government and counsel, and the importance of fiscal stability in ensuring effective royal government. That these arguments were accepted by both foreign princes and the English was testimony to the efforts of the Lancastrian court in exile and the complexity of European politics. That these same arguments were employed by the opposition to Edward IV between 1469 and 1471, effectively turning the Yorkist arguments of the 1450s against their erstwhile champions to restore Henry VI to the throne, was testimony to the endurance of Lancastrian ideals and the extent to which they dominated the political culture of fifteenth-century England.

The Readeption and the end of the House of Lancaster

By 1469 the early promise of Edward IV's reign had faded to a distant memory. He had reneged on his promise to invade France (but kept the taxation granted for this purpose), while grasping courtiers dominated the king's council and royal patronage, keeping other lords from their rightful position in the realm. The individual who felt this situation most acutely was none other than Richard Neville, earl of Warwick, one of the original 'Yorkist lords' and Edward's most important lieutenant in the capture of the throne. Warwick's relationship with Edward had been strained in 1464 by the latter's clandestine marriage to Elizabeth Grey *née* Wydeville, a widow whose father had been one of the leading Lancastrian lords during the 1450s. The problem had been exacerbated by Edward's pro-Burgundian foreign policy (culminating in the marriage of his sister Margaret to Duke Charles the Bold in 1468) and the growing influence of his queen's Wydeville and Grey relations at court. Warwick made his move in June 1469. In the April of that year there had been a popular uprising in Yorkshire, led by one Robin of Redesdale. The rebels' grievances were the familiar ones (taxation, evil counsellors, and local misgovernment) and the uprising was suppressed without difficulty. Yet, as soon as this rebellion was over the county rose again, this time led by one Robin of Holderness. The principal grievance this time was local clerical taxation, but the rebels also demanded the restoration of the Percy family to the earldom of Northumberland.

This second insurrection was also easily put down, but a third rising in June, almost certainly engineered by the disgruntled Warwick, was far more serious. The rebel leader was a member of the influential Conyers family. The head of the family, Sir John, was Warwick's steward in Richmondshire and the rebellion in effect mobilised the Nevilles' Middleham affinity against the king. Warwick now put the second part of his plan into action. On 6 July he crossed to Calais in the company of Archbishop Neville, his daughter Isabel, and the king's increasingly disgruntled brother, George, duke of Clarence. Five days later he married his daughter to Clarence against the king's express wishes, and on the following day the rebel lords issued a manifesto against those who sought to subvert the commonwealth.[11] It condemned the king's evil counsellors, naming the queen's father Earl Rivers, William Herbert, the new Yorkist earl of Pembroke, and Humphrey Stafford, the new earl of Devon, and several other courtiers. Warwick and Clarence summoned their supporters to meet them at Canterbury on 16 July and from there they marched to London and onwards to Coventry. Edward seems to have been caught unawares and he hastily despatched the earls of Pembroke and Devon north to meet the rebels. On 26 July Pembroke was routed at Edgecote near Banbury and later taken to Northampton and executed. Devon had fled before the battle but was soon afterwards murdered by a mob in Bridgwater. Worse followed: Earl Rivers was taken and put to death, and then the king, whose followers seem to have deserted him, was intercepted by Archbishop Neville and taken to Warwick castle.

Now Warwick and Clarence attempted to impose their rule on Edward IV. In an attempt to give their coup an air of legitimacy they summoned a parliament to meet at York on 22 September. Unlike Henry VI, however, Edward IV was not prepared to rule as a puppet. Warwick's regime lacked any real mandate from his fellow lords and the Kingmaker's inability to govern was demonstrated by escalating local disorder and, most seriously, a new pro-Lancastrian rebellion in the north led by Sir Humphrey Neville, Warwick's kinsman from the senior branch of the Neville family. Edward and Warwick moved north together to suppress the rising, executing Sir Humphrey and his brother Charles at York on 29 September. By October, Warwick and Clarence were forced to admit their failure: some sort of settlement was reached and Edward was able to return to London, his royal power restored. Despite the ostensible air of reconciliation, there seems little doubt that by the spring of 1470 Edward had finally resolved to break Warwick's power. Warwick's animosity towards the Wydevilles and his murder of Earl Rivers proved an insurmountable obstacle to any lasting settlement, just as the duke of York's rivalry with the duke of Somerset had dashed any hopes of reconciliation in the early 1450s. One contemporary observer noted ominously that while 'the king himself has good language of the lords of Clarence, Warwick, the archbishop of York, and earl of Oxford, saying they are his best friends, his household men have other language'.[12]

By early 1470 local disorder had again become endemic as men took advantage of the instability of royal government to pursue their private quarrels with violence. One such dispute occurred in Lincolnshire, where Richard, Lord Welles, his son, Sir Robert, and his son-in-law attacked Sir Thomas Burgh's manor house at Gainsborough. Burgh, however, was also master of the king's horse and Edward chose this dispute to reassert his royal authority. Lord Welles obeyed the king's command to appear before him, but Sir Robert refused and instead instigated a general rebellion. Warwick and Clarence fuelled the uprising by spreading rumours of the king's intention to crush the rebels without mercy. On 12 March the Lincolnshire men were routed by Edward's army at the battle of 'Losecote Field', near Empingham in Rutland. Welles was captured and his confession damned the rebel lords, claiming that they planned to make Clarence king.[13] Edward now moved north to confront Warwick's supporters, receiving the submission of Lord Scrope of Bolton and Sir John Conyers. On 24 March the king declared Warwick and Clarence traitors and promoted Warwick's brother, John Neville, to the title of Marquess Montagu, partly in compensation for his loss of the earldom of Northumberland but also in recognition of his continued loyalty. Warwick and Clarence, however, escaped Edward's wrath. They set sail from Devon and, after failing to drop anchor at Southampton, were refused entry to Calais. Finally, on 1 May, the rebel lords landed in Honfleur, where they sought the assistance of the king of France, Louis XI.

It was against the backdrop of these turbulent events in England that Warwick made his accommodation with the exiled Lancastrians at Angers. Since the summer of 1469 the rebels had used the now traditional rhetoric of evil counsellors and the maintenance of the commonwealth to attack Edward IV and the queen's family. Warwick and Clarence had explicitly appealed to the commons in a series of letters and manifestos that recalled the Yorkist lords' complaints against the government of Henry VI in the 1450s. Following the treaty at Angers, the rebel lords composed an open letter addressed to the 'true commons' of England, justifying their actions in supporting Henry VI not in terms of dynastic legitimacy but through an appeal to the language of the 1450s. They highlighted their commitment to the 'wealth of the crown and the advancing of the commonwealth of England and for reproving of falsehood and the oppression of poor people'.[14] There can be little doubt that this was empty rhetoric, although the concern shown by the authorities back in England to suppress the letter demonstrates the durability of these Lancastrian ideals. Edward IV was right to be concerned. Early in August rebellion broke out again in the north of England, led by Warwick's ally, Henry, Lord Fitzhugh. The king responded quickly, marching north with his household. The rebels faded away and on 10 September Edward granted pardons to the rebel leaders, but three days later, with the king still in York, Warwick and Clarence landed in Devon.

Once in England, Warwick moved quickly. He recovered his artillery and marched to Coventry. His return to England was marked by a popular show of enthusiasm and the commons of Kent rose in support of the earl, while the earl of Shrewsbury and Thomas, Lord Stanley also joined the rebels' banner. Most important of all, Marquess Montagu (who had recently been replaced as warden of the East and Middle March by the earl of Northumberland) initially raised men on Edward's behalf but then ignored the king's summons and joined his brother. Edward's position was now hopeless; he was in no position to give battle to Montagu, let alone Warwick's growing army. Accompanied by Anthony, Earl Rivers, William, Lord Hastings, William, Lord Saye and perhaps 3,000 followers he fled to King's Lynn and from there took ship to the Netherlands on 2 October. Meanwhile, on 3 October Bishop Waynflete escorted the feeble Henry VI from his prison cell to the King's Lodgings within the Tower and, two days later, Warwick led his army into London and submitted himself to the restored king.

Henry himself cut a pathetic figure: one chronicler noted he was 'not so cleanly kept as should seem such a prince'.[15] His 'Readeption' had been proclaimed at St Paul's Cross on 30 September, and on 13 October he made his first public appearance for some five years at a solemn crown-wearing at St Paul's cathedral. Henry spent the five months of his second reign largely confined to the bishop of London's palace, awaiting the return of Queen Margaret and Prince Edward; indeed, as Wolffe concludes, 'there is no evidence that Henry did anything at all'.[16] Meanwhile the Readeption regime in England struggled to assert its authority. Warwick presided over the government, while George Neville, archbishop of York, was reinstated as chancellor and Marquess Montagu was again appointed warden of the East and Middle Marches. There were, however, few other demonstrations of partisanship. Several prominent Yorkists (including Queen Elizabeth) fled to sanctuary, but many more, including the duke of Norfolk, the Bourchiers, Lord Dynham, and even the queen's younger brother, Sir Richard Wydeville, were reconciled with the new regime. The duke of Clarence occupied a more ambiguous position and it was not until February 1471 that he was appointed lieutenant of Ireland.[17] Warwick summoned a parliament in Henry VI's name to assemble at Westminster on 26 November 1470. Its records have not survived, but only Edward and his brother, Gloucester, were attainted and little else seems to have been achieved. Indeed, the political nation looked anxiously to the Continent for Edward's next move.

Initially at least Edward had received a lukewarm reception from his brother-in-law, the duke of Burgundy. He and his father had supported the Lancastrian cause in 1459–61 and, despite his marriage to Edward's sister, the ducal court still played host to the exiled dukes of Somerset and Exeter. Duke Charles, however, feared, quite rightly, that Warwick had promised Louis XI to commit England to war with Burgundy. By November the duke appears to have been warming towards his Yorkist guests. The following month Louis repudiated the treaty of Péronne and declared Charles's French lands forfeit. The duke was left with no choice: on 31 December he granted Edward £20,000 to assist in his recovery of his throne and Edward soon set about assembling an invasion fleet. Edward and his small band of supporters (probably fewer than 2,000) set sail from Holland on 11 March. The following day they were prevented from landing at Cromer by forces loyal to the earl of Oxford, but two days later they finally dropped anchor at Ravenspur at the mouth of the Humber. The regime's hopes of thwarting Edward's return lay initially with Marquess Montagu and the earl of Northumberland, but neither moved against the former king. Edward began to draw his supporters to his banner and he marched to confront Warwick, then at Coventry. Crucially, on 3 April, just outside the town of Warwick, Edward met and was reconciled with Clarence. Faced with overwhelming force, the Kingmaker refused battle and retreated south.

The Lancastrian regime's response was dilatory in the extreme. On 11 April, Maundy Thursday, Archbishop Neville paraded Henry on horseback around London. Wearing 'a long blue gown of velvet', the archbishop led Henry by hand along Cheapside and Cornhill before returning to the bishop of London's palace on the north side of the cathedral. One London chronicle stated that the king was accompanied by 'divers lords', but according to the later London *Great Chronicle* he was accompanied by only a small band of menial servants, while his sword was carried before him by 'Lord Zouche'. The procession was a disaster, 'more like a play than the showing of a prince to win men's hearts', and its hastily conceived nature and ambiguous symbolic message probably explains the confusion in chroniclers' accounts of the event. While the London *Great Chronicle*, almost certainly correctly, states that Henry processed on Maundy Thursday, *Warkworth's Chronicle* gives the previous day. Similarly, the 'old blue gown' Henry wore was the royal colour of mourning, suited to Maundy Thursday and Good Friday, and not necessarily a sign that 'he had no more to change with'.[18] Finally, even the identity of his sword-bearer is confused by the chroniclers: William, Lord Zouche, a Lancastrian supporter who had been pardoned by Edward IV in March 1461, had died in 1468, while John, his son and heir, was only twelve years of age. The sword-bearer may, in fact, have been that old Lancastrian stalwart, Ralph Boteler, Lord Sudeley.[19] Whatever the truth of the matter, Henry's appearance certainly failed to rally the Londoners to the Lancastrians' cause. The Yorkists entered London on the same day as Archbishop Neville's ill-judged public procession. Henry VI was soon captured and returned to the Tower. His reaction underlined how removed he had become from the reality of politics: according to one eye-witness, on meeting Edward, Henry approached him saying 'Cousin of York, you are very welcome. I hold my life to be in no danger in your hands'. Edward assured him of his safety.[20]

With Henry once again incarcerated in the Tower, thoughts turned to the defeat of the Kingmaker. On 13 April Edward IV marched out of London to confront Warwick, then at St Albans. On the morning of the next day, Easter Sunday, both armies were arrayed just outside the town of Barnet. Edward took the initiative, displaying the prowess and vigour that had characterised his actions in 1461, and attacked, despite a thick fog. The battle was savage: on the Yorkist side Lords Cromwell and Saye were killed in the mêlée and Gloucester and Rivers injured, while for the Lancastrians Montagu was cut down and the duke of Exeter left for dead. At the height of the battle Warwick's men had mistaken the earl of Oxford's badge of the 'star with streams' for Edward's 'sun with streams' and attacked, causing Oxford's contingent to cry 'Treason' and flee. The Kingmaker himself was killed while attempting to flee the field as the battle turned against the Lancastrians. In three hours of fighting Edward had reasserted his kingly authority through a stunning demonstration of his own personal prowess.

Now there was still the small matter of Queen Margaret and her Lancastrian supporters to deal with. On the same day as Edward had defeated Warwick at Barnet, the Lancastrian exiles had finally returned from France, making landfall at Weymouth. Hearing of the Kingmaker's demise, Margaret resolved to fight on and marched for Wales to join forces with Jasper Tudor. Once again, Edward demonstrated remarkable energy. Those who had fought at Barnet were tired and many were injured, but the king galvanised his supporters by celebrating St George's Day in the Garter Chapel at Windsor. From there he left for the West Country with an army of some 5,000 men. The Yorkists were at Malmesbury by 1 May, with the Lancastrians encamped at Bristol, where Margaret received reinforcements and artillery. There then followed a race to prevent the Lancastrians from crossing the Severn into Wales. The city of Gloucester refused them entry and Margaret was forced to attempt the crossing at Tewkesbury. Edward had kept pace with his enemies and when the Lancastrians found the ford at Lower Lode impassable they were obliged to give battle. The battle of Tewkesbury, fought on 4 May 1471, was a decisive victory for Edward IV. The Yorkist host was deployed in the customary three 'battles' or formations: the vanguard commanded by Gloucester, the centre by the king himself, and the rear-guard by Lord Hastings. The Lancastrians were similarly deployed: Edmund Beaufort, duke of Somerset, commanded the battle facing Gloucester; Warwick's former lieutenant at Calais, Lord Wenlock, stood opposite Edward; while John Courtenay, the recently restored Lancastrian earl of Devon, was arrayed against Hastings. A heavy artillery bombardment by the Yorkists goaded Somerset into the attack, the duke moving against Edward's own battle in search of a quick and decisive outcome. An attack by Yorkist cavalry appears to have halted Somerset's advance, and before long their attack faltered. Devon and Wenlock were killed in the fighting (Wenlock perhaps by Somerset, who, enraged at his failure to support his attack, accused him of treason), while, most significantly of all, Edward, Prince of Wales, was cut down as he fled the field. Somerset himself sought sanctuary in Tewkesbury Abbey but two days later he was dragged out and summarily executed, along with other prominent Lancastrian prisoners. Queen Margaret, her cause finally lost, attempted to find sanctuary but by 14 May she too was in Edward's custody. The battle of Tewkesbury did not immediately end opposition to Edward's restoration. At the end of April the men of Richmondshire rose in support of Henry VI, but on hearing the news of the Lancastrian defeat they submitted themselves to the earl of Northumberland as Edward prepared to march north against them. More serious was the rebellion of the Bastard of Fauconberg, Warwick's illegitimate cousin. He had been charged with patrolling the Channel, and on hearing the news of Warwick's defeat at Barnet he had returned to Calais. With 300 men of the garrison he had crossed to Kent, where he recruited support in the Cinque Ports and Canterbury, and on 12 May he attacked the city of London. The Tower and London Bridge were well defended and Fauconberg retreated to Blackheath. Six days later he and his followers withdrew at the approach of the king's army. Edward entered the capital in triumph on 21 May.

Just one piece of outstanding business remained: what to do with Henry VI? The former king was lodged in the Tower and, according to the pro-Yorkist *Arrivall*, on hearing the news of the death of his son at the battle of Tewkesbury 'he utterly despaired of any manner of hope or relief'. In fact, 'he took it so great despite, ire and indignation, that of pure displeasure and melancholy he died the 23rd May'.[21] The truth is probably less melodramatic. Edward could not allow this alternative source of royal legitimacy to continue and almost certainly on his return to the capital ordered Henry to be put to death. The identity of Henry's killer remains uncertain, but by the 1480s it was rumoured that Richard, duke of Gloucester, the future Richard III, was responsible. Certainly to Shakespeare and his Tudor audience, the murder of the saintly Henry VI was a suitable addition to the Black Legend of England's most notorious king, but there is no firm evidence of Richard's guilt. The body was first laid in an open coffin in St Paul's and then at the Blackfriars, where a funeral mass was said. Then, accompanied by soldiers from the Calais garrison, Henry's body was carried by barge up-river to the Chertsey Abbey, where it was buried in the Lady Chapel. Queen Margaret, a prisoner in the Tower, was soon transferred to the custody of her old friend, Alice Chaucer, the dowager duchess of Suffolk at Wallingford, where she remained until 1475, when she was ransomed by Louis XI. She died on 20 August 1482 and was buried in her father's tomb in the cathedral of St Maurice in Angers.

Conclusion

There is little doubt that Henry VI cut a forlorn and impotent figure during the last decade of his life. This was perhaps most apparent during the few months of his ill-fated Readeption in

1470–71, when the king's public appearances seem to have further undermined royal authority. Henry continued to attract men to his banner, although how far this represented a personal commitment to him or a more general commitment to the House of Lancaster and Lancastrian ideals is unclear. Interestingly, however, there is no evidence that the Readeption regime made any moves to resurrect formal institutions, whether conciliar or otherwise, to mitigate the king's obvious shortcomings. Perhaps the revival of Henry's personal rule was a necessary fiction in 1470–71 to counter the rival claim of the virile and capable Edward IV. Whatever the truth, it is clear that Henry did nothing to prevent the collapse of the Lancastrian dynasty: he was not present at either Barnet or Tewkesbury and died ignominiously in captivity.

Yet Lancastrianism remained strong throughout the 1460s. On an individual level many men retained their loyalty to the House of Lancaster. Even within the Yorkist regime the opposition to Edward IV, led by the earl of Warwick, used language that was distinctly Lancastrian in origin, even to the point of reissuing one of Cade's manifestos of 1450. Edward's response to the crisis of 1470–71 was to promise to live up to widely held Lancastrian ideals of good government and it is no surprise that he enlisted the support of that most committed of Lancastrian theorists, Sir John Fortescue, to legitimise the Yorkist regime in the 1470s. In 1470–71 Henry VI briefly transcended personal monarchy; his personal fitness to rule as king was secondary to his symbolic role. Despite his proven inadequacy, he epitomised the values of good government that had been the hallmark of the Lancastrian revolution of 1399 and which were the longest-lived aspect of the Lancastrian legacy in fifteenth-century England.

Notes

1 *The Paston Letters*, ed. James Gairdner (6 vols, 1904), iii, 307.

2 Michael Brown, *The Black Douglases* (East Linton, 1998), 183–99.

3 John Warkworth, *Chronicle of the First Thirteen Years of the Reign of King Edward IV*, ed. J.O. Halliwell (Camden Society, 1839), 5.

4 John Blacman, *Henry the Sixth*, ed. M.R. James (1919), 44.

5 *The Politics of Fifteenth Century England: John Vale's Book*, ed. Margaret Kekewich Coilin Richmond, Anne E. Sutton, Livia Visser-Fuchs and John L. Watts (Stroud, 1995), 223.

6 John Fortescue, *De Laudibus Legum Anglie*, ed. S.B. Chrimes (Cambridge, 1949), 2–3.

7 *Calendar of State Papers . . . Milan, Volume 1*, ed. A.B. Hinds (1912), 117.

8 Fortescue, *De Laudibus Legum Anglie*, ed. Chrimes, 12–13.

9 Rosemarie McGerr, *A Lancastrian Mirror for Princes: the Yale Law School New Statutes of England* (Bloomington, IN, 2011), 102–21.

10 *The Politics of Fifteenth Century England*, ed. Kekewich *et al*, 215–18.

11 Warkworth, *Chronicle*, 47.

12 *Paston Letters and Papers of the Fifteenth Century*, ed. N. Davies (2 vols, Early English Text Society, 1971–6), i, 245.

13 'Chronicle of the Rebellion in Lincolnshire, 1470', ed. J.G. Nichols, in *Camden Miscellany I* (Camden Society, 1847), 10.

14 *The Politics of Fifteenth Century England*, ed. Kekewich *et al*, 215–18.

15 Warkworth, *Chronicle*, 11.

16 B.P. Wolffe, *Henry VI* (1981), 342.

17 *The History of the Arrivall of King Edward IV, A.D 1471*, ed. J. Bruce (Camden Society, 1838), 10.

18 C.L. Kingsford, *Chronicles of London* (Oxford, 1905), 184; *The Great Chronicle of London*, ed. A.H. Thomas and I.D. Thornley (1938), 215.

19 I owe this suggestion to Hannes Kleineke.

20 Wolffe, *Henry VI*, 345.

21 *The Arrivall*, ed. Bruce, 38.

11 Conclusion

John Blacman and the saintly king

Following his murder in the Tower of London on the night of 22/23 May 1471, Henry VI's body was moved to St Paul's cathedral before a funeral service at the Blackfriars. It was then transported by river, guarded by a contingent of soldiers from the Calais garrison, to Chertsey Abbey. The king was buried in the Benedictine abbey's Lady Chapel. Edward IV clearly hoped that the low-key burial would mean that the last Lancastrian king would fall into obscurity, but he could not have been more wrong. Within a couple of years of his death Henry was being venerated as a saint and martyr, and during the last two decades of the fifteenth century a cult developed around his tomb, first at Chertsey, then from 1484 at Windsor, which rivalled that of St Thomas Becket in popularity. Miracles resulted from prayers to the dead king, while mentions of his name in the liturgy and his depiction in statues and stained-glass windows were testimony to his cult's popularity. In death Henry's reputation was transformed. During the reign of Henry VII efforts began to officially canonise him, a goal not yet realised when the Reformation under Henry VIII broke the relationship between the English Church and the Church of Rome.

The popularity of Henry VI was, as far as we can see, spontaneous. Yet Henry's cult and his reputation as a royal martyr were part of the Lancastrian legacy that had shaped English politics and culture throughout the later Middle Ages. Henry's piety, and how his servants and contemporaries viewed and wrote about it, were later accommodated into a framework of belief that accepted him as a saint and martyr. These reactions can all be partly understood in terms of the forms of religious practice that were closely associated with the House of Lancaster. Two sources are vital to understanding the posthumous reputation of the king. First, there is the account of Henry's life, and particularly of his religious beliefs and character, written in the early 1480s by John Blacman, a fellow of Eton College and intimate of the king. Second, there is the compilation of miracles supposedly performed by the late king and other evidence, material and liturgical, that documents Henry's popularity and reputation in the decades before the Reformation. Taken together they provide an important insight both into the nature of Henry's kingship and how his rule had been understood by his servants and subjects.

John Blacman's Henry VI

John Blacman was an Oxford graduate who resigned his fellowship at Merton College, Oxford in 1443 to enter Eton College. He served there as precentor until 1452, when he was appointed warden of the King's Hall in Cambridge. At Windsor he knew the king personally, celebrating mass for the community there and administering to the king himself on several occasions. It is clear from his writings that he was a personal companion and spiritual guide to Henry VI. In 1453 Blacman resigned his positions at Eton and Cambridge and three years later he became dean of Westbury-on-Trym in Gloucestershire. By 1458, however, he had abandoned his living and entered the London Charterhouse, an austere Carthusian monastery. Although he never became a full member of that order, in 1465 he had moved to the Witham Charterhouse in Somerset. His status as a *clericus reditus* (a monk who had not yet abandoned his worldly goods) allowed him to acquire a large library, composed principally of devotional works, and to acquire a reputation as a scholar. Probably at some point in the 1470s he set about writing his *Collectarium Mansuetudinum et Bonorum Morum Regis Henrici VI* ('A Compilation of the Meekness and Good Life of King Henry VI'). Its intended audience is unknown, but it was certainly not written as part of an official attempt to canonise the late king by Henry VII. Indeed, it may have been written for Blacman's fellow Carthusians as a comment on ideal models of lay piety.[1] Blacman was probably dead by the end of 1485 and his text was not widely known until 1510, when it was printed by Robert Copland. Thomas

Hearne reprinted Copland's text in 1732, but it was not translated into English until 1919.[2]

Blacman's portrait of Henry VI is that of a king above the everyday concerns of politics and government, driven by his own spiritual needs and those of his household. The king's piety is clear in Blacman's account. He was ostentatious in his devotions: 'he was never pleased to sit upon a seat or to walk to and fro as men of the world; but always with bared head, at least while divine office was being celebrated . . . kneeling one may say continuously before his book, with eyes and hands upturned, he was at pains to utter with the celebrant (but with the inward voice) the mass-prayers, epistles, and gospels'.[3] He would frequently act as server while the priest sang mass and marked his devotion to the Five Wounds of Christ by insisting that 'a certain dish . . . as it were red with blood, should be set on his table by his almoner before any other course'.[4] Henry even experienced visions and heard voices: 'his privy servants say that the king often saw our Lord Jesus presenting Himself in human form in the sacrament of the altar in the hands of the priest', while other household servants reported that 'he was wont almost at every moment to raise his eyes heavenward like a denizen of heaven or one rapt, being for the time not conscious of himself or those about him, as if he were a man in a trance or on the verge of heaven'. The king also claimed to have had revelations from the Virgin, from John the Baptist, and from the former archbishops of Canterbury, SS. Dunstan and Anselm.[5] Henry also complained of how the demands of royal life took him away from his devotion. Blacman relates the tale of how 'a mighty duke' knocked on the door of the king's chamber while Henry was engaged with him discussing 'holy books'. The king said: 'They do so interrupt me that by day or night I can hardly snatch a moment to be refreshed by reading of any holy teaching without disturbance.'[6]

According to Blacman, Henry's devotion was as apparent in his public life as it was in his personal piety. Blacman approved of his chastity, claiming he was never unfaithful to Queen Margaret and that he had even 'made a covenant with his eyes that they should never look unchastely upon any woman'. This concern he extended to his household and the boys being educated at Windsor. When bare-breasted dancing girls appeared to entertain the court, the king stormed out of his chamber, while he 'would keep watch through hidden windows of his chamber, lest any foolish impertinence of women coming into the house should grow to a head, and cause the fall of any of his household'.[7] Similarly, he would rebuke any of the boys being educated at Windsor who might wander into the court 'lest his young lambs should come to relish the corrupt deeds and habits of his courtiers'.[8] Henry's piety was also evident in the way he eschewed princely extravagance. He disapproved of his courtiers' practice of bringing their hawks into church, apparently disliked hunting himself, and appears to have considered the court luxurious and corrupting. Blacman recalls that the king often wore round-toed shoes and boots 'like a farmer's' and that he usually wore a long, hooded black gown 'like a townsman'. He also claimed that the king habitually wore a hair shirt under his robes during crown-wearing ceremonies.[9]

In Blacman's account Henry's 'public vices are redefined as private virtues'.[10] In other words, he does not gloss over the king's obvious shortcomings but presents them as actions consistent with a recognisable and laudable spirituality. Henry was aware, Blacman argued, of the 'pest of avarice'. He eschewed personal wealth, was generous to the poor, and 'enriched very many others with great gifts or offices'. Similarly, he did not 'oppress his subjects with unreasonable taxes' but 'relieved them from his own resources . . . and . . . preferred to live uprightly among them, rather than that they should pine in poverty, trodden down by his harshness'. This generosity operated on both a national level and a very personal one: on hearing that one of his servants had been robbed of twenty gold nobles, the king reimbursed the unfortunate man, warning him to take better care of his belongings in future and urging him to forgive the thief.[11] Thus one of the key complaints levelled against Henry – that his largesse reduced the crown to poverty – was represented as a Christian, princely virtue. Similarly, Henry's willingness to pardon those who had wronged him was redefined in positive terms. His decision in 1447 to pardon the four servants of the duke of Gloucester as they stood on the gallows awaiting execution was provided as evidence of his 'patience' and 'kind compassion'. Similarly, his well-attested desire to accommodate the Yorkist lords in 1459 was cited in support of his merciful nature. Again Blacman related specific incidents in support of his general claims: to the man who had wounded him at the first battle of St Albans Henry offered forgiveness, stating 'Forsothe and forsothe, ye do fouly to smite a king anointed so.' In all this Blacman was keen to present Henry in imitation of Christ himself. By turning the other cheek to those who sought his deposition and ultimately his death, the king had assured his place in heaven alongside the saints.[12]

As Roger Lovatt demonstrated, Blacman's account of Henry VI is a valuable historical source, the fullest pen portrait we have of the king from one who knew him personally between 1443 and the mid-1450s. Moreover, several of Blacman's assertions about the king's personality and behaviour are corroborated by other accounts. He claims, for instance, that Henry was 'continually occupied either in prayer or the reading of the scriptures or of chronicles'.[13] In 1460 parliament appealed to the king's knowledge of the chronicles when asking him to adjudicate on Richard, duke of York's claim to the throne, while Abbot Whethamstede recalled how on the eve of the battle of Blore Heath Henry occupied himself in reading chronicles.[14] The king's practice of reading the Bible and other theological tracts was unusual enough to attract the attention of others. Whethamstede observed how, in 1448, Henry had contemplated the political divisions in the realm by meditating upon the scriptures. His ability to recite parts of the liturgy was commented upon as early as the 1420s, while his recovery from illness in 1454 was marked by a rediscovered ability to say matins and evensong. The king's own vernacular Bible, in itself a remarkable possession for a fifteenth-century layman, is preserved today in Oxford's Bodleian Library.[15] Other aspects of Henry's behaviour as described by Blacman, such as his habitual use of the oath 'Forsothe', are similarly repeated in other contemporary sources, while his disapproval of naked bathing at the spa in Bath earned the city an official rebuke from Bishop Beckington within a year of the king's visit.[16]

The real value of Blacman's collection, however, is that it reveals Henry to have been a proponent of a particular brand of late medieval piety, one that would have been recognisable and acceptable to many of his Lancastrian servants and subjects. Blacman himself was a proponent of this brand of devotional piety, characterised by its 'fervent, puritanical moralism', a disregard for worldly possessions, an asceticism reminiscent of the monastic life, and a yearning for self-improvement through individual reading and understanding of scripture and other spiritual writing. This piety was devotional, as it sought to inspire feelings of awe and reverence in the individual, and elitist, as only a few had the means to devote their lives entirely to it, but it also reached out, through a programme of translation into the vernacular, to a wider lay audience. Blacman's own commitment to this austere form of devotional piety was evident in his choice to enter the Carthusian order, but also from the surviving list of his books. It contains the works of the Church Fathers alongside classics of the new forms of lay piety popular in Europe in the later Middle Ages. They included the *Imitatio Christi* ('The Imitation of Christ'), written in the early fifteenth century by the German theologian Thomas à Kempis, and the fourteenth-century *Horologium Sapientiae* ('The Clock of Wisdom'). His library also contained works by St Bridget of Sweden and St Catherine of Siena, two of the most prominent female visionaries of the later Middle Ages. The interest among wider Lancastrian circles in St Bridget was evident in Henry V's foundation of the Bridgettine monastery at Syon.

Blacman also owned a copy of Richard Rolle's *Incendium Amoris* ('The Fire of Love'). Rolle was a mid fourteenth-century mystic and hermit. 'The Fire of Love' describes his own mystical experiences and provided a guide to achieving such states of spiritual rapture. In some part Rolle based his work on the instructions written for monks by the twelfth-century archbishop of Canterbury St Anselm, but he also drew on biblical, patristic, and other traditions. Rolle was one of the most widely read authors of the early fifteenth century: his 'Fire of Love' was translated into English in the mid 1430s and some manuscripts suggest that his work had earlier been read within Lollard circles.[17] The type of ascetic piety Rolle advocated, one in which a retreat from the everyday was advocated as the only true means of salvation, was controversial on both theological and practical grounds. Another popular late fourteenth-century author, Walter Hilton, distanced himself from Rolle and those who measured the closeness of their relationship to God through dramatic visions and a life lived in seclusion. In *The Scale of Perfection*, written in the early 1390s, Hilton argued that an individual's knowledge of God was best achieved through the sacraments of the Church and, like pilgrimage, involved a long and arduous journey of devotion and self-discovery. Moreover, this process had to be achieved while negotiating the challenges of everyday life. There is evidence to suggest that Rolle's view of a mystical union with God fast-tracked through an intense contemplative and meditative process proved attractive to a Lancastrian audience. His work was certainly read at Henry V's foundation at Syon and an English translation of 'The Fire of Love' from around 1440 appears in a manuscript life of the Lancastrian saint, St John of Bridlington.[18] Rolle's exhortation to experience God through intense prayer and devotion certainly seems to fit the model of piety that Henry VI followed. In so doing Henry was not out of step with one of the mainstreams of late medieval English lay piety. Much Middle English devotional writing of the fifteenth century 'does not simply recall Rolle's themes but is frequently quotational, recycling Rolle's own words for new audiences'.[19] Henry's piety, as described by Blacman, would thus have been recognisable to his contemporaries. Whether or not the majority of them considered it suitable behaviour for a king is open to debate.

Henry VI: saint and martyr

In the years after his death Henry VI's reputation was transformed. His failures as king were largely forgotten (in fact he developed virtues he had plainly never enjoyed during his lifetime) and he emerged as one of the most popular saints in late medieval England. The development of his cult appears to have been spontaneous, but it was later championed by successive monarchs, leading to a serious, albeit ultimately futile, attempt to have him canonised in the first decades of the sixteenth century. Henry's posthumous reputation reveals much about how the Lancastrian regime had been regarded by its subjects, and the strength of the king's cult is testimony to the durability of aspects of the Lancastrian legacy into the sixteenth century.

The rapid growth of Henry VI's cult was without parallel in late medieval England. While other 'political' saints, such as Simon de Montfort, Thomas of Lancaster, Archbishop Scrope, and even Edward II, and purely religious figures, like St John of Bridlington and Richard Rolle, encouraged cults that had a strongly local identity, Henry's popularity appears to have been nationwide. While it was naturally focused on his burial site, first at Chertsey and later at Windsor, the late king apparently performed miracles throughout the south-east of England and East Anglia. Even where the saintly Henry is not recorded to have intervened, there is evidence of popular devotion to him. As early as 1473 offerings were being made in York Minster, a practice so popular that within six years Archbishop Booth had banned it, claiming it to be in contempt of both the Church and the reigning monarch, Edward IV. From the 1480s there were numerous examples of statues and likenesses of the king appearing in parish churches throughout England. In 1480 Henry appeared alongside kings Edmund, Olaf, and Edward the Confessor on the rood screen of Barton Toft's Church in Norfolk. Henry appeared boyish and unsaintly, in contrast to the bearded and haloed Anglo-Saxon kings. Thirteen years later he appeared in another East Anglian rood screen, this time at Ludham in Norfolk, and by the Reformation at least six, and possibly eight, other East Anglian churches featured painted images of Henry. Similar regal representations of the king, holding an orb and sceptre and depicted alongside Lancastrian royal beasts, appeared in rood screens at Stambourne in Essex and Ashburton and Whimple in Devon. Statues or other images of the king are recorded in the parish churches of Alton (Hampshire), Ashton-under-Lyne (Lancashire), Houghton Regis (Bedfordshire), Alnwick (Northumberland), Toft (Cambridgeshire), and Oddingley (Worcestershire), but these probably represent only a fraction of the number of late fifteenth- and early sixteenth-century churches in which Henry was venerated.[20]

The widespread popularity of Henry's cult is also evident from the evidence of prayers composed invoking his assistance and mention of him made in liturgical books and calendars. He was referred to as 'Harri sant' in Welsh bardic poetry, while at least twelve liturgies or hymns written in his honour survive from as far afield as Dublin, the West Midlands, and Yorkshire.[21] More telling perhaps are the large number of pilgrim badges that survive from those who visited or planned to visit his tomb. Almost four hundred badges, a number exceeded only by those depicting St Thomas Becket, survive. They have been discovered mainly in the south of England, but examples have been found in Shropshire, Lincolnshire, Oxfordshire, Warwickshire, Northamptonshire, and even in Rouen. Wills also record evidence of devotion to the late king: in 1484 a Norwich woman instructed her executor to travel to Chertsey, where 'King Harry lies', on pilgrimage, while testators in Kent were still making bequests for lights before images of the king into the 1530s. Henry appealed to a wide cross section of English society. Ordinary men and women travelled to his shrine and remembered him in their wills, and aristocratic families commissioned expensive manuscripts containing liturgies and hymns, while in 1502 even Queen Elizabeth of York paid for three proxy pilgrimages to Henry's tomb at Windsor.[22]

The image of Henry VI portrayed by followers of his cult was, at first sight, very different from the reality of his reign as king. In visual terms they portrayed a king of exemplary regality: frequently crowned, carrying the orb and sceptre, and depicted alongside other royal saints. These located Henry within a well-established tradition of kings who had been martyred, conferring upon him a dignity and authority which had been lacking in the latter years of his reign. This allowed his devotees to rewrite his princely attributes, arriving at the image of a virtuous king replete with the qualities that had been conspicuously absent during his lifetime. In 1492 the poet James Ryman described him as 'a king 'of royall fame/ And of full worthy gouernance' and of 'grete renowne/ And of virtue more excellent'.[23] A prayer composed in his honour in the north-east of England celebrated him as the 'blessed king so full of virtue, the flower of all knighthood that never was defiled'. To its author, Henry was 'a crowned king with sceptre in hand, most noble conqueror' who had 'conquered I understand a heavenly kingdom most imperial'. Each verse ended with the plea 'Now sweet King Henry pray for me'.[24] Yet this emphasis on Henry's regality was not entirely incongruous. During his lifetime, Henry's subjects had been aware that his dual coronation as king of England and France had conferred upon him an imperial dignity. A mid fifteenth-century pen-and-ink drawing of the king mounted and wearing armour depicts him wearing the closed imperial crown of England atop that of France, while the 1441 foundation charter of King's College shows him wearing a closed imperial crown, the first such depiction of an English king.[25] The king himself was well aware of his divinely sanctioned royal status and his perception of his own dignity may have contributed to his aloofness and sense of separation from even his closest servants.

Henry's royal characteristics were, however, only one aspect of his popular cult. As Tom Freeman has reminded us, the popular Henry was also a political leader, healer, and a holy martyr.[26] The late king soon developed a reputation as one who had patiently endured long periods of suffering, humiliation, and unjust punishment. This view of Henry was reflected in chronicles and histories written from the 1480s: the Tudor historian Polydore Vergil, writing in the first decade of the sixteenth century, observed that there was in Henry an 'honest shamefacedness, modesty, innocence and perfect patience, taking all human chances, miseries and afflictions of this life in so good part as though he had justly by some offence of his deserved the same'.[27] It was not Henry's murder as such that led to his popular veneration as a martyr, but his long and patient suffering during his lifetime. He thus gained a reputation as a friend and patron of those who had been unjustly punished or suffered great adversity. This aspect of the cult of Henry VI is apparent in the surviving prayers dedicated to the king. One characterised him as a 'school of patience/ to those oppressed by force/ to the sad and desolate'. Another prayer stated that Jesus 'had willed that [His] beloved servant King Henry should be afflicted by the weight of many tribulations, in order that by the merits of his patience and most innocent life . . . the copious sweetness of [His] grace may be displayed to the people by the glory of miracles'.[28]

An account of the miracles supposedly performed by the saintly Henry was compiled by the custodians of his shrines at Chertsey and Windsor and presented to the papal curia in 1503. This was part of an official process of canonisation, which required that accounts of the miracles he had supposedly wrought be scrutinised by papal officials. The process was pursued by the canons of Windsor and given royal backing by Henry VII. The surviving *miracula* in the British Library contains 174 separate miracles annotated by the papal officials, some of which are marked 'probatum' ('proved').[29] Taken together, they are a varied assortment of stories, relating how Henry 'healed traumatic injury, freed prisoners, protected people from fire, shipwreck and drowning, repaired inanimate objects, healed animals and even helped to find lost property', alongside more obviously Christ-like interventions such as restoring the blind to sight and raising the dead. Henry seems to have been able to assist those who had been unjustly punished, such as the two convicted felons saved on the gallows by the king's intercession or the four occasions when Henry freed men wrongly imprisoned. Unlike many other popular late medieval saints, he does not appear to have gained a reputation for healing a particular ailment or helping a particular group in society, such as pregnant women. Instead, the king appears to have been 'a patron saint for emergencies', frequently intervening when people were in mortal danger or suffered great adversity. Moreover, Henry's intercession more often than not resulted from a call made at the moment of greatest need, not as a result of a considered vow of pilgrimage. In more than half of the miracle stories the king intervened at the supplication of parents of dead or injured children, family members, friends, or bystanders.[30]

The nature of the miracles attributed to Henry VI might seem to suggest that his cult was not primarily motivated by any political adherence to the displaced House of Lancaster. Indeed, suggestions that the cult was developed and popularised as part of a conscious effort on the part of Henry VII to identify his regime with the Lancastrian past can be discounted.[31] Yet in one crucial way Henry's cult was political. Its very popularity made it political and connected it to one of the main pillars of the Lancastrian legacy. Like those of the political saints Thomas of Lancaster and Archbishop Scrope, Henry VI's cult identified itself with the Lancastrian tradition of defending the rights of the commons and caring for their welfare. While Thomas of Lancaster had resolutely defended the political freedoms of the commons during his lifetime and thus emerged as a political saint in death, Henry VI's life of patience, mercy, and charity translated into a genuine concern for the well-being of his former subjects in death. It was no coincidence that a large proportion of the miracles attributed to Henry were identical in form to those performed by another Lancastrian saint, St John of Bridlington. In 1450 Henry had registered his own 'great affection and singular devotion' to St John, exempting the priory from the terms of the Act of Resumption that year, and devotees of the king's cult recognised him as one of a long tradition of Lancastrian saints.[32] Henry's cult therefore reflected the durability of one aspect of the Lancastrian legacy. It also revealed the controversial nature of that legacy. Blacman's account of Henry's piety may have been designed not to further popularise the cult but 'to both counter and correct the popular image' of the king as a man of the people. Blacman's ascetic, contemplative king was purposefully made aloof from the everyday concerns of his former subjects, reminding his readers of another aspect of Lancastrianism, the deep and characteristic piety that had been associated with the House of Lancaster since the fourteenth century. The different interpretations of Henry VI's cult demonstrate that Henry, like the identity of the dynasty as a whole, was 'a nebulous and ill-defined character who was many things to many people'.[33]

Popular and official interest in Henry VI's cult reached its zenith during the reign of Henry VII. In 1498 the monks of Westminster Abbey petitioned the king to have Henry's body removed from Windsor to Westminster. The abbot of Westminster claimed that Henry VI had wished to be buried there, that it was the traditional place of burial for English kings, and that he should be entombed there alongside his father. Henry's council found in favour of the abbey, probably encouraged by the king, who was planning his own magnificent sepulchre there, but negotiations over the precise details of the move (and especially the cost) proved long and difficult. In his will, written in March 1509, Henry VII expressed again his desire 'right shortly to translate . . . the body and reliquaries of our uncle', but the plan appears to have died with him later that year. Henry VIII was to give express instructions to make the tombs of both Henry VI and Edward IV at Windsor 'more princely, in the same place where they are now, at our charge'.[34] As late as 1529 he even visited Henry's tomb at Windsor and made offerings. Efforts to pursue Henry's canonisation at Rome also slowed after 1509, despite a brief flurry of activity in the late 1520s, before Henry VIII's divorce from Catherine of Aragon changed the nature of Anglo-Papal relations for ever. Yet there is evidence that there was interest in the popular cult of Henry VI up to the Reformation. As late as 1538 a chapel in Caversham run by the Augustinian monks of Notley Abbey claimed to have 'the holy dagger' that had been the instrument of Henry's murder (alongside the 'holy knife' that had allegedly accounted for the Anglo-Saxon King Edward the Martyr). The royal commissioners duly seized the offending items and sent them to Thomas Cromwell.[35] As late as 1577 the antiquarian

William Lambarde expressed his alarm that relics associated with Henry VI were still being venerated at Windsor. By the later sixteenth century Henry's reputation was ambiguous and accounts of his life sometimes contradictory. *The Mirror for Magistrates*, a mid sixteenth-century account of the lives of various historical figures that was instrumental in informing Shakespeare's history plays, portrayed Henry as both virtuous and incompetent. He was 'a silly weak king' whose misdeeds were responsible for the civil wars of the fifteenth century, but he was also a Christian ruler who struggled to reconcile his piety with the demands of kingship.[36] In all probability the complexities of Henry's character proved as perplexing for early modern audiences as they do for historians today.

Conclusion

Henry VI's posthumous reputation reveals much about the strength of the Lancastrian political and cultural legacy into the sixteenth century. His piety was recognised and to some extent celebrated both at an elite level by John Blacman and at the popular level by those devoted to his cult. Blacman's account of the king located him within an important, if controversial, strand of late medieval devotional practice, underlining how the Lancastrian kings both reflected and shaped the piety of the fifteenth century. On the other hand, popular devotion to his cult reflected the widespread appeal of ideas associated with the Lancastrian dynasty and how they had long been identified with the welfare of the commons of England. There can be little doubt that Henry's qualities as a king were better regarded in the early sixteenth century than they had been at the time of his death. The general attitude towards him was summed up by John Rous, writing in the late 1480s: 'a most holy man, shamefully expelled from his kingdom, but little given to the world and worldly affairs which he always committed to his council'.[37] This image of a saintly king wronged by evil counsellors and blameless for the wars that had seen the destruction of the Lancastrian dynasty suited both the agenda of the new Tudor monarchy and the sensibilities of the king's former subjects.

Yet, as this book has argued, this was a simplistic verdict on a king whose two reigns spanned six decades. Throughout his adult life, apart from those brief periods when he was affected by illness, Henry VI involved himself in the great political issues of his day. First and foremost, this meant a personal commitment to securing a peaceful settlement of the war in France. In 1439 this involved advocating the release of the duke of Orléans and after 1445 it manifested itself in a determination to surrender the counties of Maine and Anjou in the face of uncertainty among his councillors and resistance from the men who held the English strongholds there. It also meant a conscious rejection on Henry's part of his role as the leader of the nation in war, one of the pillars upon which the image of Lancastrian monarchy had been built. In 1436 and in 1452/53 serious consideration appears to have been given to the possibility of the king leading an army to France in person, but in rejecting this course of action Henry and his councillors turned their backs on the legacy of John of Gaunt, Henry IV, and, most importantly of all, the king's father, Henry V. Henry's desire for peace also shaped the Lancastrian regime's response to its domestic critics and rivals during the 1450s. In 1455 his willingness to work with the Yorkist lords in the wake of the first battle of St Albans did nothing to halt the deep-seated personal feuds among his lords that would characterise English politics until 1461. The long and painful descent into civil war was characterised by Henry's periodic interventions in the cause of peace: the ill-fated 'Loveday' of 1458 was so preposterous an idea that it could only have originated in the naïve Christian optimism of the king himself. Similarly, the arguments made by the author of the *Somnium Vigilantis* on the eve of the Coventry Parliament in 1459 were in reaction to the king's well-known propensity to forgive his enemies, even when such actions smacked of a weakness that would only strengthen the Yorkists' hands.

These interventions in the cause of peace in the 1450s were characteristically idiosyncratic. To Bertram Wolffe they represented the 'perverse wilfulness' that lay at the heart of Henry's character.[38] For all his consistency in the cause of peace and reconciliation, Henry was at times fickle, with disastrous consequences. This was the king who stood by the duke of Suffolk in 1450, banishing him from England for five years, against the stated advice of his lords, when the Commons wanted him to suffer the penalties of treason, but who, later that year, deserted Lord Saye and Sele, his chamberlain, leaving him to the tender mercies of Cade's rebels.

It may have been the same character trait that moved Henry to have his uncle Gloucester arrested at the Bury Parliament in 1447, an event which, with hindsight, was a defining moment in the history of the Lancastrian monarchy. It was possibly behind the exuberance with which he greeted the French ambassadors in 1445 and the certainty with which he lectured bishops and lords on proper moral behaviour and the teachings of the Church.[39]

At times, however, the king appears more consistent and measured in his approach. Much has been made of the lackadaisical way he approached the everyday business of government, particularly in handling requests for the king's patronage. His unfortunate habit of making the same grant twice or allowing offices and rewards to accumulate in the hands of a few favoured courtiers earned him the condemnation of contemporaries and later historians alike. Yet the evidence of those petitions that bear his sign manual or some other evidence of his personal intervention reveals that Henry did pay attention to matters that concerned him. These primarily related to the Church, diplomacy and the concerns of the Lancastrian royal family, and to suits arising from or concerned with his closest household servants. During the 1440s these concerns combined in his great project to establish his colleges at Eton and Cambridge. In achieving this he was assisted by a dedicated group of servants, both clerical and secular, who made the king's aspirations a reality and who were suitably rewarded for their loyalty and efforts. We should not doubt the nature of Henry's personal commitment to his foundations nor fail to recognise that in so doing he was acting in a way that was entirely at one with the actions of many of his leading servants and subjects.

We should also recognise that in a reign so long and complex as Henry's the nature of the king's government and the effectiveness of his rule changed over time. The Henry who presided over the descent into civil war during the late 1450s was clearly a very different man from the energetic, driven individual who pursued a policy for peace, established the colleges at Eton and Cambridge, and who resisted the opposition of his uncle Gloucester during the mid 1440s. We can only hazard a guess at the psychological and physical effects of the crisis of 1449–53, a period that saw the collapse of the Dual Monarchy, the loss of close, personal friends, and the end of the political consensus that had characterised the Lancastrian polity for as long as Henry could remember. It is equally futile to speculate on the precise nature of the illness that afflicted the king in the summer of 1453, rendering him incapable of rule, or anything else for that matter, until Christmas 1454. It is sufficient to say that there had been no signs of so catastrophic an illness previously and that subsequently Henry's involvement in the affairs of state was at best sporadic and at worst virtually negligible. Yet he was still king and his presence and opinion mattered until the defeat at Towton, perhaps sustained by the memory of his personal rule during the 1440s. During the years after 1454 the king developed a physical and mental resilience, perhaps assisted by the ascetic devotional practices that he clearly followed, that allowed him to later survive almost a decade of exile and imprisonment. The Henry who emerged from the Tower of London in September 1470 to begin his 'Readeption' rule was completely transformed from the man who had pursued his policies with determination in the 1440s, or even the one who had still provided a hint of leadership at times during the 1450s. During this brief period the king, who now left the government of the realm entirely to his councillors, was apparently oblivious to the crisis around him. He suffered passively and silently the death of his son and heir, his own imprisonment and finally murder. In so doing he had at last met the expectations of his subjects.

Notes

1 Katherine J. Lewis, "'Imitate, Too, this King in Virtue, Who Could Not Have Done Ill, and Did It Not'": Lay Sanctity and the Rewriting of Henry VI's Manliness', in *Religious Men and Masculine Identities in the Middle Ages*, ed. P.H. Cullum and Katherine J. Lewis (Woodbridge, 2013), 126–42.

2 Roger Lovatt, 'John Blacman: Biographer of Henry VI', in *The Writing of History in the Middle Ages: Essays Presented to R.W. Southern*, ed. R.H.L. Davis and J.M. Wallace-Hadrill (Oxford, 1981), 415–44.

3 John Blacman, *Henry the Sixth*, ed. M.R. James (1919), 28.

4 Ibid., 35.

5 Ibid., 36, 38, 42, 43.

6 Ibid., 38.

7 Ibid., 29–30.

8 Ibid., 34–35.

9 Ibid., 36.

10 Roger Lovatt, 'A Collector of Apocryphal Anecdotes: John Blacman Revisited', in *Property and Politics: Essays in Later Medieval English History*, ed. A.J. Pollard (Gloucester, 1984), 182.

11 Blacman, *Henry the Sixth*, ed. James, 31–33.

12 Ibid., 39–41.

13 Ibid., 27, 37.

14 *Registrum Abbatiae Johannis Whethamstede*, ed. H.T. Riley (2 vols, Rolls Series, 1872–3), i, 338.

15 Lovatt, 'A Collector of Apocryphal Anecdotes', 187.

16 Blacman, *Henry the Sixth*, ed. James, 30; *The Register of Thomas Bekyngton, Bishop of Bath and Wells, 1443–1465*, ed. H.C. Maxwell-Lyte and M.C.B. Dawes (Somerset Record Society, 1934), 116–17.

17 *The Middle English Translation of The Incendium Amoris of Richard Rolle of Hampole*, ed. R. Harvey (Early English Text Society, 1896).

18 Yale University Beinecke Rare Book and Manuscript Library, Beinecke MS 331.

19 R. Hanna, 'Rolle and Related Works', in *A Companion to Middle English Prose*, ed. A.S.G. Edwards (Cambridge, 2004), 28.

20 Richard Marks, 'Images of Henry VI', in *The Lancastrian Court*, ed. Jenny Stratford (Donington, 2003), 117–24.

21 Leigh Ann Craig, 'Royalty, Virtue and Adversity: the Cult of Henry VI', *Albion* 35 (2003), 187–209.

22 Marks, 'Images of Henry VI', 113; Danna Piroyansky, *Martyrs in the Making: Political Martyrdom in Late Medieval England* (Basingstoke, 2008), 74–80.

23 *Historical Poems of the XIVth and XVth Centuries*, ed. Rossell Hope Robbins (New York, 1959), 199–200.

24 Blacman, *Henry the Sixth*, ed. James, 50–51.

25 Dale Hoak, 'The Iconography of the Crown Imperial', in *Tudor Political Culture*, ed. Dale Hoak (Cambridge, 1995), 57–64.

26 Thomas S. Freeman, 'Ut Verus Christi Sequester: John Blacman and the Cult of Henry VI', in *The Fifteenth Century V*, ed. Linda Clark (Woodbridge, 2005), 134.

27 *Polydore Vergil's English History*, ed. Sir Henry Ellis (Camden Society, 1844), 70–1.

28 Craig, 'Royalty, Virtue and Adversity', 200–2.

29 BL, Royal MS 13.c.viii printed as Paul Grosjean, *Henrici VI Regis Miracula Postuma* (Brussels, 1935).

30 Craig, 'Royalty, Virtue and Adversity', 204–9.

31 J.W. McKenna, 'Piety and Propaganda: The Cult of Henry VI', in *Chaucer and Middle English Studies in Honour of Rossell Hope Robbins*, ed. Beryl Rowland (1974), 72–88.

32 *PROME*, xii, 157.

33 Freeman, 'John Blacman and the Cult of Henry VI', 127–42.

34 McKenna, 'Piety and Propaganda', 80–84.

35 *Three Chapters of Letters Relating to the Suppression of the Monasteries*, ed. Thomas Wright (Camden Society, 1843), 222.

36 Thomas J. Moretti, 'Misthinking the King: the Theatrics of Christian Rule in *Henry VI, Part 3*', *Renascence* 60 (2008), 275–94.

37 B.P. Wolffe, *Henry VI* (1981), 5.

38 B.P. Wolffe, 'The Personal Rule of Henry VI' in *Fifteenth-Century England 1399–1509*, ed. S.B. Chrimes, C.D. Ross, and R.A. Griffiths (Manchester, 1972), 44.

39 Blacman, *Henry the Sixth*, ed. James, 28, 32, 38.

Suggestions for further reading

Ralph Griffiths's magisterial *The Reign of King Henry VI* (1981; 2nd edn, Stroud, 1998) is the essential starting point for any serious study of the reign. Although somewhat confusing at times in its structure, the breadth of its coverage of every aspect of the reign is unmatched. B.P. Wolffe's *Henry VI* (1981) was published in the same year and is a much more manageable, if less comprehensive, account of the reign. Wolffe's portrait of the king has proved controversial, something explored by John Watts in his introductory essay to the 2nd edition (New Haven, CT, 2001). Watts's own *Henry VI and the Politics of Kingship* (Cambridge, 1996) is less a biography of the king and more of a study of late medieval political culture. It is, nevertheless, essential reading. Katherine Lewis's *Kingship and Masculinity in Late Medieval England* (2013) provides a different approach to the reigns of Henry and his father. Henry's queen is the subject of Helen E. Maurer, *Margaret of Anjou: Queenship and Power in Late Medieval England* (Woodbridge, 2003). More general accounts of the reign can be found in Gerald Harriss, *Shaping the Nation: England 1360–1461* (Oxford, 2005) and Maurice Keen, *England in the Later Middle Ages* (2003).

Christopher Allmand's *Henry V* (1992) is the standard scholarly biography of Henry's father, but see also John Matusiak, *Henry V* (2013) and the essays collected together in *Henry V: The Practice of Kingship* (Oxford, 1985). Another important recent collection is *Henry V: New Interpretations*, ed. Gwilym Dodd (Woodbridge, 2013). Henry IV is less well served by biographers, but see Ian Mortimer, *The Fears of Henry IV: The Life of England's Self-Made King* (2007). Lancastrian culture, particularly literature, has been the subject of much recent scholarly attention. One of the most important contributions, again controversial, is Paul Strohm's *England's Empty Throne: Usurpation and the Language of Legitimacy 1399–1422* (New Haven, CT, 1998). Other important studies include Jenni Nuttall, *The Creation of Lancastrian Kingship: Literature, Language and Politics in Late Medieval England* (Cambridge, 2007) and Maura Nolan, *John Lydgate and the Making of Public Culture* (Cambridge, 2009). Various books serve as introductions to the literary and religious culture of the fifteenth century, but a good starting point is *A Companion to Medieval English Literature and Culture c.1350–1500*, ed. Peter Brown (Oxford, 2009). Similarly, V.J. Scattergood's *Politics and Poetry in the Fifteenth Century* (1971) remains a classic introduction.

The first three decades of Henry's reign were dominated by the French war. The most accessible introduction to the Hundred Years' War remains Christopher Allmand, *The Hundred Years War: England and France at War c.1300–1450* (Cambridge, 1998), but see also Anne Curry, *The Hundred Years* (Basingstoke, 2003). The struggle to establish and maintain the Lancastrian Dual Monarchy is without doubt the least well-known aspect of the war, but see Juliet Barker, *Conquest: The English Kingdom of France* (2010). For the duchy of Normandy see Christopher Allmand, *Lancastrian Normandy, 1415–1450* (Oxford, 1983). The significance of the battle of Agincourt continued to be felt throughout Henry's reign, and for three very different accounts of the battle see Anne Curry, *Agincourt: A New History* (Stroud, 2006), Michael K. Jones, *Agincourt 1415* (Barnsley, 2005) and Juliet Barker, *Agincourt* (2005). A detailed case study of John Talbot, earl of Shrewsbury, the most distinguished of Henry VI's commanders in France, can be found in A.J. Pollard, *John Talbot and the War in France 1427–1453* (1983).

Henry's domestic rule (or lack thereof) is another important theme among historians who have studied his reign. Principal among them is R.L. Storey's *The End of the House of Lancaster* (2nd edn, Stroud, 1999). The particular challenges faced by the Lancastrian regime in the duchy of Lancaster are the subject of Helen Castor's *King, Crown and the Duchy of Lancaster: Public Authority and Private Power, 1399–1461* (Oxford, 2000). The domestic crisis of 1450 is explored in Isabel Harvey, *Jack Cade's Rebellion of 1450* (Oxford, 1991). The Percy/Neville dispute, one of the personal noble feuds that contributed to the breakdown of public order in the 1450s, is explored in R.A. Griffiths, 'Local Rivalries and National Politics: The Percies, the Nevilles and the Duke of Exeter, 1452–1454', in his collected essays, *King and Country: England and Wales in the Fifteenth Century* (1991). Much detailed work has been published in the form of articles and essays and many of these are contained in the edited collections arising from the annual Fifteenth Century Conference, first established in 1970, with the essays published as *Fifteenth Century England 1399–1509*, ed. S.B. Chrimes, C.D. Ross, and R.A. Griffiths (Manchester, 1972). Since 2000 they have been published annually by Boydell & Brewer as *The Fifteenth Century*, ed. Linda Clark.

The study of the fifteenth century is still dominated by the insights of K.B. McFarlane. His most important published work was gathered together as *England in the Fifteenth Century*, ed. G.L. Harriss (1981). His legacy was felt especially at the universities of Oxford and Bristol, where his students and his students' students completed their PhDs. For an important collection of essays that deal with his impact on fifteenth-century studies see *The McFarlane Legacy: Studies in Late Medieval Politics and Society*, ed. R.H. Britnell and A.J. Pollard (Stroud, 1995). Much of that work has concentrated on prominent individuals or families. G.L. Harriss, *Cardinal Beaufort: A Study of Lancastrian Ascendancy and Decline* (Oxford, 1988) is a monumental biography of one of the leading figures of the Lancastrian period. Other work concentrates on the nobility. Richard, duke of York, is the subject of Paul Johnson's biography, *Duke Richard of York 1411–1460* (Oxford, 1991), but see also Carole Rawcliffe, *The Staffords, Earls of Stafford and Dukes of Buckingham, 1394–1521* (Cambridge, 1978), A.J. Pollard, *Warwick the Kingmaker: Politics, Power and Fame* (2007), and M.A. Hicks, *Warwick the Kingmaker* (Oxford, 1998). Another strand of McFarlane's legacy was the detailed study of local society. Among the best of these are Simon Payling, *Political Society in Lancastrian England: The Greater Gentry of Nottinghamshire* (Oxford, 1991) and Christine Carpenter, *Locality and Polity: A Study of Warwickshire Landed Society* (Cambridge, 1992). A rich and complex view of local society in the fifteenth century is afforded by the Paston letters, published in three parts as *Paston Letters and Papers of the Fifteenth Century*, ed. Norman Davis, Richard Beadle, and Colin Richmond (Oxford, 1971–2004). For the background to this important collection see Helen Castor, *Blood and Roses* (2004).

The Wars of the Roses have seen a huge increase in recent scholarly and literary attention. Some of this is good, some of it less so. Recent historical studies include David Grummitt, *A Short History of the Wars of the Roses* (2013) and Michael Hicks, *The Wars of the Roses* (New Haven, CT, 2010). A more controversial approach is to be found in Christine Carpenter, *The Wars of the Roses: Politics and the Constitution in England, c.1437–1509* (Cambridge, 1997), while an important collection of essays can be found in *The Wars of the Roses*, ed. A.J. Pollard (Basingstoke, 1995). A.J. Pollard, *The Wars of the Roses* (3rd edn, 2013) continues to be the best thematic introduction, while a good military history is John Gillingham, *The Wars of the Roses* (1981). An interesting study of some of the factors that motivated men to fight in the Wars can be found in Malcolm Mercer, *The Medieval Gentry: Power, Leadership and Choice during the Wars of the Roses* (2010).

Index